Praise for
Run for Cover

"*Run for Cover* is a captivating study of what it means to experience the safety, confidence and comfort of a life completely surrendered to God. Rhea Briscoe has written a book that's rich in biblical content and personal applications. Her stories are riveting and her words will challenge you to grow a faith that turns fear into faith. If you apply the truth inside these pages, your life will be transformed."

—Carol Kent
Speaker and Author of *When I Lay My Isaac Down* (NavPress)

"Rhea Briscoe's book, *Run for Cover*, is an insightful, authentic journey through her relationship with Christ. The book offers hope and is filled with practical lessons on dwelling with God on a day-to-day basis. Rhea Briscoe is honest in her approach to life's issues and points to God's enduring faithfulness. Her testimonies and teaching will inspire you to find stability in your own walk. You will be encouraged—filled with hope and a desire to deepen your relationship with God. I highly recommend this amazing book. You will want to read *Run for Cover* over and over again as each page, story and lesson will propel you into God's destiny for your life."

—Steve Swanson
Friends of the Bridegroom Worship Ministries

"I knew Rhea Briscoe long before I actually met her. I was ministering in Wisconsin for most of 2003 and I continually came across so many amazing, unshakeable, Jesus-loving people. Sure enough, I found out they were disciples of Rhea and her teachings and were greatly impacted by her life. Jesus said that people would know us by our fruits. Rhea is passionate for Christ and the power of the Holy Spirit; that comes forth right off these pages. By the time you finish this book, you will be far better off for it. You will be inspired to dive into the bottomless, intense, sweet presence of God and experience all that He has for us."

–Tommie Zito
Evangelist

RUN
for
COVER

RUN
for
COVER

Finding Intimacy
in the Presence of God

RHEA BRISCOE

PUBLICATIONS

Fort Washington, PA 19034

Run for Cover
Published by CLC Publications

U.S.A.
P.O. Box 1449, Fort Washington, PA 19034

UNITED KINGDOM
CLC International (UK)
Unit 5, Glendale Avenue, Sandycroft, Flintshire, CH5 2QP

ISBN (paperback): 978-1-61958-223-1
ISBN (e-book): 978-1-61958-224-8

Dedication

This book is lovingly dedicated to Anna Mae Bickhart, the one who instilled in me a love for the Word of God, consistently modeled faithfulness before me and taught me to run for cover and take shelter in the trustworthiness of God. Thank you for taking a little girl and stirring up the gift of God that was in her—your labor has not been in vain.

Contents

Preface 15

Acknowledgements 17

Introduction: The Vision. 21

1 God's Promise for Us 29

2 Hidden Securely in God's Shelter 47

3 He Is Our Safe Zone 61

4 Surely He Will Deliver Us 81

5 Avoiding the Enemy's Traps 93

6 Finding Refuge under His Wings. 111

7 Fear Not! 123

8 Angels to Guard Us 141

9 Made for Authority 155

10 Stomping on Serpents 173

11 Holding Fast to God and
        Giving Place Only to Him .193

12 God's Conditional Promises 213

13 He Will Deliver Us from Trouble 231

14 Satisfied with Long Life. 245

    Afterword: Will We Be Found Faithful? 263

    Notes 269

Preface

For those of you who don't know me, permit me to introduce myself. I am an itinerant minister who travels extensively, ministering the love of God and preaching the truth of His Word through Snowdrop Ministries. I am not ashamed of the gospel of Jesus Christ, for I am absolutely convinced that it is the power of God unto salvation. My life is evidence of His power at work, and I pray that the book that you hold in your hands substantiates that power in even greater measure.

I am a pastor's wife, married to the most tender shepherd I have ever known. He is a mighty man of God who loves me and his Lord deeply. I am grateful.

I am incredibly blessed to be the mother/stepmother of seven children. They are polished arrows in my quiver, and I am thankful. I pray every day that the Lord uses them for His glory and makes them mighty weapons of warfare for His kingdom. All seven of them have stolen my heart, and each one is a tremendous gift to me from God. I am honored to be their mother.

I am a woman with a past that she's not proud of living in a present that she knows has been redeemed. My life testifies to God's overcoming power and His ability to bring beauty from the ashes of our lives. He truly is a redeemer and deliverer—a close investigation of my life proves that fact.

I am first and foremost a lover of God, and I pray that my life is a reflection of Him in everything that I say and do.

I am not kooky, nor do I fall for "every wind of doctrine" (Eph. 4:14). I am a blood-bought child of God who passionately studies His Word to show myself "as one approved, a worker who has no need to be ashamed, rightly handling the word of truth" (2 Tim. 2:15). I want nothing more in my life than to bring God glory and to represent Him with authenticity and a pure heart. I aim to live a life like Nathanael in which God can affirm that I am one in whom there is nothing false (see John 1:47).

The book that you hold in your hand was written after I taught an extensive study on Psalm 91. The truths that God unveiled to me while studying this passage have changed thousands, and I pray that they will affect your life deeply as well. Please keep in mind that this is not an exegetical treatment of Psalm 91 from a theological scholar. It is simply my personal revelation and insight. I pray that it's a blessing to you.

Please don't think it accidental that you have chosen to read this book. I have prayed for you, the reader, asking God to reveal Himself to you at deep levels as you meditate on the truths that you will find in these pages. Be expectant as you read, for Scripture promises that those who hope in the Lord will not be disappointed (see Isa. 49:23). His Word is "living and active" (Heb. 4:12). I have purposefully saturated this book with His Word, because I know that my words do not hold power, but His words are the words of eternal life (see John 6:68).

Now may God "give you the spirit of wisdom and revelation" as you read "so that you may know him better" (Eph. 1:17, NIV). I pray that you will encounter God in this book in a way that you never have before. Be blessed and encouraged as you listen for His voice in the pages that follow.

Acknowledgements

First and foremost, to my heavenly Father, the King of Kings and Lord of Lords, to the One my soul loves, I am deeply humbled and undone by Your goodness to me. Thank You, gracious Father, is all I can say. My heart overflows with thanksgiving for all You have done and all You are doing. How I want You to receive glory and honor and praise from my life and from the pages of this book. Be glorified, my King, and draw each person who picks up this book to your magnificent self. Amplify and anoint each word with your sweet Holy Spirit, and grant each reader a sense of Your powerful presence as he or she digests the words on these pages. I love You with my whole self and long to see Your kingdom come and Your purposes revealed on this earth. "Maranatha" is my heart's cry; come quickly, I pray, Lord Jesus.

To my precious husband, Dave: Thank you for loving me the way you do. You are a constant reminder to me that God can restore the years the locusts have eaten, that He gives beauty for ashes and that He will always take what the Enemy means for evil and use it for good. He did that for me when He brought you into my life! I see Jesus in you at every turn. You are a wonderful father, an incredible husband and the most tender shepherd I have ever known. Thank you for loving Jesus the way you do. There aren't enough words in this world to describe the love that I have for you. I'm so proud to be your wife.

To my children—Danny, Tyler, Mike, Christy, David, Brooke and Kendal—and to my precious son-in-love, Steve: Psalm 127:3–5 says, "Children are a heritage from the LORD. . . . Blessed is the man whose quiver is full of them" (NIV). My quiver is full, and each one of you is a gift from God to me. I love you so very much. I pray daily for you that you will be taught by the Lord, that your peace will be great and that you will know His power and presence all the days of your life. I am so deeply proud of each one of you. May you always know that you are accepted by the Beloved—dearly loved by Him—and that there is no safer place than the shelter of the Most High God.

To my father, Richard Shaffer, the man who raised me and taught me what unconditional love and acceptance truly means: Your love for me gave me a glimpse of my heavenly Father. You will never know what your sacrificial love and unselfish commitment has meant to me. I pray that when you walk through the gates of heaven, you hear His "Well done." I love you dearly, Daddy.

To Stuart and Jill: Thank you, first and foremost, for the gift of your son. He is God's biggest blessing in my life, and I promise you, I will love him forever and honor him always. Thank you for the way you model godliness before me—for the way you love me and radiate Jesus to me. Stuart, you always believed that there was a book in me. Thank you for calling it forth and for encouraging me in the call of God on my life. I love you and Jill so much.

To Rick, Pickle, Robin, Ron and Denise, my precious nieces and nephews, and to their children: You are the epitome of family, and I love you all so much. Thank you for your love and support. You teach me about loyal love and undying commitment. I'm so glad that I was born into your family.

To Leslie Hook: You are my Jonathan—my armor bearer and my dearest friend. Words can't summarize my thankfulness for you and for all you do. Your covenant friendship is priceless to me. Thank you for believing in me and for believing in the call of God on my life. I love you dearly and am eternally grateful for you and for your service to the Lord. You, without a doubt, give yourself fully to the work of the Lord, and I'm so thankful to be co-laboring with you. Two are better than one. We are a side-by-side, dearly loved dynamic duo. Anthony and Susie down the street think so too.

To Don Hook: Humility and a servant's heart describe you best. Thank you for your commitment to Snowdrop Ministries. God sees what you do so faithfully and quietly behind the scenes to promote His kingdom. Proverbs 28:20 says, "A faithful man will abound with blessings." I pray that you abound greatly, my friend.

To the Monday night Bible study team—Jill, Karen K., Karen M., Karen V., Kelsey, Leah and Sandy: You are indeed watchmen on the wall. Thank you for being co-laborers in the gospel with me, for your undying service, for your tireless commitment to the Lord's work and for your passionate desire to promote the gospel of Jesus Christ. You are the real deal! I love ministering beside you, and I'm so grateful for each one of you.

To the Aline United Methodist Church: They say that it takes a village to raise a child. Thank you for raising me in the fear and admonition of the Lord.

Introduction: The Vision

I was enjoying a weekend at home—a much-welcomed rarity for me, since I traveled nearly every weekend as an itinerant minister. I had spoken at a local event on Saturday and now, on Sunday morning, I was looking forward to attending worship service with my husband and daughter and then spending a leisurely afternoon at home with them.

My husband, Dave, serves as a pastor at Elmbrook Church in Brookfield, Wisconsin. In addition to his normal workweek, he ministers at the Saturday evening service as well as our three Sunday morning services. This particular weekend he and our youngest daughter, Kendal, quietly slipped out of the house in the early morning hours while I slept soundly and went to the early services without me. I would join them for our third service at eleven. I awoke soon after their departure and trekked downstairs to indulge in some quiet time with the Lord. An atmosphere of solitude filled our home, and I spent sweet time in His presence. Oh, how I cherish such times!

I eventually journeyed back upstairs for a quick shower. As I entered my bedroom, I turned on the television to create some background noise. I paused momentarily, transfixed by my favorite Food Network chef preparing what looked to be an utterly scrumptious entrée. Captivated, I sat down on the bed and leaned back against the headboard, hoping to glean from her culinary expertise. I'm still unclear about what transpired immediately following.

The details that I am about to share may sound preposterous or far-fetched, but I assure you, they happened just as I describe them— and my life was forever impacted as a result. I hope that yours will be as well!

As I leaned against the headboard, I suddenly lost awareness of my surroundings. I don't remember closing my eyes, and I'm certain that I didn't drift back to sleep. In fact, I was mesmerized by the fact that although I could still distinctly hear the voice of the chef rattling off instructions, her voice was becoming strangely more distant, and eventually it faded into the background. I immediately became conscious of music—the most amazingly beautiful music I had ever heard. Mozart himself would have had difficultly recreating and putting it to score. It was breathtaking and peaceful, filled with exquisite harmonies that enveloped and soothed my soul.

Remarkably, I found myself standing before a line of what I instantly knew were angels, and I passed before them like a general surveying his troops. Oddly enough, my feet never touched the ground, but I moved in suspended motion, gliding and being carried along by some gentle force.

There are countless books and artistic representations depicting angels, but none of them accurately depict those I saw that day. What I saw were not angelic beings with feathered wings and cherub faces, nor were they colossal in size. But I somehow knew instantaneously that they were angels. As I passed before them that day, a heavenly sound reverberated from them—a sound not heard by my ears but one that echoed in the core of my being.

As I moved down the ranks, I noticed that the skin color of all the angels was white. I stopped before the last angel. This one was different from the rest. His skin color was black, and he held a higher place of authority than the others. As I paused before him, the music stopped, and he began to emit the most beautiful sound of all. No sound on earth could compare to the melodies and harmonies I heard that day.

I was flooded with feelings of warmth and acceptance as this angel sang. At one point he lifted his hand and with one smooth stroke went from my mouth to my heart, where he paused. Suddenly my body was swept from a vertical to a horizontal position; I was now levitating, prone. I felt no fear or apprehension nor any desire to leave that place.

In 2002 my friend Leslie's mother had died of ovarian cancer. In the days leading up to her passing, she had appeared fearful and apprehensive about her impending death. Because Leslie was certain of her mother's salvation, she had approached the hospice nurse and inquired about this seeming lack of peace. The hospice nurse had replied, "Oh, that's understandable; she's just nervous about being the new kid on the playground."

I used to have my own fears about being the "new kid on the playground." Although I knew that I was saved by grace and was confident that I would be going to heaven, it wasn't fear of death that shook me but fear of the unknown. In addition, I am the mother of seven children, and while I look forward to being absent from the body and present with the Lord, I have always been concerned about leaving my children behind after my death. But things changed for me that day.

As I lay in that prone position, I thought, *This must be what death feels like. My husband is going to come home from church and find my body lying lifeless on the bed, and everything is going to be okay.* All fear was gone. There was no "new kid on the playground" kind of feeling at all. I knew that my children would be just fine, and *nothing in me* wanted to leave this extraordinary place.

As I lay prostrate, someone approached me from behind. I knew instantaneously that it was God. I can't tell you how I knew it, but I did. Suddenly I was enveloped with what seemed to be wings; they completely covered me from the back of my head to my waist. I was hidden, shielded, and protected. I felt a divine sense of safety and security, the very things I'd struggled to find all my life. My feelings of insecurity and fear were swallowed up in His presence that day. I was safe and securely hidden in Him.

I felt as though a blanket of peace had been thrown over me. I was overcome not just with the most incredible sense of peace but also with a depth of love that I had never encountered before. It was an indescribable love, the magnitude of which no love in this world could compare.

As I lay enraptured, I had a sense of being pulled into the center of whatever had enveloped me. I didn't speak my concerns out loud but simply thought, *What's happening?* Immediately I received the answer. It wasn't an audible reply. The communication that took place that day was all done through my thoughts; I would think something and immediately receive the answer. "You are hidden with Christ in God, Rhea" (see Col. 3:3), came the reply. Yes! I was familiar with that scripture verse, but now I was experiencing it at a level that I had never dreamed possible. It was clear that I was hidden in the depths of God. Safe in His presence. Saturated by His love. Immersed in His peace. Captivated by His very being. I never wanted it to end!

I had absolutely no concept of time as I lay there. In fact, it seemed as if time didn't exist. But suddenly, without notice, I felt what I knew was my spirit slipping away from this place of peace. *No! No! I* thought. *I don't want to go back.* As I slipped back into regular consciousness, I observed that in the vision, my body was still lying in the prone position, at rest in God's presence. *What is that, Lord? Why is my body still there?* God's reply was that this is the position I am always in—securely hidden with Christ in God. I may be walking on the earth, but I am in the heavenlies with Him, securely hidden and safely protected by Him. I could now live with a greater sense of freedom because of this newfound understanding. The fact that I was secure in Christ was no longer only head knowledge—the feelings of security I experienced that day were burned deep within me.

I was startled as, with a heavy thud, my spirit reentered my body, now lying flat on the bed. My body shook from the impact, and I knew, as Paul describes in Second Corinthians 5:6, that I was back "at home in the body." Straightaway I jumped up from my bed and bolted into the bathroom. I sat there with my head in my trembling hands. The memory of the incredible music was already fading. The sense of overwhelming peace and deep contentment was vanishing. The depth of love—the likes of which I had never sensed before—was drastically diminishing.

My first thought was, *Please don't let it fade, Lord*. I wanted desperately to hang on to that feeling. I prayed that it would be etched into my memory. I was undone. All I knew was that I never wanted to forget what had just happened to me, yet the incredible sense of love that I never wanted to forget was already lessening. However, what remained was the ingrained knowledge that I was indeed *hidden* with Christ in God, that I was safe in His presence and that *nothing* could happen to me outside His perfect will for my life. This was a place of safety.

Although at the time I wasn't sure what was happening, I know now that I experienced a heavenly vision. Some people are not comfortable with the term "vision," but Scripture speaks clearly about the subject. In Joel 2:28 God spoke a promise through the prophet Joel, saying, "I will pour out my spirit on all flesh; your sons and your daughters shall prophesy, your old men shall dream dreams, and your young men *shall see visions*." John experienced a vision on the isle of

Patmos, Ezekiel experienced many visions and Peter describes a vision about the Gentiles that appeared as a great sheet being let down from heaven by its four corners. Paul said that he could boast of his visions; he wrote about a time when he had a vision and didn't know whether he was "in the body or out of the body," but he knew that he was caught up to the third heaven and shown many things (2 Cor. 12:2).

So visions exist. But to say that I was caught off guard for this one would be an understatement. I could believe that God would speak in visions to Peter, Paul, the prophets of old and, of course, to the disciple whom He loved most, but I was totally unprepared when a glimpse of His glory interrupted my everyday life to speak to the depths of my heart.

As I began to seek the Lord regarding the vision I had received, He led me to a study of Psalm 91. This book that you are holding is a compilation of the truth that I discovered while seeking a deeper understanding of that psalm and its relationship to the vision I received that unforgettable Sunday morning—the truth that if we dwell in the shelter of the Most High and abide in His shadow, we will rest utterly secure, free from the fear of man and the attacks of the enemy and flooded with God's promises of peace, safety, security, honor and eternal life.

> He who dwells in the shelter of the Most High will abide in the shadow of the Almighty. I will say to the LORD, "My refuge and my fortress, my God, in whom I trust."
>
> For he will deliver you from the snare of the fowler and from the deadly pestilence. He will cover you with his pinions, and under his wings you will find refuge; his faithfulness is a shield and buckler. You will not fear the terror of the night, nor the arrow that flies by day, nor the pestilence that stalks in darkness, nor the destruction that wastes at noonday.

A thousand may fall at your side, ten thousand at your right hand, but it will not come near you. You will only look with your eyes and see the recompense of the wicked.

Because you have made the LORD your dwelling place—the Most High, who is my refuge—no evil shall be allowed to befall you, no plague come near your tent.

For he will command his angels concerning you to guard you in all your ways. On their hands they will bear you up, lest you strike your foot against a stone. You will tread on the lion and the adder; the young lion and the serpent you will trample underfoot.

Because he holds fast to me in love, I will deliver him; I will protect him, because he knows my name. When he calls to me, I will answer him; I will be with him in trouble; I will rescue him and honor him. With long life I will satisfy him and show him my salvation. (Psalm 91)

ONE

God's Promise for Us

He who dwells in the shelter of the Most High will abide in the shadow of the Almighty.

Psalm 91:1

When our children were growing up, my family loved to attend the circus when it was in town. On one of our excursions, our daughter, Brooke, who at three years old had always been fiercely independent and never wanted to be carried, walked just ahead of her dad and me, exploring her new surroundings and thrilled to be enjoying a little freedom.

As we rounded a corner, a clown approached. He greeted Brooke in typical circus-clown fashion. Startled, she spun around and ran back to her daddy as quickly as her little feet would take her, her arms raised high. It was clear that Miss Independent wanted to be picked up. She had confidence in her daddy and knew that he would protect her in her time of need. She knew where to run for safety.

Do we exhibit the same kind of confidence in our heavenly Father? Do we turn to Him in our time of need? Does fear send us running into His arms? Do we trust, as Scripture so clearly tells us, that He will be our "very present help in trouble" (Ps. 46:1)? Do we know that our life is safely guarded in Him?

We get to choose the place where we are going to dwell. Are we going to live in mediocrity and bitterness, in unforgiveness and anger, in insecurity and feelings of worthlessness? Or will we decide to dwell in the shelter and protection of the Most High God? It's a choice and one that we must be purposeful about making.

The Promise of Psalm 91

Psalm 91, whose rich promises we will examine in this book, is a reassuring picture of God's divine protection. It's a comforting psalm about God being our refuge and our shelter. It highlights the assurance of His protection and the safety that we can find in His presence. Psalm 91 is a promise from God, and as people of God, we can rest in His promises.

The Word of God says that "all the promises of God find their Yes in him" (2 Cor. 1:20). In other words, God means what He says, and He'll do what He promises. Scripture says that His Word is already "settled in heaven" (Ps. 119:89, NKJV), and therefore we can count on Him to fulfill His Word in our lives. That should give us great comfort. He is a trustworthy God, and He keeps His Word!

We live in a world of broken promises. We don't need to look beyond our own experiences to know that people don't always keep their word and that promises don't always hold much weight. A promise is only as good as the integrity of the one making it. In much of society today, wedding vows are no longer held sacred, election promises go unfulfilled, parents fail to follow through on commitments to their children and the corporate world guarantees promotions or raises that never materialize.

As the parents of seven children, my husband and I learned early on the importance of saying something to our children (either in the form of a promise or a command) only if we intended to follow through with it. Children learn very quickly whether or not their parents can be counted on to mean what they say. With every promise kept, our children learn that we can be trusted to do what we say we will do, and that kind of faithfulness is important to them. The opposite is true as well—with every promise broken, we teach them to disregard our words and to put little weight on what we say.

Although my husband, Dave, and I endeavored to always mean what we said when dealing with our children, we were not always perfect. Our Father in heaven, however, is perfect 100 percent of the time, and He absolutely, positively can be trusted to mean what He says.

Lamentations 3:23 describes God's faithfulness as "great," Psalm 36:5 exclaims that it "reaches to the heavens" (NIV), Psalm 100:5 promises that it endures "to all generations," and Second Timothy 2:13 says that God can't help but be faithful, even when we are faithless, because He can't deny Himself.

The Old Testament word for "faithfulness" is *emunah*; it means "firmness, security, fidelity, stability and truth." Its origin is in the word *aman*, which means "to support, uphold, be faithful, made firm, established, sure, verified."[1] In other words, God can be trusted; He is established and sure, and He will always be faithful and completely trustworthy. Establishing this truth firmly in our hearts is a prerequisite to understanding and receiving the promises of Psalm 91.

Psalm 91: A Conditional Promise

While it's important that we understand the faithfulness of God and know that He will keep the promises He makes to us in Scripture, it's also important that we realize that Psalm 91 is a chapter-long conditional promise.

You see, we need to distinguish between two types of promises in the Bible: conditional and unconditional. An example of an unconditional promise is God saying, "I will never leave you nor forsake you" (Heb. 13:5). This promise is not dependent upon us meeting any requirements before it can be fulfilled. It's God saying, "I give you My Word, and I mean it when I say that I will *never* leave you and *never* forsake you."

A conditional promise, on the other hand, requires *our* faithfulness, or *emunah*. The Bible is full of these. For example, in Matthew 11:28 Jesus says, "Come to me, all who labor and are heavy laden, and I will give you rest." The condition to be met for those who are weary and heavy laden is that we *come* to Jesus. It is a conditional promise.

Psalm 91 is an entire chapter detailing a conditional promise of God. It's vital that we understand this if we hope to receive the benefits listed in this psalm.

The psalm is full of promises, but in order to appropriate those to our lives, we have an overarching condition to fulfill, and it is specified in the first verse: "He who *dwells in the shelter of the Most High* will abide in the shadow of the Almighty."

The word "dwell" is a verb meaning "to live, inhabit, dwell, stay, be settled, cause to settle, cause to sit, marry [with a focus on the spouses living together], stay, sit down, at rest."[2] We must take careful note—the passage says "he who dwells," not one who visits once in a while. So often we want to visit the shelter of the Most High—give Him our ten minutes of quiet time or read a word that He spoke to someone else instead of seeking Him with all our heart and requiring Him as a vital necessity.

We want the benefits of salvation, the assurance of heaven and we want to be able to run to that place of protection occasionally, but too often we are content to follow the Lord at a distance, never fully realizing the intimate fellowship that is available to us when we dwell in His presence.

The promises outlined in Psalm 91 are not possessed by all believers but only by those who walk in close fellowship and deep communion with God—those who are intentional about dwelling, abiding and living in the awareness of God's presence.

Dwelling with God—Something to Take Seriously

Dwelling implies a permanency, a residing—a place of habitual fellowship. But do we truly understand what it means to walk in habitual fellowship with God? To have our abode in Him? To linger in His presence, walk in close communion with Him and bask in His glory, fully aware that His presence lives inside us and that we carry that presence wherever we go?

My husband and I dwell in the same house, but what would happen if I greeted him in the morning but then did not communicate or spend any time with him the rest of the day? We would share a dwelling place but be like two ships passing in the night. We would never know true intimacy or the comfort of one another's presence. Sadly, this is the case with many Christians today when it comes to relationship with Christ.

Many of us have made Jesus our Lord and Savior and invited Him to dwell with us, but we live without the awareness of His presence in our lives—always falling short of the depth of intimacy that He longs to share with His people. Many of us have prayed a "fire insurance" prayer—understanding that there is a hell to shun and a heaven to embrace—but we never truly walk in habitual fellowship and sweet communion with God. My son, Tyler, is particularly fond of saying, "We want heaven, but we want to live like hell to get there." With our lips we declare Jesus Lord, but we don't exemplify evidence of that lordship. When this is the case, we miss out on the benefits promised to believers in Psalm 91.

Jesus Himself said,

> Not everyone who says to me, "Lord, Lord," will enter the king-
> dom of heaven, but only the one who does the will of my Father
> who is in heaven. Many will say to me on that day, "Lord, Lord,
> did we not prophesy in your name and in your name drive out
> demons and in your name perform many miracles?" Then I
> will tell them plainly, "I never knew you. Away from me, you
> evildoers!" (Matt. 7:21–23, NIV)

That verse scares me a bit. It scares me to think that we can call
Jesus "Lord" and believe with all our heart that He is, yet still not
know Him. The people Jesus referred to in this passage prophesied in
His name, cast out demons and did many signs and wonders. I'll bet
that they were good religious people who never missed church and
truly believed that they were saved and going to heaven! After all,
they were calling Him Lord—they obviously believed that He was! It
is sad to realize that Jesus used the word "many" when He referred to
them, implying that in the day that we stand before Him, it will not
be just a few whom He sends away—it will be many.

Those believers who do not dwell in the shelter of the Most High
will miss out on the promises of Psalm 91—one of which includes
salvation! I don't want to be one of the "many" He sends away. We
must be careful that we are not just going through the motions of
Christianity; instead we must seek the Lord with all our heart and
endeavor to dwell in a place of intimacy and deep connection with
Him. God wants us to *know* Him. He desires a deep and abiding relationship with us—not mere lip service.

Jeremiah has something to say about this:

> "Like their bow they have bent their tongues for lies. They are
> not valiant for the truth on the earth. For they proceed from
> evil to evil, and they do not know Me," says the Lord. . . . "They

have taught their tongue to speak lies; they weary themselves to commit iniquity. Your dwelling place is in the midst of deceit; through deceit they refuse to know Me," says the Lord. (Jer. 9:3, 5–6, NKJV)

God was telling Jeremiah that he was living in the midst of deceit. He was not referring to Jeremiah himself but to the people surrounding the prophet. God's people were living in falsehood, behind a façade of lies. As a result of this sin, His people didn't truly know Him and therefore went from evil to evil, sin to sin, wearying themselves to commit iniquity. God told Jeremiah that they were no longer valiant for the truth on Earth or passionate for Him.

Are we guilty of that? Are we no longer valiant for the truth because we love our sin more than we love dwelling in His shelter? Do we play religious games and try to make people think that we are more spiritual than we are? None of us has time for that in our lives.

Lip Service

The *American Heritage Dictionary* defines lip service as a "verbal expression of agreement or allegiance, *unsupported by real conviction*; hypocritical respect."[3] It's so easy for us to express allegiance with our mouth because we know that it's the right thing to do yet lack the true conviction that produces fruit and brings change into our lives.

Jesus once said, "Isaiah was right when he prophesied about you hypocrites; as it is written: 'These people honor me with their lips, but their hearts are far from me'" (Mark 7:6, NIV). He was implying that some people simply give Him lip service—they talk a good talk *about* God but never truly *know* Him. According to Jesus, this is hypocritical! If you and I are going to talk the talk, we must make sure that we walk the walk! God notices the difference, and frankly, so does everyone around us.

Not long ago my husband and I purchased a new desk for our home office. The rest of our office furniture was cherry wood, so it only made sense that the desk we purchased should be cherry as well. The day we decided to go furniture shopping was during a particularly hectic time in my life. Truthfully, my workload was so heavy and I was so frenzied that furniture shopping was not high on my list of priorities. Consequently, I was willing to settle for just about anything. I wanted to get a desk and get back home!

As we entered the furniture store, I was a woman on a mission. I quickly made my way to the home-office section and in record time located a desk that I thought was perfect—and, surprisingly, the price was right. *Hallelujah,* I thought, *Let's get this thing paid for so I can get back to work!* My husband, however, wasn't convinced. After a thorough examination, he explained that while the desk I had chosen looked good at first glance, it was merely covered by a wood veneer and not made of genuine cherry wood. It was a cheap imitation of the real thing.

As Christians, we should strive for authenticity in our relationship with Christ. We need to be the real thing, not a cheap imitation or a "spiritual veneer." Many churches are filled with people who at first glance look great but upon thorough examination are exposed as frauds. My mother used to say, "Rhea, you are the only Bible some people are ever going to read, so be careful in the way you are living." Are we genuine or imposters? Are we dwelling in the shelter of the Most High or living as imitations of the real thing?

Jesus did not have a lot of tolerance for spiritual frauds; in fact, He had plenty of negative things to say about them. At times He referred to them as "whitewashed tombs" (Matt. 23:27)—people who work really hard to look good on the outside but on the inside are full of death and everything unclean. We need to be intentional about examining our lives daily, tearing down façades, purifying our hearts and minds before the Lord and refusing to live in falsehood but rather in authentic, wholehearted devotion to Him.

As we saw in Jeremiah 9, God's people were dwelling in the midst of deceit. The word "dwell" there is the same word that God uses in Psalm 91:1—the word that means "to make your abode" or "reside." Is it possible that we could be making our abode in a place of deceit?

We shouldn't be quick to dismiss that possibility until we get a grasp on what the word "deceit" means—it means "fraud" or "a fraudulent man."[4] God rebuked His people in Jeremiah's day for living in a place of fraudulence—they were fakes and not the real deal (like the desk at the furniture store!). I don't want to be a fraudulent person—I want to be the real deal or nothing at all. I don't want to put on a mask of spirituality and miss out on the power of God's presence. I don't want to choose sin over intimacy with God and lose my passion for God's truth. I don't want to be a fraud—a cheap imitation of the real thing! I want to be valiant for the truth.

It takes a lot of energy to live in the midst of deceit, to maintain an impeccable spiritual exterior while the interior is less than desirable. I know—I lived there for a long time!

God Desires Intimacy with Broken Sinners

But here's the good news: no matter where we are in our walk with the Lord, even if we have made our abode in a place of deceit, God is calling us to a place of intimacy with Him. God knows everything that there is to know about us—the good and the bad. Psalm 139 tells us that. He knows when we sit and when we rise. He knows our thoughts and what motivates them. He knows what we are going to say before we say it. He knows what makes us tick and why we do the things we do, and here is the amazing part—He loves us anyway and wants us to live in His presence!

Romans 8:39 tells us that *nothing* can ever separate us from the love of God—nothing we've done, nothing we could ever do and nothing that has ever been done to us. That's amazing love. That's a place of rest and security, and the One who knows us so well invites us to come just as we are and dwell with Him in that place of refuge. He wants us to know Him and experience Him fully.

I love my husband dearly. Our relationship is a place of safety for me. I love that I can be myself with him, makeup or no makeup, overweight or thin, wrinkles or no wrinkles, dressed to the nines or in my sweatpants, with a smile on my face or tears in my eyes. I love that when he wakes up next to me each day with my messy hair, morning breath and sleeper dirt in my eyes, the first words he utters to me are about his great love for me. He loves me just as I am—no façade needed.

God wants us to experience that same kind of intimacy and depth of love with Him. We don't need to appear super spiritual, put on a mask of perfection or try to amaze Him with our spiritual façade. So many of us feel that we need to impress the Lord with our undaunted church attendance and flawless commitment to serving and ministering in the church. We work hard to pretend that we have it all together. But we don't need to have it all together or be on our best behavior! We have a God who loves us just as we are and never wants us to hesitate to come to Him that way.

Many years ago I was ministering at a conference in California and preaching on the scripture in Luke 5 where the Pharisees, feeling smug in their self-righteousness, were grumbling and questioning Jesus' conduct because He was meeting with tax collectors and sinners. Jesus, ever aware of His mission to seek and save the lost, responded gently to them, saying, "It is not the healthy who need a doctor, but the sick" (Luke 5:31, NIV).

As I spoke that day, I drove home the point that the church should be functioning as a hospital—a place where people who are sin sick can safely come and meet with Dr. Jesus and be healed. I stressed that sometimes the church functions instead as a courtroom in which people are judged and that this should not be.

At the end of that service, a young woman named Kayla approached me and told me that she'd had firsthand experience with the church functioning as a hospital. I encouraged her to share her story with me.

Kayla was a recovering heroin addict who had been clean for six months. But in years past heroin had overtaken her life and stolen everything from her. It had stripped her of her dignity, her home, her job, her children, her marriage, her finances and her health. It had left her homeless on the streets of California, and she had felt powerless over it. She had tried everything to get free—treatment centers, drug rehabilitation programs, twelve-step groups—but nothing had worked.

One day as she walked the streets on a heroin high, a passerby shared the gospel with her. She thought, *I've tried everything else—why not try this Jesus?* The following Sunday she wandered into a local church. She waited to enter until after the service began and was purposeful to leave before it ended. She felt that she knew what people would think of her and wanted to avoid their cruel judgments. Strangely enough, she was captivated by what she heard that day and drawn by the irresistible love of Jesus. She returned to that church week after week, each time high as a kite but desperately longing to know this One who seemed to accept her right where she was, in the condition she was in.

As I listened intently to her story, Kayla reached over to take the hand of an elderly lady sitting close by and, drawing her into our conversation, introduced the woman to me. "Rhea," she said with feeling, "one Sunday morning I went into that church, and this woman here was waiting for me in the back row where I normally sat. She took me by the hand and led me to her seat in the front row, and I am standing here six months clean of a horrible addiction because this woman understood that the church is a hospital and loved me enough to introduce me to Dr. Jesus!"

We don't need to clean ourselves up before we come to Jesus. (If that were the case, I would still be trying to clean myself up!) He loves us just the way we are and invites us to come to Him in the condition we are in. We can approach Him boldly, free of spiritual façades, free of masks and clever pretenses, with the knowledge that He knows everything about us and loves us anyway! That's a breeding ground for intimacy—for dwelling in the shelter of the Most High.

Many of us can pray up a storm, quote lots of Scripture and would never dream of missing church on Sunday morning, but do we truly know what it means to dwell in a place of intimacy with God and live in freedom with Him? Or are we content being frauds—putting on a good exterior and keeping up false fronts? God isn't impressed with our church attendance or our Scripture memorization. He longs for relationship with us. Jeremiah so gently reminds us that living in a place of deceit keeps us from intimately knowing the lover of our soul—the only One in whom true intimacy and safety can be found.

Intimacy Requires Vulnerability—but It's Worth It

I once heard someone describe intimacy as into-me-see. I like that, because that's what intimacy requires you to do—allow someone to "see-into-you"—and that's not always comfortable or safe. When we are intimate with someone, we risk exposure. "What will they think if they find out who I really am?" "What if I'm not good enough?"

"What if they reject me when they discover how deeply flawed I am?" Yes, intimacy is risky. It requires vulnerability, but when it's truly attained, it is a place of great comfort and safety.

I have a cherished friend named Leslie. We share an intimacy in friendship that many people never obtain with a friend, and I am grateful for that. Having been friends for almost twenty years, we have a lot of history together. Leslie is my dearest friend, most intimate confidante and my faithful partner in ministry. Our families vacation together, celebrate together, walk through pain together and share many happy memories together.

Our friendship is a safe place. Leslie knows all about me—and she loves me anyway. I'm not afraid to be myself around her.

I don't have to impress her (I can't—she knows too much), and she sticks by me even when I disappoint her. She knows my deep, dark secrets, has shared in my joys and walked closely with me through much heartache.

We've cried together and prayed together, and we are masters at shopping together. She's not embarrassed to be seen with me even when I'm wearing raggedy sweatpants and looking ghastly without my makeup.

I can call her at any hour of the day or night, and she will be happy to talk with me. Our friendship is a place of security; I have no doubt that my secrets are safe with her. Our relationship is reciprocal—Leslie shares her life with me in much the same way that I do with her.

We are often asked if we are sisters because we act so much alike, and people tell us all the time that they wish they could have a friendship like ours. We've even had people admit that they are jealous and deeply envious of us! What they don't understand is that we work hard at the intimate friendship we share; we are intentional about it. It's silly for others to be jealous of what we have when they could have the same thing with someone else—it just requires work. And, of course, risk taking!

To have an intimate relationship with someone requires a willingness to share ourselves, take risks and let down walls so that we can be real with another person. It requires self-disclosure, an investment of energy and emotional susceptibility. Intimacy doesn't just happen. Leslie and I are purposeful about creating a safe atmosphere—one in which we can share and have freedom to be real—and the glue that holds it all together is intimacy.

When we are intimate with someone, we allow that person to know us at a level that is up close and personal. We allow them to see into us, which could lead to rejection but has the potential to bring about the beauty of unconditional acceptance.

Knowing and Being Known

True intimacy is deeper than a physical connection—it takes us to a place of connection and fulfillment found in truly being known. Intimacy requires work. It requires us to be purposeful about staying available and connected and resolute in keeping communication open and vulnerable. You and I were created for intimacy with the One who created us.

As we saw earlier, God knows everything about us and is not turned off by it! The writer of Psalm 139 exclaims, "O LORD, you have searched me and known me!" (139:1). The word "search" means "to dig," or, my favorite definition, "to excavate," which carries the connotation of God digging through the garbage of our lives to uncover the treasure that He knows is buried deep within us.[5] Remember, *He* created us and put the treasure there in the first place. He knows what is buried beneath our brokenness and hidden behind our sinfulness. He is intimately acquainted with us!

Yet we often try to hide and cover our imperfections from the One who knows us best. Shockingly, things haven't changed much since the Garden of Eden. As you know, when God created man in the garden, He created man to walk with Him in intimacy, but sin entered the picture and separated man from God, and intimacy was lost. Genesis 3:8 tells us that because of their sinfulness, Adam and Eve hid themselves from God. We haven't learned much from their mistake, because, like Adam and Eve, we continue try to hide ourselves from the One in whom nothing is hidden. We fool ourselves that hiding is a better solution than risking exposure and allowing ourselves to be fully known.

When Christ died on the cross for us, He came to repair what had been lost at the fall and to restore relationship between us and God. As a result, we can now come boldly into His presence and find comfort in our time of need (see Heb. 4:16). First Corinthians 1:9 says that we have been called into fellowship with Christ. The word that Paul uses for "fellowship" in this passage is *koinōnia*, which means "intercourse, fellowship, intimacy, communion."[6] Think about that! God wants us to enjoy the safety of knowing that we are fully known and completely accepted by Him.

God is like my friend, Leslie, is with me; He knows the deepest, darkest things about us and still sticks by our side. We can come to Him boldly—not fearing rejection or condemnation—but in the freedom of being completely and totally known and loved by a covenant-keeping God.

Intimacy, however, is a two-way street. It needs to be reciprocal. God told Jeremiah that he was dwelling in the midst of a fraudulent people, people who, because they insisted on maintaining a lifestyle of lies and falsehood, did not know Him. And the same is true of us; dwelling in a place of deceit keeps us from knowing Him.

God knows us, but do we know Him? I don't mean do we know *about* Him. I know a lot *about* President Barack Obama. I know that he is the forty-fourth president of the United States. He was born in Hawaii, his wife's name is Michelle and he has two beautiful daughters. I even know that his favorite food is broccoli. But I don't *know* Barack Obama. The same can be true of our relationship with God. We can know a lot about Him but never truly know Him. We can follow the Lord and confess His lordship in our lives but never truly dwell with Him intimately.

We can't get to know someone unless we spend time with him or her, getting to know what the person loves, discovering what makes that individual's heart beat, finding out what brings him or her joy. Why do we spend so much time putting up spiritual façades when the Creator of the universe wants us to truly *know* Him? He wants to fellowship with us and take us to a place of deep communion with Him.[7]

Dwelling Requires Action

I want to learn to dwell in God's presence, in His shelter. But living in that place is a choice every day of our lives, every moment of our day. We must be intentional about where we dwell.

Psalm 91 calls us to live in God's presence: "He who dwells in the shelter of the Most High will abide in the shadow of the Almighty." But as we saw earlier, "dwell" is a verb, and a verb conveys action. It puts a motionless subject into motion.[8] That's important, because you and I are the implied subjects of this verse, and if we are going to meet the condition behind the promise of this passage, it requires action on our part, not a passive waiting. We, the subject of the verse, must be put into motion instead of sitting idly and waiting for God to instantaneously zap us!

We must make a *choice* to dwell in the shelter of the Most High—to direct our thoughts toward Him and remain in intimate communion with Him—becoming daily conscious of His presence with us. We must be intentional about living under the protection of His covering.

In her book *Psalm 91*, Peggy Joyce Ruth uses the illustration of an umbrella in a rainstorm to help her readers gain deeper insight into the psalm.[9] It's a brilliant example, because just as an umbrella affords protection from a rainstorm, so dwelling under the umbrella of God's protection provides us with shelter from the storms of life. It goes without saying that an umbrella is only useful if we choose to remain under its covering. The moment we step out from under its protection, we are exposed to the elements and immediately affected by them.

The same is true of our relationship with God. We have a choice to remain firmly tucked under the shelter of His protection; or we can choose to remove ourselves from it, but we will always feel the effects of stepping out from under cover. Proverbs 22:3 says, "The prudent see danger and take refuge, but the simple keep going and pay the penalty" (NIV). We have to choose to take cover when we see danger.

When we truly understand the safety found in the shelter of the Most High, we will run for cover, taking refuge in His presence, and intentionally guard against anything that entices us to remove ourselves from it. Just as my three-year-old daughter, Brooke, ran to the safety of her father's arms, so we must abandon our independence and run to the Lord, knowing that He will take care of us in our time of need. As we increasingly learn to dwell in God's presence, we will be blessed with the amazing abundance of promises that He has made to us in Psalm 91.

TWO

Hidden Securely in God's Shelter

He who dwells in the shelter of the Most High will abide in the shadow
of the Almighty.

Psalm 91:1

When I was a little girl, I spent a lot of time visiting with my grandparents in Pennsylvania. My cousins, Doug and Dave, lived across the street from my grandparents' house, so a visit there almost always guaranteed playtime with my cousins!

Doug and Dave had a rustic red playhouse tucked away in their picturesque backyard—it was our hiding place. We spent countless hours hidden away in that backyard paradise. It was a refuge for us where we could be sheltered from the cares of the world, safe from the neighborhood bullies and protected from Grandma's endless list of chores that was waiting for us.

I can still picture that little hideout in my mind—the handcrafted exterior painted bright red, the roof covered with weather-beaten asphalt shingles, the windows meticulously trimmed in white and strategically mounted on the door a hand-painted sign with a stern warning for anyone who dared to approach uninvited: "DO NOT ENTER—THIS MEANS YOU!" There we could be hidden away and concealed from the tyranny of the world around us.

The secret place of the Most High provides that same kind of refuge for us as believers. God is our hiding place, and we can run into His presence and find safety in our time of trouble (see Ps. 32:7). We need to understand this, because the enemy of our soul understands the protection that we find in God's presence—he once enjoyed the shelter of that protection himself—and he does not want us dwelling there. He is fully aware of that place of safety and security and will do all he can to lure us from it.

But Second Corinthians 2:11 reminds us that we should not be unaware of the Enemy's schemes, because he desires to take advantage of us. In other words, the Enemy uses cleverly devised plots and strategies to gain advantage in our lives—worries, cares, concerns, busyness, pride, self-sufficiency, ignorance, bliss, laziness—and he does that with the hopes of drawing us out from under cover.

We'll discuss these things at length in a later chapter, but as we move into this one, stop for a moment and ask God to increase your spiritual radar, giving you a greater awareness of the plots and devices of the Enemy so that you will not be caught unaware, unprotected and vulnerable to his attacks.

Hiding in God's Shelter

In Psalm 91's original language, the shelter, or "the secret place," as the King James translates it, is defined as a covering, or as "the hiding place" of God.[1] I like that! I understand hiding places.

Psalm 91 encourages us not just to visit but to dwell in God's hiding place—the secret place of the Most High. It's a great hideout, and God's hiding place doesn't need a "Do not enter" sign for the Enemy to know that he's not welcome there.

Hidden away in God, we are free from the devil's access and sheltered from the tyranny of the world. Psalm 61:3 says that God is a shelter and a refuge for us and "a tower of strength against the enemy" (NASB). We need to run into that strong tower and be safe. From there we are insulated from the Enemy's assaults, safely tucked away from his schemes, sheltered from his destruction and free from his devices. It's like coming under an umbrella in a rainstorm—we can still see the rain falling, we just aren't overwhelmed by the effects of it!

We have a lovely community park near my home in Wisconsin where I enjoy walking a scenic path that surrounds a quiet and serene river. I visit this park often to exercise and enjoy the leisurely two-mile trek around the river.

One day as I walked, the sky abruptly filled with black storm clouds, and I found myself caught in a torrential downpour. Much to my chagrin, my car was parked on the other side of the river, so I quickly ran for cover to the nearest rain shelter. Strangely enough, I'm not sure that I had ever noticed or appreciated the strategic locations of those shelters scattered throughout the park before, but that day they were a welcome gift.

As I sat under the safety of that cover, isolated from the effects of the storm raging around me, I couldn't help but think about Psalm 91. God is my shelter—a protection from the storms that rage around me. As I set sequestered in that refuge, the storm around me didn't stop, but I was insulated from its effects. I had chosen to run for cover, and I experienced the benefits of that decision!

The same is true of God's shelter of protection. There is no promise that the storms of life will cease—in fact, Jesus Himself said, "In this world you *will* have trouble" (John 16:33, NIV)—but when we choose to run for cover to the shelter of His protection, we will be insulated from the effects of life's storms that rage around us, safely tucked away in the hiding place of God. But tragically, so many of us, when caught in the storms of life, fail to run to God for shelter. Instead we seek refuge in the counsel of a friend or in the arms of a lover, or we try to wait out the storm. A shelter can only provide refuge for those who are willing to utilize it and who make the decision to flee to it for protection. We have to make the choice to run to the Lord in our time of need and be willing to admit our powerlessness, willingly responding to His open invitation to find refuge in Him, our strong and sturdy shelter. There is no safer hiding place to run for cover.

Voles Under Cover

My husband is a great gardener. He's British, so I think that gardening is an unwritten requirement for him! He takes great delight in a well-manicured lawn, and the gardens surrounding our home are breathtaking. I love nothing more than to sit on my front porch and soak up the beauty of the surroundings.

Some time back I noticed that the turf appeared to be dying off in certain areas of our lawn, and I was shocked by what seemed to be multiple underground tunnels forming under the grass. The beautiful yew trees that bordered the front of our home had begun to whither and dry up, and the twigs that remained on them no longer held their recognizable evergreen needles.

As I perused the rest of the landscape, I noted numerous burrow openings both in the lawn and in the mulched shrubbery. Upon closer examination, I noticed the head of a small, black, mouse-like creature dart out one of the openings and then quickly duck back in, disappearing before my eyes. I wondered if I had imagined the look of satisfaction in his beady little eyes and was sure that I had noted a smirk of delight on his furry face. Yes, a positive identification had been made; it was quite clear that my lawn had been invaded by voles! I had read about the culprits online and the extensive damage that they could cause, and I knew that I had to act quickly!

In the days that followed, I began a plan of attack that eventually played out like a scene from the movie *Caddyshack*. I read all I could about the varmints and visited every hardware store and pest control center in the area, applying each of their suggestions with meticulous detail. Nothing worked! I was on a search-and-destroy mission—me against the voles.

It seemed, however, that the voles were on a mission of their own—to aggravate the daylights out of me—and it was working! I had declared all-out war on the voles, and quite frankly, it appeared that they were winning! My husband would say that "obsessed" was an accurate description of my behavior, but I prefer to consider myself the conquering hero.

In the evenings while I watered my shrubbery, the unwelcome visitors emerged from their burrows, only to duck back under cover as soon as I made a move toward them. I provided countless hours of entertainment for my neighbors as I literally darted in and out of my shrubbery beds, aiming my hose full throttle at the five-inch beasts taking over my lawn! There seemed to be no solution to my all-consuming vole problem.

I considered dynamite, but my sweet husband thought that it might be overkill. No poison, no traps, no enticement to lure them out worked, and after months of frustration, the voles hadn't vacated, and my lawn remained a mess. But God in His faithfulness used those voles to provide me with a very accurate description of our need to run for cover and the protection afforded to us in His presence.

Just as I tried every way I could to catch those voles, the Enemy of our soul has declared all-out war against us, and Psalm 91:1 tells us that God is our refuge, and no weapon that the Enemy forms against us can prosper (see Isa. 54:17). No trap, no poison, no enticement of his can prevail in our lives as long as we stay under cover, safely burrowed away in the shelter of God's protection. Even my voles understand that concept!

A dear friend of mine struggles with a cyclical sin that seems to master his life. He loves Jesus, tries to live for Him, reads his Bible regularly and never misses church. How then does sin have a stronghold on him, you ask? Because he tries to fight it in his own strength instead of running for cover and trusting his battles to God. He white knuckles it. He has an incredible will and does well for a period of time, but then in a moment of weakness, he takes the enemy's bait and cycles downhill into the stronghold of sin at an alarming rate. He hates what this sin does to him and to his family, but he feels utterly powerless against it.

Recently I shared my vole illustration with him, and we talked about my inability to access those vexatious voles as long as they remained safely tucked away in their undercover burrows. I shared my frustrations about how the clever little varmints knew better than to indulge in the poisons I put out and refused to be lured into the live traps I set for them but especially about how much I hated how smart they were to duck under cover when I pursued them.

My friend immediately caught the parallel. He, like so many of us, ducks occasionally, but in his moments of weakness, he eyes the tasty bait or is lured out from under cover by the toxic poison disguising itself as a captivating delicacy that he can't live without. As a result, he is ensnared by the enemy of his soul in a trap that sucks the life out of him and his family.

We must not be unaware of the Enemy's schemes. "A prudent person sees trouble coming and ducks; a simpleton walks in blindly and is clobbered" (Prov. 22:3, MSG); or, as the Holman Christian Standard Bible puts it, "A sensible person sees danger and takes cover, but the inexperienced keep going and are punished." We need to run for cover into the shelter of the Most High God as if our lives depended on it, because they truly do.

Stable and Fixed

When I study the Word of God, I like to read several translations of the verse I'm studying. I am particularly fond of the Amplified Bible's classic edition for Psalm 91:1. It says, "He who dwells in the secret place of the Most High shall remain *stable and fixed* under the shadow of the Almighty [Whose power no foe can withstand]."

Our youngest daughter, Kendal, is a dynamic, confident four-teen-year-old. As the youngest of seven children, she has never lacked attention; each of her six older siblings have taken her under their wing and are intentional about sowing into her life. She is strong and self-assured. When she does something embarrassing or something that would make most people uncomfortable, she laughs and says, "I'm stable; I'm secure." I love that she can laugh at herself! I love even more that she is secure and confident in who God made her to be.

I wonder what *our* lives would be like if we were truly stable and secure in the person God created each of us to be. So many of our issues are rooted in insecurity, which leads to things like hatred, jealousy, envy, timidity, discord, low self-esteem and worthlessness. Insecurity is usually the root beneath gossip and the reason we can't celebrate other people's successes. It's time that we learn to be *stable and fixed* in who God says we are. That can only happen when we discover the truth of who we are in Him, which comes from being intentional about dwelling, living and abiding in the safety of His presence.

Remember, that word "dwell" doesn't just mean a casual relation-ship or someone who gets an occasional glimpse of God's glory. God is talking about a dweller, someone who is intentional about positioning himself in the presence of God. I've often pondered what Paul meant when he commanded us to "pray without ceasing" (1 Thess. 5:17). Is that even possible? It must be! But Paul didn't have nonstop verbal conversation in mind when he told us to pray continually. Rather, he meant for us to live in a place of uninterrupted communion and intimacy with God. That's the picture we see in Psalm 91—a place where we are intentional about dwelling, living and abiding in God's presence as we maneuver through this thing called life.

We need to be purposeful about being connected to and aware of God's presence as we walk through our day. We can be conversing with Him or praying quietly in our mind while we're washing dishes, cleaning our house, grocery shopping or sitting at our desk at work. We can ask the Lord about how to reply to a conversation we're having with someone even as we listen to that person speak. We can converse with God as we are exercising or out on a run. That's what Paul had in mind. He is exhorting us to be purposeful about living in a place of constant communion with God, because it is in that place of true connection that we realize that He alone is the giver of life (see Ps. 36:9, NET) and that it can be found in no other.

If you find yourself lacking life and vivacity at times, do a spiritual inventory and determine whether you are truly abiding in that place of uninterrupted communion with the giver of life or are seeking life from counterfeit and ineffectual sources that leave you empty and longing for more.

Finding Our Life in Him

The Bible says that we have died and that our real life "is hidden with Christ in God" (Col. 3:3). The word for "life" in this verse means "the absolute fullness of life,"[2] and while it points to eternal life, it conveys the idea of eternal life that began the moment we accepted Jesus Christ as our Lord and Savior. We can't find life in any other source. I've checked! I looked everywhere—under every rock, in every crevice and in all that the world has to offer. It's only found in Jesus.

No man or woman will ever love us enough—I have the best spouse, and he still doesn't do it for me. No child will ever fulfill us enough—I have seven (that's a perfect number), and they don't do it for me. No drug can make us high enough, no addiction can numb us enough.

We will never be successful enough or have enough money in the bank. When we finally get that bigger house that we've been dreaming of, we will just want someone to clean it for us. Only Jesus can give us what we need. Our *real* life is hidden in Him—in the secret place of the Most High.

Something that is hidden has to be discovered. We discover life when we seek God with all our heart and learn to dwell in His presence. My mother used to tell me, "You've got to get under the spout where the glory comes out!" It was good advice, and she knew it, because like me, she had tried everything else and had learned by experience that nothing could satisfy like Jesus. We must be intentional about positioning ourselves under the spout where the glory comes out—becoming purposeful about dwelling, living and abiding in the Lord's glorious presence—for it is there and only there that we will discover *true life* in its absolute fullness.

The International Standard Version renders Colossians 3:3 this way: "You have died, and your life has been *safely guarded* by the Messiah in God." I love that! If we truly believed that we were "safely guarded" in Him, would it change the way we lived?

If we really knew that we were secure in God, the way with interact with people would change drastically. We could take more risks in sharing our lives with others. It would no doubt impact our willingness to be real in our relationships.

It would cause us to be bolder in sharing our faith and in stepping out with God. If we really believed that we were guarded by the power of God, fear would have no place in our lives, and anxiety could have no impact on us. Oh, the value of understanding the "safe place" that we have in Him and the knowledge that nothing can touch us outside His perfect will.

Many of us look for security in everything other than a relationship with the Lord. We think that security and life can be found in the perfect job, the right salary, a certain someone, a loyal friend, a bigger bank account or perfect looks, when in reality those things are empty and unfulfilling. Only Jesus can make us secure. Only Jesus can satisfy. Jesus is the true source of our life and the One who can make us stable and secure.

Finding Our Security in God, Not Man

Prior to the vision that I had on that life-changing Sunday morning, my life was dominated by an insecurity that was rooted in the fear of man. I had a desperate longing for approval and a deep need to be accepted by those around me. I was filled with insecurity and never really felt safe. I did not understand who I was in Christ, and as a result, I looked for validation from sources other than the One who truly loved me and had promised to fulfill me.

I was a diehard people pleaser and worked tediously to earn the love and respect of everyone with whom I came into contact. This superwoman complex that drove my life was further fueled by the perfectionism that dominated everything I did.

I lived for the accolades and praise of man, even though I eventually realized that at best they only momentarily silenced the deep feelings of worthlessness that perpetuated the cycle that repeated itself over and over again. Living like this was draining, and I quickly found myself in shackles, realizing the truth of the proverb that says, "Fear of man will prove to be a snare" (Prov. 29:25, NIV).

My emotions were as unstable as shifting sand. Trying to obtain value and security from any source other than God was like trying to grasp a cloud with my hand. I worked laboriously to obtain the approval of man, performing tirelessly, serving endlessly, but it was like chasing after the wind. I longed to feel secure, to be at rest in who God said I was and to know the safety that could be found in no other source than Him.

The thing that impacted me most about the vision I received was the intense sense of safety and security I felt while in God's presence. I cannot find adequate words to explain the feeling. The knowledge that I was safe because my life was hidden with Christ in God, safely guarded by Him, burned like a fire within me in the months following the vision. He was my protector.

Head knowledge no longer motivated me; instead I learned by experience that being nestled away in His presence was a place of great safety and security, a place where I was already accepted in the Beloved and dearly loved. I didn't need to perform or earn my acceptance. I was deeply cherished and treasured by Him. I didn't need to protect myself or worry about all that loomed around me. In that secret place I knew that He was my stability and security and that there was no better place to reside. I no longer needed to fear confrontations or tiptoe around "porcupine" people. I was safe in Him. I could find no better hiding place.

My New American Standard Bible titles Psalm 91 "Security of the One Who Trusts in the Lord." Do we know that our security resides in Him? We need to establish that truth in our minds, because when trouble comes or something threatens our security, we will make the choice to run to the thing in which we trust.

When We Dwell, We Will Abide

The Hebrew word used for "Most High" is *elyown*. It means "highest, most high, supreme."[3] It is a title for the sovereignty of God. When we dwell in the shelter of the Most High, we abide with the God who is sovereign over all.

Notice that the word "sovereign" contains the word "reign." In other words, God is sovereign, and He reigns over all. He is in absolute control. There is no force greater, no power mightier. That is comforting. Kay Arthur says, "If God is not sovereign, if He is not in control, if all things are not under His dominion, then He is not the Most High, and you and I are either in the hands of fate (whatever that is), in the hands of man, or in the hands of the devil."[4]

I am glad that we are in the hands of a God who is sovereign over all and that our lives aren't left to fate. Anything that happens to us is under His dominion. When we are under the protection of the Most High God, the Almighty, the strongest of the strong, nothing can assail us, and hidden in His secret place, nothing can defeat us. And "if God is for us, who can be against us?" (Rom. 8:31). If the strongest of the strong is on our side, what do we have to fear? The transforming truth of Psalm 91 is that we are in a place of great security when we are intentional about positioning ourselves under God's shadow and abiding in His presence. "He who dwells in the shelter of the Most High *will abide* in the shadow of the Almighty."

The word "abide" means "to lodge, stop over, pass the night, remain, cause to rest or lodge." But this word has a negative connotation as well: "to show oneself obstinate, to be stubborn, to murmur against someone, to grumble, to harbor bad thoughts."[5] In other words, we can choose to abide in God's presence and remain in a place of rest, or we can stubbornly persist in thought patterns and behaviors that keep us from that place of rest.

Where do we abide? Do you pass our time living in bitterness and unforgiveness? Do we remain in a place of victimization and self-pity? Do we persist in grumbling and complaining and harboring bad thoughts and therefore find ourselves lacking rest and peace of mind? We serve a God who is supreme over all, sovereign and all-powerful. He rules over that thing that we refuse to let go of; He reigns over that situation that has made us bitter and unforgiving; He is above any pain or addiction that seems to dominate our lives. He is Most High!

We have a choice as to where we will abide. If you are stuck in bitterness or pain, instead of stubbornly persisting in a place of powerlessness, run for cover and begin to lodge in God's place of rest.

The opportunity to dwell in God's secret place is available to everyone, but as we noted in chapter 1, this promise of God is conditional. Not all of us will do what is necessary in order to be able to dwell there. Some of us are happy to be shallow Christians living out in the open, exposed to the Enemy's defeat—like the friend I mentioned earlier—never truly walking in the victory Christ secured for us. It takes work and intentionality to get to the place of dwelling. For some of us, it's just too much work; instead we are content to live mediocre, mundane lives.

I have lived on both sides of the fence, and I have found that our *real life* is truly hidden with Christ in God. We can't find abundant life in any other source. Run for cover to the secret place of the Most High God, and begin to experience the fullness of life that Christ died to secure for you.

THREE

He Is Our Safe Zone

I will say to the LORD, "My refuge and my fortress, my God, in whom I trust."
Psalm 91:2

In my basement is a chair that my husband and I have owned for over thirty years. Initially it was one of four matching oak chairs purchased with our kitchen table, part of a beautiful set designed by a carpenter.

As our family grew in size, we purchased a larger kitchen table. We gave the older table and three of the chairs to a friend of ours, retaining one chair for a built-in desk in our newly remodeled kitchen. Our kitchen was painted country blue, so we painted the chair the same shade of blue.

Years later I changed the kitchen décor, and we repainted the desk chair forest green. As our children grew older, our daughters requested a desk for their bedroom. We purchased a desk for them, painted the chair white, and moved the chair to their room.

Two of our sons are die-hard Manchester United fans, and when they were in their early teens, we redecorated their bedroom in a way that would have made even Wayne Rooney green with envy. Then— you guessed it—we painted the chair from the girls' room bright yellow to complement the team colors and moved it into the boys' room.

Eventually the chair was no longer needed. We stuffed it away in a corner of our basement, and for many years it went unnoticed, until I caught a glimpse of it one day as I was retrieving something from my basement freezer. Its paint was peeling, and I saw glimpses of country blue and forest green peeking through the layers. The bright yellow and red Manchester United colors were fading but still visible, and the specks of white brought back fond memories of my sweet girls sitting at their desk studying.

But underneath all those layers of paint was a beautiful oak chair that had been originally crafted by a carpenter. Tears filled my eyes as I realized how often I had done the very same thing to my own life that my family had done to this chair. I had been beautifully created and crafted by a Carpenter with a unique purpose and plan for me, but my fear of man and longing for acceptance had caused me to adapt to whatever environment in which I happened to find myself.

Like the chair that had been painted so many times, I had been guilty of "painting myself" to fit in, changing to become the person man wanted me to be instead of being content with the unique creation that God had made me to be. I had once been in the same condition as that battered chair hidden away in our basement, no longer resembling the Carpenter's original design, feeling discarded and of little value.

I knelt on the basement floor that day, undone by the fact that once again God was showing me that my fear of man was a snare and thankful that He was freeing me from that trap.

Created for a Purpose

God created us. He knit us together in our mother's womb. We are not accidents; we have been purposed and planned by God, fearfully and wonderfully made. We have been created in the image of God, and He doesn't want us recreating ourselves to bear the image of another. Each of us is His "masterpiece" (Eph. 2:10, NLT). But sadly, when we fear man more than we fear God, we will conform to the image that man wants us to be instead of resting in who God created us to be, forgetting that God is already pleased with us.

Somewhere along the line I began to believe the lie that I was not acceptable the way God had created me and that I needed to reinvent a Rhea that was more acceptable to others. Fear of rejection ruled my life, and I longed for a place where I truly felt safe and accepted for who I was—a place where I didn't need to "paint myself" to fit in and be free to be me! I desperately wanted to feel stable and secure, and that was the cry of my heart and the focus of my prayer life when God mercifully sent the vision that so impacted my life!

In the weeks following my vision, God spoke powerfully to me about being sheltered and protected in His presence. He showed me that by taking refuge in Him, I was safe and secure to be who He had created me to be. I didn't need to prove myself or make a good impression on others.

After my unexpected experience with the Lord, I suddenly became aware that nothing could happen to me outside His sovereign will and that He truly was my protector and defender. I didn't have to fear man any more. I was accepted in the Beloved and dearly loved by Him. I was indeed safe with Him.

How about you? Is God your refuge? Is He God in whom you trust, or do you put more value in man's opinion of you? God wants us to find refuge in Him and to rest securely in what He says about us. He does not want us to be constantly shaken by man's critical judgments or defined by man's opinion of us. He wants us to live securely in who we are in Him, understanding the immense value and worth that He has put inside us.

Putting too much weight in man's opinion is a snare, a carefully concocted trap by the Enemy to keep us from resting securely in the Lord. We must stop trying to be what other people want us to be and learn to be content with the magnificent creation that God created us to be.

Safe from the Enemy

All of us need a safe place where we feel protected, sheltered, and secure—a place where we can run in the midst of trouble or distress and find protection and safety. We look for that safe place in so many sources, but Psalm 91 tells us we can only find it in God. He promises to be our refuge and strength, our "ever-present help in times of trouble" (Ps. 46:1, GW). We just have to choose to run to Him.

When I was in elementary school, we used to play tag on the playground. Sometimes we made the game a little more challenging by adding "safe zones"—as long as a player was in the safe zone, he or she could not be tagged. However, the minute we left the safe zone, we were fair game.

Psalm 91 paints a picture of the safe zone that we have in Christ—a place where we can run and not be touched, where the enemy of our soul cannot access us. First John 5:18 in The Message expresses this beautifully: "The God-begotten are also the God-protected. The Evil One can't lay a hand on them." You and I are the God-begotten, and therefore in this game of "tag, you're it," we win, hands down! It's not even a competition as long as we stay under cover in the safe zone!

The Bible says, "The name of the LORD is a strong tower; the righteous run to it and are safe" (Prov. 18:10, NKJV). When we run to God and all that He is for cover, He becomes our safe zone—the fortress surrounding our life. Psalm 4:8 reminds us that it is God *alone* who makes us dwell in safety. There is no other means of defense.

We can install the most advanced in-home security system, bolt our doors, and sleep with a gun under our pillow. We can choose friends wisely, isolate ourselves, hold people at a distance and shield our hearts in order to keep from being wounded. We can cover our pain with humor and work day and night to excel. We can put up a wall of denial and refuse to look at the pain and trauma of our past. But our futile attempts to protect ourselves will fail miserably. God planned it that way, because He wants to be our safe zone, the One in whom we take refuge. It is God alone who makes us dwell in safety.

In Numbers 35 (see also Josh. 20; Deut. 19) God told Moses to command the children of Israel to appoint six cities of refuge. He told Moses that a criminal could flee to those cities and find protection from the avenger. These were cities of hope where someone who had done wrong could safely anticipate a new beginning. As long as he remained in the confines of that city, no one could touch him. The cities of refuge are reminders to us that God is our place of refuge—our very present help in times of trouble.

The word "refuge" is used three times in Psalm 91, and with each mention of the word, God doesn't promise to *provide* a refuge, He promises to *be* the refuge. There's a big difference! Hebrews 6:18 says that God is like those cities of refuge to whom we "have fled for refuge to lay hold of the hope set before us" (NKJV). We can run to Him for cover and be safe. Our souls are secure with Him. He shelters us from the punishment we deserve and provides us a place of safety from the destroyer, but like the children of Israel, we must choose to flee to Him for refuge and protection.

Making God's Promise Personal

The author of Psalm 91 was convinced that God is his refuge (his safe place) and His fortress (his stronghold and protection). Notice that he went from making a general statement in verse 1, "He who dwells in the shelter of the Most High will abide in the shadow of the Almighty," to a very personal statement in verse 2: "I will say to the LORD, '*My* refuge and *my* fortress.'" There is a vast difference between saying that the Lord is *a* refuge and that He is *my* refuge.

It's not unlike the day I married my husband so many years ago. On our wedding day David Briscoe became *my* husband. We are intimate; we have deep, personal connection; we love each other passionately. To me Dave is not just *a* husband, he's *my* husband. The author of Psalm 2 is making his statement personal by saying, "The Lord is *my* refuge and *my* fortress." It implies intimacy and a personal connection.

It is vital that we come to the place in our walk with Christ that His Word and His promises become personal for us. His Word cannot just be something we read and quote in order to look super spiritual; rather it must be truth applied, lived out and experienced daily in our lives.

We must not just read the Bible for information but meditate on it and seek God for revelation from it. The revelation we receive from Him makes His Word come alive to us, and as a result, it becomes personal and applicable to our everyday life.

The writer of this psalm took a truth about God and made it his own—it was personal revelation to him. He had learned by experience that God would be who He said He will be. The author had firsthand knowledge that God is the Great I Am and would be everything we need Him to be when we need Him to be. The author of Psalm 91 confidently believed that God was his refuge and his fortress and had absolute faith that he could put his trust in Him.

Can you confidently say that God is your refuge? Are you able to declare by personal experience that He is your fortress?

Building Walls

The problem that we have with trusting God is that we learn very early on that life can be a painful place. People who we trust to carry us drop us, and those who should be our protectors sometimes become our perpetrators. We feel vulnerable, unprotected and exposed, and rather than putting our trust in God, we learn very quickly to protect ourselves. Every hurt, every pain, every betrayal becomes a brick in our hand to begin creating the emotional walls that we erect to keep ourselves safe. Maintaining those walls becomes a full-time job and requires more emotional energy than most of us have.

One of my favorite scriptures is Isaiah 49:15–16: "Can a mother forget the baby at her breast and have no compassion on the child she has borne? Though she may forget, I will not forget you! See, I have engraved you on the palms of my hands; *your walls are ever before me*" (NIV). It's so comforting to know that God is familiar with our walls and that they are ever before Him. Others might not know that we have an emotional wall up, but God does. All our brokenness and woundedness lay open before Him. He's fully aware of it all.

A number of years ago, I happened upon a scripture from Lamentations 2 that read, "The LORD determined to tear down the wall around Daughter Zion" (2:8, NIV). The passage is talking about the devastation and desolation of Israel due to the judgment of God, but as I meditated on that scripture, I saw clearly that God was able to tear down our walls. Being aware of Isaiah 49:16, which says that our walls are ever before God, I knew that God was familiar with my walls, so I gave God permission to deconstruct the barriers that I had subconsciously constructed around my life.

Because over the years I had been deceived by the pride of my heart (see Obad. 1:3), I was not even aware that I had put up walls to keep myself safe. Walls to protect my heart and keep people from wounding and rejecting me. Walls to hold people at a distance and isolate myself from further pain. Walls that may have been necessary to protect me as a little girl but were no longer serving me well as an adult woman.

In Bible times the walls surrounding a city were built to defend it from attack. The walls that I had subconsciously constructed around my own heart functioned the same way, but little did I know that the same walls that kept people from hurting me also kept people from loving me. They severed me from the fullness of life and insulated me from intimacy with God and with others.

God Is Our Protector

I was trying to protect myself, but Scripture was clear: God wanted to be my safe zone, my protector, the One in whom I took refuge. He wanted to tear down my walls. But God's promise to be my refuge was conditioned upon my choosing to run to Him for cover and letting Him deliver me from patterns of behavior that provided me with a false sense of security.

I desperately wanted to be free but didn't know where to begin. But the fact that Lamentations 2:8 declared that God had *determined* to tear down the walls around the daughter of Zion brought me great comfort. The word "determined" reverberated in my mind. Being a determined woman myself, I understood the significance of the word, since nothing could stop me once I had firmly decided to do something. If I was like that in my humanity, what must the all-powerful God be like when He gets determined? I was encouraged! I was not able to bring down my own walls, but I could choose to take refuge in the One who was "determined" and put my trust in Him.

Lamentations 2:8 goes on to talk about the "ramparts" surrounding the walls of the daughter of Zion. Ramparts are fortifications that reinforce the walls, making them even stronger and less penetrable. I realized that each time I had been wounded or hurt, I had subconsciously fortified the walls in my life and made them even more impenetrable. Every time I was rejected, my walls were reinforced by vows that I purposefully made, declaring never to allow anyone close enough to hurt me again. Years of pain and heartache, rejection and abandonment had left my life more impenetrable than Fort Knox.

How do we risk allowing God to bring down the walls that have given us the illusion of safety for so many years or, for some of us, most of our lives? As I pondered Lamentations 2:8 and asked God about His determination to tear down Israel's walls, He led me to a verse in Zechariah: "'Jerusalem will be a city without walls. . . . And I myself will be a wall of fire around it,' declares the LORD" (2:4-5, NIV).

As we saw earlier, walls provided protection for a city. Why then would God declare that Jerusalem would be a city *without* walls? Because He wanted them to know that *He* would be their protection—a wall of fire around them.

A wall of fire cannot be penetrated. Anyone trying to break into a city through a wall of fire would put himself in danger and end up being consumed before he could get inside. One commentator thinks that this picture from Zechariah 2:5 of God being a wall of fire around Jerusalem "alludes to shepherds making fires about their flocks, or travelers that made fires about their tents in desert places to frighten wild beasts from them."[1] No matter how we look at it, it's a beautiful picture of God's protection.

The Apple of God's Eye

Proverbs 30:5 says that God "is a shield to those who take refuge in him." A beautiful picture of this is seen in Psalm 17:8, which tells us that we are the apple of God's eye. The apple of the eye refers to the pupil, and every bone in our faces is structurally formed to protect our eyes.

The eye is precious and needs to be shielded at all costs. As the apple of God's eye, we are precious to Him, and He promises to shield and protect us.

Additionally, the pupil is the center of the eye and the part of the eye that provides focus. Being the apple of God's eye means that we are always in God's focus and in the center of His vision; His eye is continually on us.

It gets even better, because Zechariah 2:8 says, "Whoever touches you touches the apple of his eye" (NIV). I especially like the New Living Translation: "Anyone who harms you harms my most precious possession." We are God's "treasured possession" (Deut. 7:6). Anybody who messes with us messes with God. It's a picture of God's deep loyalty and tender love toward us. We are the apple of His eye!

In the Hebrew language the word for "apple" (in terms of the apple of one's eye) is literally translated the "little man of the eye."[2] How great is that!

See, when we look someone in the eye, we can see a tiny reflection of ourselves in the person's pupil, and that's just good, because when we dwell closely with God in the secret place, we get close enough to Him to catch a glimpse of ourselves in His eye!

He becomes a mirror for us to view ourselves. The mistake I made for so many years of my life was to look to the world as my mirror and allow the reflection I caught of myself in others to define and hinder me.

Distorted Images

Our mirrors can be many things: parents, spouses, friends, coworkers, teachers, in-laws, the media, even our culture. Sometimes we allow our experiences and the circumstances of our life to act as mirrors for us. We catch a reflection of ourselves in the way others see us, in the way they treat us, in the things they say about us. We look to people to reflect an image that says, "This is who you are," and sadly, many of us receive that image as truth and rarely challenge it.

The Enemy of our soul, the one who comes to steal, kill and destroy, uses people as instruments to deposit lies into our hearts, and because we value people's opinion, and because they *should be* good mirrors, we believe the reflection that we see and allow our lives to be defined by it. Many times the people we use as mirrors are broken themselves or bent by sin, and as a result, the mirror in which we view ourselves is distorted and inaccurate.

A house of mirrors at a state fair or an amusement park is usually a maze-like attraction, the mirrors set up in such a way as to become obstacles to keep people from seeing themselves clearly. Many times the mirrors are designed to distort people's reflection in order to confuse them and limit their ability to successfully navigate the maze. Because of this people may find themselves stuck, paralyzed with fear, full of anxiety and unable to maneuver freely.

Some mirrors are concave or bent a certain way in order to make a person appear either super skinny (I like those best!) or super fat. If we look into a mirror like that and believe what we see, we will be misled by a lie and taken captive by a fraudulent representation of who we truly are.

What if a super skinny woman looked in the mirror that made her look super fat and assumed that the reflection she saw was accurate? She would probably begin dieting and exercising like a mad woman to try to make that image more acceptable and beautiful.

Then what if, after dieting successfully for a number of weeks, she returned to that distorted mirror and, believing that nothing had changed, returned to her dieting and exercising and became anorexic? It wouldn't matter how much the woman changed—as long as she used that same mirror, the image reflected back to her would be distorted, because the problem was never with her image but with the mirror.

As long as we use a distorted mirror, we will never have an accurate reflection of who we are.

We will never measure up if the mirror in which we see our reflection is broken or warped. We will always want to paint ourselves to fit in and use walls to protect ourselves. To get a truthful reflection, we need to change the mirror.

James calls the Word of God a mirror:

> If you listen to the word and don't obey, it is like glancing at your face in a mirror. You see yourself, walk away, and forget what you look like. But if you look carefully into the perfect law that sets you free, and if you do what it says and don't forget what you heard, then God will bless you for doing it. (James 1:23–25, NLT)

The only mirror we can totally trust is the Word of God. It is a perfect mirror. It's the only place where we can catch a true reflection of who we are in Him. It's accurate and life giving, but as with a mirror, in order to catch our reflection from it, we have to look into it.

It's vital that we spend time daily in the secret place of the Most High God, looking into His Word and meditating on it. We must take refuge in Him and what He says about us.

The truth of His Word is a place of protection for us. All other sources are distorted mirrors, bent by the same distorted truth that is warping us. We can't trust that refection; we must take refuge in Him instead.

When We Make Lies Our Refuge

When we allow others to define us, so much of what forms and molds us is lies—deceiving words that we believe as truth. Isaiah 28:15 says, "We have made lies our refuge, and under falsehood we have hidden ourselves" (NKJV). The New English Translation makes it even clearer: "We have hidden ourselves in a deceitful word." When we allow the things that people speak over us, the unfair judgments and distorted opinions that they mirror to us, to form us and shape our beliefs, we make lies our refuge—and we don't even realize it.

The word "lies" in Isaiah 28:15 means "anything that deceives."[3] The *Oxford Dictionary* defines "deceive" as "to cause someone to believe something that is not true, typically in order to gain some personal advantage."[4] So many of us have been made to believe something that is not true by the Enemy of our soul, and he has gained advantage over us as a result. We have allowed Susie down the street to define us instead of the King of Kings and Lord of Lords. We've been grossly misled.

The Bible identifies Satan as the Deceiver and the Father of Lies. Lies are his native language (see John 8:44). We do not fight "against flesh-and-blood enemies, but against evil rulers and authorities of the unseen world, against mighty powers in this dark world and against evil spirits in the heavenly places" (Eph. 6:12, NLT).

Our battle is not against people. The words that were spoken over us, the hurtful things that people said and did to us, the abuse that we endured, the heartache that we survived were never about flesh and blood. It was about the Enemy of our soul. Any place that reeks of deception surely has the Enemy behind it.

We must learn to identify the voice of the Father of Lies in our lives. The Enemy knows that if you and I get a revelation of who we truly are in Christ, we will be a force to be reckoned with, so he whispers his lies to entice us away from believing God's truth. His goal is to keep us from the destiny that God has for us and to paralyze us so that we will not manifest all that God created us to be.

The Enemy's lies are dangerous. If we believe a lie as truth, it forms a false belief, and all behavior is birthed from belief. If a lie is spoken over a child and embedded in him as truth, he will form a false belief about himself, and his behavior will flow from it.

Our lives and behavior will never be any better than the lies we believe about ourselves, and the treasure in us will never be manifested—it will be put in mothballs and hidden from the world—until the false belief is uncovered and conquered.

That's why it's so important that we allow God to examine our lives and to identify and tear down the refuge of lies that we have put our trust in.

Destroying Lies with the Truth

After telling us that "we have made lies our refuge," Isaiah 28 goes on to say that "hail will sweep away the refuge of lies" (Isa. 28:17). Hail is responsible for billions of dollars in property loss every year. In a hailstorm an unreliable or dilapidated property is more susceptible to destruction than a property standing on a firm foundation.

God wants to bring a hailstorm of truth to knock down the refuge of lies that we have put our trust in and put us back on a firm foundation. We might think that this is impossible or that it will require too much work, but God says that the lies that you and I believe are unreliable and defective and therefore will easily be destroyed by the truth of His Word.

Every belief we have about ourselves must be run through the test of His Word. We must ask ourselves, *Is this thought based on truth or birthed from a false belief whispered by the father of lies?* I like to run every thought and belief about myself through the criteria of Philippians 4:8. Is what I believe and think about true, noble, right, pure, lovely, admirable, excellent or praiseworthy? If not, it needs to be discarded.

I will allow my mind to be fixed only on thoughts that fit that criteria. We must learn to mind our mind and demolish any argument that sets itself up against the knowledge of God. We must "take captive every thought to make it obedient to Christ" (2 Cor. 10:5, NIV). I like that!

I have to personally take responsibility for my thoughts and *make* them obedient to Christ. We have a choice as to what we think on and believe; we do not need to receive the Enemy's lies as truth.

Perhaps the lies we believe were not whispered by the Enemy but rather spoken to us by someone we loved or respected. Or maybe someone who was extremely broken and wounded themselves spoke careless words to us, and we believed them and have been hurt by them ever since. We need to forgive that person and move on. It's time that we rise up and take responsibility for the things that we think on, the memories that we cherish, the lies that we allow to have prime real estate in our minds. God will not do for us what His Word commands us to do for ourselves. We have to choose to take our thoughts captive and make them obedient to Christ.

Refusing Others' Assessments of Us

David, a shepherd boy and the youngest son of Jesse, once had to evaluate what someone else wanted to put on him—and he had the courage to discard it immediately.

One day, when David was at home with his father in Bethlehem, his father summoned him to deliver food to his brothers at the Israelite camp, where they were in battle with King Saul. David arrived at the camp just as the Israelites were going out to battle against the

Philistines. Running to greet his brothers, he overheard a giant by the name of Goliath talking smack and intimidating the Israelites with his words. The Bible describes their reaction to the giant: "All the men . . . fled from him and were dreadfully afraid" (1 Sam. 17:24, NKJV).

David was shocked that an uncircumcised Philistine could defy the army of the living God, so the young shepherd boy volunteered to fight the giant. Everyone thought the idea was crazy, but David had seen God deliver him from the paw of the lion and the attack of the bear, and he was confident that God would do the same with this giant.

He understood, "If God be for us, who can be against us?" (Rom. 8:31). David had no doubt that he was under the shelter of the Most High and that God would be a refuge for him.

King Saul, however, was not as confident. He pointed out David's obvious youth and inexperience, but David refused to be moved by what man said about him. He knew to whom he belonged. He refuted the lies and continued in the strength of the Lord.

Eventually King Saul agreed to let the young shepherd fight Goliath, but he insisted on clothing David with his armor. The Hebrew word for "armor" in this passage doesn't just mean a defensive garment but additionally "measure" or "portion measured out to someone."[5] In other words, Saul didn't think that David measured up—so he gave him his armor.

David wanted to please Saul, so he agreed to wear the armor. It didn't take long, however, for David to realize that Saul's gear was heavy and cumbersome. He knew that it would hinder him, so he took it off: "David fastened his sword to his armor and tried to walk, for he had not tested them. And David said to Saul, 'I cannot walk with these, for I have not tested them.' So David took them off" (1 Sam. 17:39, NKJV).

The Hebrew word for "test" means "to try, to prove, to put to the proof."[6] Do we ever take the time to test or approve (or even better, disprove) what other people try to put on us? Do we take the time to determine if what they have said and done is the good and perfect will of God for our life? Do we take what they say and do to us as truth and allow it to become embedded in our mind, or do we keep our mind renewed with the truth of what God says about us and test and prove people's opinions against God's Word? Romans 12:2 tells us, "Do not conform to the pattern of this world, but be transformed by the renewing of your mind. Then you will be able to test and approve what God's will is—his good, pleasing and perfect will" (NIV).

I love that David rejected what Saul was trying to put on him and "put them off" (1 Sam. 17:39). In other words, he refused to let Saul's armor have any place in his life. He wasn't going to carry what someone else had tried to clothe him with and let it hinder his ability to fight.

Casting Off Dead Weight

Too often we allow others to point out our shortcomings and clothe us with an image that they think is acceptable, causing us to walk through life burdened and restricted by unkind words, unfair expectations, hurtful memories and tainted judgments. But this only happens when we do not stay in the refuge of God's truth and keep our minds renewed with the reality of who we are in Christ. It's time that we put off those things that keep us from fighting the good fight and allow God to bring a hailstorm of truth to demolish any lies in which we have taken refuge.

Hebrews 12:1–2 tells us,

> Let us strip off and throw aside every encumbrance (unneces-
> sary weight) and that sin which so readily (deftly and cleverly)

clings to and entangles us, and let us run with patient endur-
ance and steady and active persistence the appointed course of
the race that is set before us, looking away [from all that will
distract] to Jesus. (AMPC)

Now "the sin which so easily and cleverly entangles us" is not
always *our* sin—it can sometimes be the sin of others that clings to us
and hinders us from running our race well. We must stop allowing
others to clothe us and begin to test what people say to us against the
truth of the Word of God.

I have a friend whose mother buys all her clothing. I would love
that, but my friend does not. She's a full-grown adult, capable of
buying her own clothing, and she resents that her mother insists
on doing it for her. I always chuckle, though, because she accepts
the clothing and wears it anyway, even though the clothes her mom
buys are not my friend's style, and they never fit her. Whenever she
wears them, her whole day is impacted negatively . Why then doesn't
she refuse to wear them? Why, like David, doesn't she put them off?

I don't know, but this is exactly what we do with other people's
expectations, opinions, preferences, memories, even their dreams
and desires instead of resting in who God says that we are! We need
to put off those "uncomfortable clothes" and refuse to accept them
as truth in our lives.

God is our only true refuge and the One in whom we can put our
trust. Psalm 62:8 says, "Trust in him at all times, O people; pour out
your heart before him; God is a refuge for us." "Trust" here means "to
have confidence in, to set one's hope and confidence upon any one,
to be secure and fear nothing for oneself."[7] It's a picture of having a
secure, bold confidence in and reliance upon God. It's a trust so strong
that when we exercise it, we fear nothing, because we are secure in
Him.

God wants to be a refuge for us—a safe place where we can pour out our soul, spill out our emotions and shed some of the stinking thinking and false beliefs that hinder us. In Hebrew the word "pour" in Psalm 62:8 is translated "to spill, to shed, to pour out."[8] We are to "shed" our soul before God. With Him we can be ourselves; we don't have to perform for Him. We are accepted in the Beloved and dearly loved by Him. We can rest, letting go of any spirit of intimidation and relish unashamedly and unapologetically all that He created us to be.

Let's run for cover to the safe place of the Father's protection and let Him tear down any refuge of lies in which we have previously taken cover. He is a reliable, steadfast refuge in whom we can completely place our trust.

FOUR

Surely He Will Deliver Us

He will deliver you from the snare of the fowler.

Psalm 91:3

My mother died in late 2009. She was my closest friend and confidant, and I loved her dearly. Her passing marked the culmination of a year that was without a doubt the worst year of my life.

The difficulties had begun in January, when someone I loved had hurt me deeply—so deeply that I could hardly function. Quite honestly, the pain was so profound that I could say with Paul that I "despaired even of life" (2 Cor. 1:8, NKJV). I wanted to die.

Not too long after that one of our children started spinning out of control, making choices that were not good and reaping the negative consequences. I was devastated by some of the decisions he was making and felt powerless to stop it.

As if that was not enough, I developed an eating disorder that just about destroyed my life. Looking back now, I see that the eating disorder stemmed from the fact that my life was completely out of control and the only thing I *could* control was my eating.

Ironically, it turned out that my eating controlled *me*! I would look at a plate of food, and panic would seize me. I was obsessed with calculating the number of calories that each morsel contained and knew exactly how long I would have to exercise to burn off each precious bite of food.

I was compelled to exercise, sometimes getting up in the middle of the night to spend an hour or two on the treadmill—just in case I had miscalculated the calorie count or forgotten to account for something I had eaten. The addiction consumed my life—the compulsion drove me. I was spiraling downhill fast on a path of destruction, like a freight train out of control.

It was in the midst of all this turmoil that I received word that my mother had developed a complication from a routine outpatient surgery and was not expected to survive. I was shocked. I had called her the night before her surgery to wish her well and had told her that I would check on her when she got home the next afternoon. She never returned home. I rushed to the hospital in time to hold her hand as she took her last breath and stepped into glory.

The pain of that loss was astronomical. The heartache from all that was happening in my life was profound. Meanwhile, my addiction intensified, and I became more desperate than I had ever been in my life. I felt defeated and without hope, and I cried out to the One who had promised to deliver.

My speaking schedule was extremely heavy during that time. My calendar was booked two years in advance, and I was speaking across the country almost every weekend. One of the things I had always prided myself in is that I would never preach something that hadn't first preached to me. I refused to proclaim something about God that I didn't believe myself. I absolutely would not step into a pulpit and declare that God was a bondage breaker if I was in bondage or talk about victory in Jesus if I was living in defeat. I refused to minister from a place of hypocrisy and falsehood. So because of the bondage that was dominating my life, I canceled every engagement that I had scheduled and began a quest—not just to study about the God who could deliver, not just to put together a good sermon about a God who was able, but to experience His deliverance firsthand in my own life.

Surely!

The King James Version of Psalm 91:3 says, "Surely he shall deliver thee from the snare of the fowler, and from the noisome pestilence." "Surely" is a powerful word. It is a statement of confidence, a declaration of certainty that God is able to deliver. I experienced this truth personally, and I can exclaim with the writer of Psalm 91 that *surely* our God is able to deliver us.

The author of this psalm was absolutely confident that what he was saying was true; he had no doubt in God's ability. His assurance came from knowing His God. He didn't just know *about* God, He obviously had a relationship with Him and had spent time with him. We know from verse 1 that he knew the importance of making the Lord his dwelling place and of abiding in His presence. He spent time with the Father and was intimate with Him.

The psalmist is saying, "I know my God; I've made him my dwelling place. You can trust me when I say that surely He will deliver you." He doesn't say that "maybe" God will deliver us, or if we are good enough He might deliver us. There is absolutely no doubt in his mind—*surely* He will deliver us.

Many reading this might find themselves in the throes of addiction, as I once did. The bondage you are in may seem more powerful than anything you've ever faced. Your fear may be paralyzing. Perhaps you've surrendered to it and think that you can just deal with the captivity, maintain it and live in it for the rest of your life. But I can testify from my own experience that *surely* our God delivers. I'm confident of it, because He did it for me, and He is not a respecter of persons. *Surely*, absolutely, indisputably our God delivers us all.

No one has to stay addicted, no one has to live in despair and no one is at the mercy of hopelessness or helplessness. No marriage is too far gone. No one is too deep in debt. Surely our God is able to deliver!

"I Do Myself!"

One of the reasons we remain stuck in hopeless situations is that we sometimes think that we don't need God—that we are able to deliver ourselves. We might think that we can fix ourselves, break that habit or overcome that addiction. Perhaps some of us have even put off surrendering to Christ until we get our lives straightened out. But no matter how hard we try, we can't fix ourselves.

Our youngest daughter, Kendal, has been fiercely independent since she was born. The youngest of seven children, she learned very quickly how to survive in a busy, chaotic household. She is now a determined and strong young woman, and I have no doubt that her tenacity and individualistic personality will serve her well in life.

One Sunday morning when Kendal was just a toddler, as we were about to go out the door to church, I directed the children to put their shoes and coats on. Excitedly our indomitable little Kendal declared, "I do myself!" and with that she grabbed her coat and shoes and dove for cover under the kitchen table. "Not today you aren't," I replied, and I sent one of her older siblings under the table to retrieve her.

Not missing a beat, she darted out from the other side of the table and scurried upstairs to her bedroom, triumphantly locking the door behind her! (This would be a good time for me to offer a bit of seasoned advice and strongly recommend that parents *not* put locks on their children's bedroom doors!) Not one to give up easily, Kendal shouted from inside her securely locked fortress, "I be right out. I do myself!"

Now my husband is a pastor, and any pastor's wife will tell you that there is an unwritten rule for ministry families: never be late for church! I have to be honest and admit that we were late every Sunday morning. I'd like to say that it was because of my teenage daughters, but it wasn't. It was because of Kendal Charis.

Week after week we went through the same routine, and Sunday after Sunday as I stood outside her bedroom door, pleading for her to let me help her tie her shoes and zip her coat, I could hear the Lord's still small voice saying to me, "Do you hear her, Rhea? She sounds just like you: 'I do myself, Lord! I got this one under control; I'll call You if I need You. I do myself!'"

Eventually little Kendal would stubbornly emerge from behind the locked door with her shoes still untied and her coat still unzipped. Why? Because she couldn't do it herself. She needed someone bigger than she was to help her. The same is true of you and me. We can't deliver ourselves. We need Jesus. And the good news is, He is able.

The Snare of the Fowler

The writer of Psalm 91 uses the picture of a fowler's snare to describe our need for deliverance from the traps of the Enemy: "He will deliver you from the snare of the fowler" (91:3). A fowler is a trained bird catcher, and a snare, of course, is his trap. The word translated "fowler" in the Hebrew language means "bait-layer" or "trapper."[1]

Most fowlers capture their prey by using nets. The goal is to lure the bird in with enticing bait. When a bird takes the bait, a trigger is released and the animal finds itself entrapped by the net. The more the little bird struggles, the more entrenched it becomes. All attempts to free itself will only cause additional injury or intensify its entanglement.

While in the trap, the bird is at the mercy of the fowler, who cleverly remained concealed until the bird took the bait.

When the writer of Psalm 91 declares that God will deliver us from the snare of the fowler, he has in mind the snares of the Enemy of our soul. My eating disorder was a trap, set by the Enemy. He was a calculated bait layer. The bait was enticing, and I became profoundly ensnared. The more I struggled to free myself, the more deeply entrenched I became. Just like a little bird caught in a snare is not able to free itself, we too need help to be delivered from the traps of the Enemy. Our struggle will only cause further entanglement and deeper bondage. We need a deliverer.

Psalm 91:3 promises that God will be just that for us. We need only stand still and watch the deliverance of the Lord. Second Chronicles 20:17 confirms this: "You shall not need to fight in this battle; take your positions, stand still, and see the deliverance of the Lord [Who is] with you" (AMPC). God wants to spring us from any trap that the Enemy uses to ensnare us; He wants our soul to be free from all that is holding us captive.

In the book of Luke we read that Jesus stood up in the synagogue and read from Isaiah 61. Applying the text to Himself, He announced that He was sent "to heal the brokenhearted, to proclaim liberty to the captives and recovery of sight to the blind, to set at liberty those who are oppressed" (Luke 4:18, NKJV). Jesus doesn't want us captive to the ploys of the Enemy.

The psalmist exclaims in Psalm 124:7, "Our soul has escaped as a bird from the snare of the fowlers; the snare is broken, and we have escaped" (NKJV). A bird caught in a snare is powerless to help itself; all it can do is cry out for a deliverer. We are no different. But God will provide a way of escape if we cry out to Him. Scripture says, "No temptation has overtaken you that is not common to man. God is faithful, and he will not let you be tempted beyond your ability, but with the temptation he will also provide the way of escape" (1 Cor. 10:13).

Do We Want to Be Healed?

We noted earlier that sometimes we stay stuck in our troubles because we try to deliver ourselves. But there is another reason we remain in our trials: sometimes God provides a way of escape, and in our ignorance we refuse to take it. Quite frankly, some of us like our bondage.

Oh, we may not identify it as bondage, and we probably don't realize that we are in a trap set by the Enemy, but we have been living as captives for so long that it has become our normal.

Jesus approached a man like this as he lay by the pool of Bethesda in Jerusalem. Scripture says that "a multitude of invalids—blind, lame, and paralyzed" (John 5:3) lay near this pool, hoping to be healed, and the man Jesus approached was one of those invalids. The King James Version uses the word "impotent" to describe these people. It means "to be weak, needy, without strength, powerless."[2]

John tells us that a great multitude of impotent people were gathered there together. Isn't it funny how we surround ourselves with people as broken as we are—people of like mind with the same type of weaknesses that we have, people who keep us stuck instead of holding us accountable?

We shouldn't surround ourselves with yes men; we need to be intentional about surrounding ourselves with people who will call us up higher instead of pulling us down lower.

Part of breaking free from our traps is being willing to look at the things that keep us stuck and then doing something different. Albert Einstein described insanity as "doing the same thing over and over again and expecting different results."[3] That's what happens when we repeat patterns of behavior that keep us impotent and powerless instead of taking the way of escape that God so willingly provides.

Why were all these invalids drawn to the pool of Bethesda? It's likely that someone was healed at some point and now others flocked to this pool, putting their hope in something that really had no ability to help.

Apparently an underground spring under the pool of Bethesda would bubble up, and tradition tells us that the people believed that an angel was stirring the water. At that point, whoever got into the pool first was healed of whatever infirmity he or she had.

Picture it in your mind! A great multitude of crippled people— that's not just one or two—all racing to get to the water *first*. I'm sure it was quite a sight. Aren't you glad that it's not first come, first serve with God?

His healing power is not in limited supply; His willingness is not biased or partial. His ability is boundless and unmatched. His arms are wide open, beckoning us closer and He longs for us to be all that He created us to be.

In the midst of this crowd, the man whom Jesus approached that day had been an invalid for thirty-eight years. The word translated "invalid" in John 5:3 means that the man had "a weakness or a want of strength."[4] The Amplified Bible's classic edition says that he'd had a "a deep-seated and lingering disorder for thirty-eight years."How many of us have deep-seated and lingering issues that plague our lives? Or a weakness that leaves us crippled, feeling powerless and without life?Perhaps it's something that has plagued us for thirty-eight years— maybe something that happened when we were a child that left us feeling paralyzed with fear or traumatized by pain.

Something had happened in this impotent man's life thirty-eight years earlier that had rendered him powerless and without hope. And he had lived that way from then on! But oh, when Jesus shows up, everything changes.

The Bible says, "When Jesus saw him lying there and knew that he had already been there a long time, he said to him, 'Do you want to be healed?'" (John 5:6). *Okay, we might think, what kind of question is that? Of course he wants to be made well! He's been an invalid for thirty-eight years!* But did he? Do we?

Jesus is walking into our lives today, asking us the same question: "Do you want to be healed?" Are we tired enough of living where we have been living, in the condition we've been in? Have we reached the point at which we are ready to say to Jesus, "Whatever it takes, whatever needs to be done, I want to be whole again?"

Jesus "saw" the man lying there. In the original language the word "saw" means "to look at, to examine, to inspect, to see and ascertain what must be done about it."[5] Jesus sees us too. We might think that nobody truly sees us, but Jesus does. He is El Roi, "the God who sees me" (Gen. 16:13, NIV). Some of us have spent our lives trying to attract attention by dressing provocatively or by excelling and achieving. But Jesus notices us!

That's scary for some of us, because we know that our life is a mess, and quite frankly, we hope that He *doesn't* see us! But He does, and He knows the condition we are in and has already ascertained what must be done about it.

Not only does Jesus see us—He also knows us. "When Jesus saw him lying there and *knew* that he had already been there a long time, he said to him, 'Do you want to be healed?'" (John 5:6). Jesus saw the man and "knew." The word "know" means "to understand, perceive, have intimate knowledge of."[6] The man may not have known Jesus, but Jesus knew him, and He approached him that day with the question that He brings to you and me today: "Do you want to be healed?"

Look how the man replied to Jesus' kind offer: "Sir, I have no one to put me into the pool when the water is stirred up, and while I am going another steps down before me" (5:7). Can you hear the whine in his response? Jesus asked the man a yes-or-no question, and he replied with an excuse as to why he was the exception to the rule. He deflected the blame for his crippled state onto someone else, pointing the finger, painting himself as a victim, assuming no responsibility in the matter.

We do the same:

- "I wouldn't be so angry if I'd had a better childhood."
- "I wouldn't be crippled with bitterness if I hadn't been sexually molested as a child."
- "I'd be a better man if my dad hadn't walked out and left me without an example."
- "I wouldn't feel so rejected if he hadn't left me for a younger, more beautiful woman."

Now many of us have been truly hurt, and I am not trying to minimize the pain. Trust me, there is very little that you could tell me that I would not be able to say, "Been there, done that, got the T-shirt." But I do know that none of us needs to stay hurt. We have to stop blaming others for the things that have happened to us and make up our mind that we really want to be made well.

The King James Version quotes Jesus as saying, "*Wilt thou* be made whole?" The Greek word translated "wilt" is *thelō* and means "to will, have in mind, intend, to be resolved or determined, to purpose."[7] In other words, our will is involved in our healing. As we noted, God promises to always give us a way of escape, but we must choose to take it. Apparently the man did just that, because when Jesus told him, "'Get up, take up your bed, and walk,' . . . at once the man was healed, and he took up his bed and walked" (John 5:8–9).

It's not possible for us to be in the presence of a holy God and remain unchanged, as this man discovered. Scripture tells us that Jesus is "the same yesterday and today and forever" (Heb. 13:8). The challenge for us is to truly believe by faith that Jesus doesn't "change like shifting shadows" (James 1:17, NIV), to believe that the same God who healed a cripple at the Pool of Bethesda can work wonders in our own lives. God said it, and that settles it! What would the church be like today if we truly took Him at His Word and believed with outrageous faith?

If we want to be made well, we have to be determined to get into the secret place of the Most High and say, "Lord, I believe that You are my deliverer. I believe that You are God and that nothing is impossible for You. I choose to line up my will with Yours, and I will begin believing that surely my God will deliver me from this trap, from this prison of my own making, from this stronghold of the enemy. I resolve to trust in You and choose to stand still and watch the deliverance of the Lord."

Surely God is able. If we remain crippled, it is because we choose to. We are not powerless; we are powerful in Him. We are not victims; we are victors in Him. The same power that raised Christ from the dead is living inside us. Get up and walk! We need to make up our mind that we want to be whole again and then leave our place of powerlessness, walking away from what has kept us comfortably crippled.

Getting Over Our Unworthiness

A final reason that some of us don't receive God's deliverance is because we don't feel worthy to ask for God's help. Maybe we blame ourselves because of choices we have made. Maybe we think that we have maxed out God's ability to forgive us or that we have stepped over the line and pushed His buttons one too many times. Perhaps we think that we've disappointed God too much to ask for His help or that our choices have completely separated us from His love. Or maybe, just maybe, we think that God could never love us—that we are too flawed or too sinful.

But God loves us with an everlasting love. Nothing we do can separate us from it. He's not angry with us or disappointed that we fell into a snare or took the Enemy's enticing bait. He's not put off or intimidated by what holds us captive. He endured the cross so that we didn't have to endure one more moment of being crippled or trapped.

During my incredibly painful year, I had many reasons to believe that I was unworthy of God's deliverance as I battled with the grip of my eating disorder. But as I sought God, I was strengthened to believe that He was a bondage breaker and that I needed to push away my sense of guilt and failure and call out to Him for help and deliverance. And you know what? He heard me and set me free, and He restored my life.

Cry out to him like a bird caught in a net. None of us is too far gone. Surely—absolutely, certainly, undoubtedly—our God will deliver us.

FIVE

Avoiding the Enemy's Traps

He will deliver you from the snare of the fowler.

Psalm 91:3

W hen I was a little girl, I loved to go muskrat trapping with my brother, Ron. Memories of rising before dawn to check and reset the traps that we had strategically placed the day before are still vivid in my mind forty years later.

My brother is an avid hunter and an outdoor enthusiast. I'm sure that dragging his little sister along with him was not high on his list of priorities, but he seemed to love teaching me the ins and outs of proper trapping and was patient with me. He taught me the importance of placing the trap correctly, but he also explained to me how paramount it is to use the appropriate bait when setting the trap.

Both placement of the trap and the correct use of bait are vital. For example, when setting a mousetrap, a person needs to place it in the proper surroundings so that the unsuspecting mouse innocently stumbles upon it and is ensnared before it realizes what has happened. The person would also need to use bait that would entice the mouse and lure it in. A reasoning person would never bait the trap with a worm—that only works for catching trout. He would use something that he knows the mouse likes: cheese.

Did you know that if you want to trap a skunk, the best bait to use is grape jelly? Who would have guessed! If you want to trap a coyote, the best way to do it is with watermelon slices. Trappers have websites devoted to helping others use the right kinds of bait in order to avoid wasting any time with the wrong bait.

Our Enemy does not waste his time using the wrong bait either. For a vulnerable woman who is not confident in herself and who seeks the affirmation of men, he will use a trap set with a good-looking man who says all the right things.

For a man living in a loveless marriage whose wife does not affirm him the way he wants to be affirmed, a woman may come up to him and say, "Oh, you work so hard for your wife. She's so lucky to have you. Talk to me about it." For a person who has a fear of rejection, watch for a trap bearing the bait of rejection by one friend after another.

If alcohol is someone's weakness, and that person is trying hard in his own strength to break free, the Enemy will bring a friend along who will lure that person to the bar on Friday night.

The Enemy will hit on our weak spot. The bait that works for you might not work for me. But he knows what will tempt each of us.

Our Enemy has studied us; he knows our weaknesses and vulnerabilities. He is keenly aware of where the trap needs to be placed in order for you and me to innocently stumble upon it, and he knows the proper bait to use. He is cold. He is calculating. He is not in any hurry to get us into the trap, because when he gets us, he wants us to be caught for a very long time. So he carefully places his traps and lays his bait to entice us so that, *snap*, we will be caught.

We need to pray constantly, "Don't let me be unaware of the Enemy's schemes," because we don't want to unsuspectingly stumble into one of his snares.

The Trap of Offense

I was grieved when I read the *International Standard Bible Encyclopedia*'s summary on the word "snare." It explains, "There was a practice of sewing a captured bird's eyelids together and confining it so that its cries would call large numbers of birds through curiosity and they could then be taken in the trap."[1] We have an enemy who does things like that!

The devil uses many types of traps to entice us away from the Lord's presence, and one of those traps is the offenses caused us by other people. Our Enemy is not omnipresent—he can't be everywhere at once—so he employs other minions to lay traps for you and me as believers. Of course he uses principalities and evil forces, but he also uses people who are ignorant of his devices or who are blinded to the things of God to help him devise and set traps for us. Like the fowler, the Enemy of our soul blinds the eyes of gullible people and traps them in his snare, and they in turn call out and lure others into bondage with them.

Think about the child molester, drug dealer or adulterer who destroys whole families because that person is blind to the trap that he or she is in. Jeremiah 5:26 says, "Wicked men are found among my people; they lurk like fowlers lying in wait. They set a trap; they catch men." We need to be careful not to allow offenses to draw us away from the Lord—and we also need to be sure that we do not make ourselves available as a tool for the Enemy to use to snare others.

Jesus makes it clear in Luke 17:1-2 that offenses will surely come:

> Then He [Jesus] said to the disciples, "It is impossible that no offenses should come, but woe to him through whom they do come! It would be better for him if a millstone were hung around his neck, and he were thrown into the sea, than that he should offend one of these little ones." (NKJV)

The Greek word translated "offense" in this verse is *skandalon*. It means "the movable stick or trigger of a trap."

In his book *The Bait of Satan*, John Bevere says that "this word originally referred to the part of the trap to which the bait was attached. Hence the word signifies laying a trap in someone's way. In the New Testament it often describes an entrapment used by the Enemy. Offense is a tool of the devil to bring people into captivity."[2]

Picture a mousetrap. The *skandalon* is the part of the trap where the bait is placed—where the cheese is attached, if you will (or, if you are from Wisconsin, where the peanut butter is placed, because we value our cheese). Now if someone sets a mousetrap, what happens when the mouse comes and takes the bait? *Snap!* He's caught and unable to get free.

Do you see the picture that Jesus is drawing for us? He is saying, "You can be *sure* that offenses will come." In other words, count on it! We can be sure that people will hurt us.

But what we need to keep in mind is that offense is bait on a trap. Don't take the bait!

Countless people are wounded and angry, filled with hatred and rage, bitterness and unforgiveness over something that someone did to them years ago, and they feel justified in their behavior. They don't realize that the offense they have nursed was a trap set by the Enemy of their soul—bait to lure them in.

Our unforgiveness, however, isn't hurting that person who hurt us ten years ago. *We* are the ones who are trapped, caught in the enemy's scheme to render us powerless and ineffective for Christ.

My momma used to tell me, "Forget vengeance, Rhea. The best revenge is a life lived well." If we have held on to an offense that someone has perpetrated against us, we need to cry out to the One who is able to deliver us and repay the person by living well!

Overlooking Offenses

As we have seen, offense can be a very effective bait of the Enemy. What do we do when someone offends us, especially when we have been deeply and seriously wounded?

Proverbs 19:11 says, "It is to one's glory to overlook an offense" (NIV). This is the point that we must endeavor to get to in our lives. If someone offends us or tries to hurt us, rather than strike back or say something nasty in return, we should seek to walk away and say, "That's a trap, and I am not taking the bait! I am not unaware. It is to my glory to overlook an offense."

In order to do this, it is vital that we keep in mind that we "are not fighting against flesh-and-blood enemies, but against evil rulers and authorities of the unseen world, against mighty powers in this dark world, and against evil spirits in the heavenly places" (Eph. 6:12, NLT). We need to change the way that we think about the people who offend us. The person who hurt us is, in actuality, a tool in the hand of an expert bait layer. The Enemy has sewn their eyes shut and blinded them to what they were doing, so we need to overlook the offense and begin fighting against the true enemy.

You might wonder how it's possible to overlook an offense that has hurt you so deeply. In chapter 2 of this book we saw that the prophet Zechariah wrote, "Whoever touches you touches the apple of [God's] eye" (Zech. 2:8, NIV). Our facial structure is designed to protect the pupil of the eye. When something dangerous comes toward our face, our first instinct is to cover our eyes—to protect what is fragile and precious to us: our sight. Whoever touches you and me touches the apple of God's eye, and He will respond to protect and cover us from injury. Knowing that makes it easier for us to walk away from offense and not take the bait. If someone hurts us, we can walk away unoffended, refusing to be caught in the trap of offense, because we know that the person has just touched the apple of God's eye, and whoever messes with us messes with God.

Have you taken the bait of offense and become trapped in unforgiveness? Have you been wounded by someone's words and become ensnared by deadly bitterness? Has someone done you dirty, and you find yourself caught in the claws of self-pity and anger? Let that person go—it was never about him or her anyway. The offense is a trap set by the Enemy of your soul. And Psalm 91:3 makes it clear that God intends to free us from the snare of the fowler. Don't take the bait! Whoever touches us touches the apple of God's eye. We need to remember that and get on with our lives. It's to our glory to overlook an offense.

The Trap of Wrong Thinking

Another area that the Enemy loves to trap us is in our thinking. He uses his lies, entices us with his whispers and ensnares us with wrong thinking. We must learn to be intentional about walking in victory when it comes to the battle for our mind, will and emotions.

So much of the overcoming power that God secured for us depends on our willingness to take every thought captive to the obedience of Christ and to mind our minds. We can't allow ourselves to have a thought that is contrary to the thoughts that *He* has about us. We must gird up our minds—sweeping them clean of thoughts that don't line up with the Word of God. We have the mind of Christ, and we must always yield to it. So many of us walk in defeat as a rule and in victory as the exception—but that flies in the face of all that God secured for us on the cross of Calvary.

Colossians 3:15 is a beautiful passage about allowing the Lord and His Word to have the final authority over the anxious thoughts and destructive lies that try to exploit our thinking:

> Let the peace (soul harmony which comes) from Christ rule
> (act as umpire continually) in your hearts [deciding and set-
> tling with finality all questions that arise in your minds, in that
> peaceful state] to which as [members of Christ's] one body you
> were also called [to live]. (AMPC)

"You" is the understood subject of this verse. Paul is saying, "*You* let the peace of God rule in your hearts." It's a command, but we have a choice as to whether or not we will obey it. Will we let God's peace rule in our mind, will and emotions, or will we let destructive and anxious thoughts reign? Will we let confusion, anxiety and unforgiveness rule our thoughts, or will we be saturated and filled with the peace of God? We must mind our minds and not fall into the trap of the enemy.

It's interesting to me that in this verse the words "let" and "rule" are the same in the Greek. It is the word *brabeuō*, which means "to be an umpire," "to decide, determine," or "to direct, control, rule." It actually comes from the Greek word meaning "to arbitrate, govern, rule."[3] If we want to avoid the Enemy's snare when it comes to our thinking, we must determine to let the peace of God "umpire" and rule our hearts—our mind, will and emotions.

As we saw in the previous chapter, Psalm 124:7 says, "Our soul has escaped as a bird from the snare of the fowlers" (NKJV). The word "soul" means "the seat of the emotions and passions, the activity of the mind, the activity of the will and the activity of the character."[4] That's where the Enemy will try to trap us. He's after our character. We need to decide what will have control of our hearts and minds. What we will allow to umpire and have the final say in our lives? Will it be the devil's accusations and lies or the peace of God?

Recently while attending a major league baseball game, I gained a deeper understanding of the importance of using an umpire to arbitrate final decisions. My husband surprised me one night with tickets to a Milwaukee Brewers home game. I loved it! That's my kind of date night.

It was early in the baseball season, and quite frankly, the Brewers were not off to a good start. This game, however, was a close one, and the fans were enthusiastic, hoping for a win. In the seventh inning one of my favorite players grounded the ball to second. As he sprinted to first base, the second baseman on the opposing team threw the ball to first at the same time that our player stepped on the bag. It was a close call, but the runner appeared to be safe at first.

The first-base umpire, however, called him out. The crowd thundered in uproar, everyone challenging what appeared to be an obvious wrong call. Did the umpire need glasses? Certainly he could see what we had seen clearly even from the nosebleed section. The crowd hissed, and boos bellowed throughout the stadium. Our attempts, however, were futile; the umpire's call stood firm. He had the final say. The umpire always has the authority to decide. When there is a dispute, his call will silence the opposition. That's the point Paul is trying to make about when there is a dispute between my flesh and my spirit, between peace and confusion, between God's truth and the Enemy's lies: the peace of God is present as an umpire wanting to make the final call. The question is, will we let it? Will we receive it? Will we allow the peace of God to have the final say, quieting the roar of lies within us and silencing the opposition that wants to trap us into thinking falsely?

That's what abiding in Him is all about, isn't it? It's refusing to leave the peaceful place of His presence, refusing to be shaken by circumstances or moved by situations. It's a determination to remain in a place of rest and peace—knowing that His faithfulness will be a shield to us. We need only be still and watch the deliverance of the Lord.

Allowing God's Peace to Rule Our Thoughts

God will not do for us what He has instructed us and empowered us to do. We are admonished in His Word to *let* the peace of God rule in our hearts. We must discipline our thinking and learn to yield to the peace of God and allow it to garrison our hearts with the peace that passes all understanding. When we submit to the lordship of Jesus Christ and let His rule have the final say in our thinking processes, the natural consequence will be peace. We must *choose* to let the peace of God rule our heart and submit to His government in our lives.

As we have noted, offenses will surely come into our lives, and these can fuel negative and hurtful thoughts in our minds. But no one has the power to take our peace. We have to willfully surrender it to anyone who offends us. But we can't afford to give people that kind of power! We can instead make the choice to let the peace of God reign in our lives.

We need to learn to take captive every thought that is contrary to the peace of God ruling our mind, will and emotions. The Enemy wants us to live in despair, not peace; in bitterness, not peace; in anger, not peace; in unforgiveness, not peace; in torment, not peace. It's a trap—don't take the bait.

No matter what we are going through, we must firmly decide to let God's peace rule in our lives and circumstances. This is not about our feelings—it's a resolve of the will. Our situation doesn't have to be peaceful for us to experience and manifest the peace of God. When we submit to the rule of the kingdom of God in our lives—letting God's Word and will have final say in spite of what we are going through—the peace of God will rule, and heaven, which lives in us, will be manifested here on Earth and made visible in and through our lives. People will be able to see the difference in us, and it will be a testimony of what God can do.

The Enemy Knows Our Weakness

Maybe the things we have discussed so far are not the bait that entices you. Perhaps the Enemy entices you with a man or woman other than your spouse—someone who says all the right things and makes you feel good about yourself. Or perhaps a promiscuous life-style has caused you to become ensnared. Some of you may be caught in the claws of an addiction or by jealousy or envy that consumes your life.

Are you trapped in memories that are haunting you? In anger that enslaves you? Does self-hatred have you in its clutches? Perhaps the Enemy's trap for you is leaving you feeling unwanted and unloved or abandoned and rejected. Some of you are trapped with overwhelming credit card bills or with a gambling or shopping addiction or by words that were spoken over you as a child. For some of you, secret sin has ensnared you, and you are filled with shame and guilt and hate yourself for your sin.

Maybe you are trapped in religiosity. You have been in church all your life, you've gone through the motions; you know more Scripture than I know, but it's not doing anything for you, it's not changing your life. Maybe you're caught in a negative thinking pattern—obsessing and mulling things over and over and can't get free.

If any of these ring true for you, are you willing to come to terms with the fact that you just might be trapped? Caught, having taken the bait of the Enemy, lured and enticed into his snare. But again, the good news: surely God is able to deliver you.

We all have areas of weakness that we are oblivious to—however, Satan is not oblivious to them. He knows our weaknesses, and he wants to use them to keep us from the will of God. Satan is called the tempter for a reason. James tells us that "each one is tempted when he is lured and enticed *by his own desires*" (James 1:14, NET), by his own lusts. The Enemy knows what our flesh craves and the proper bait to use in his trap for each of us.

God, however, has placed a limit on the tempter's ability to use our weaknesses. He promises that the Enemy will never be able to tempt us beyond what we are able to bear and that He will always provide us with a way of escape (see 1 Cor. 10:13). We must make the decision to please God and not satisfy the cravings of our flesh. We must endeavor to stay in the will of God and live a life pleasing to Him—to stay under cover in the shelter of the Most High.

We do not have to take the bait of the Enemy or be lured into his traps. God will always give us a way of escape, but we must choose to take it.

Our flesh will cry out to be satisfied; our ungodly desires will scream to be fulfilled. The devil makes the bait irresistible and enticing and sugarcoats it with a sense of entitlement. Our natural inclination is to take the bait and indulge our flesh, but we must refuse the temptation to justify and reason our desires away.

We can't think that we can indulge and just ask forgiveness later. That plays right into the Enemy's hand. The fowler wants us to focus on satisfying the flesh and remain oblivious to the trap itself. He doesn't want us to give any thought to the consequences—just immediate satisfaction.

Our Best Defense: Stay Close to God

As we saw in chapter 1 of this book, Psalm 91 is a conditional promise. As we draw near to the Lord and are intentional about dwelling and abiding in His presence, we can lay claim to the promises found in this passage. God is indeed willing to deliver us from the snare of the fowler, but we can't hope to reap this benefit if we do not fulfill its conditions. As we stay close to Him, hidden in the secret place,

He will not just deliver us out of the snare, but He will keep us from it in the first place.

When our children were younger, my husband and I took four of the kids to Israel. We were blessed to have a Messianic Jew tour guide named Sari leading the group we were with. My husband, Dave, had known this man since Dave was in his teens, since my husband's family had traveled to Israel often when he was growing up and had always requested Sari as their guide. Sari was a somber, heavyset man with a stern personality and a great love for the history of his country. He was extremely knowledgeable and made our visit to Israel a rich experience.

As gruff as Sari could be, he had a soft spot for children, and our four took an instant liking to him. One day as we toured the busy streets of Jerusalem, our family was distracted with taking in the sites, and we lagged behind the group. Merchants and peddlers approached us on all sides, trying to sell their wares. Sari stopped the tour and summoned my husband, Dave, to his side. He told Dave that he wanted the children to stick as close to him as possible as we walked through the streets of Jerusalem. Pickpockets and dangers lurked in all corners, and Sari was alert to their activity. We were not. For the remainder of the day, Sari kept the children close by his side, never more than an arm's length away, guiding and directing them through the city.

Like Sari, God is aware of dangers that we can't discern. He is an all-knowing, omnipresent God, and nothing is hidden from His sight. He knows what the Enemy is scheming and is aware of his plots. He knows where the snares are and how to render them powerless. As we draw close to Him in the secret place and walk with Him, abiding in His presence, He directs us away from dangers and warns us about and protects us from the traps of the Enemy.

When we make the Most High our dwelling place, He promises not just to deliver us from the snare but to help us avoid the snare in the first place. When we are purposeful about spending time with Him, staying close to Him, constantly aware of His presence and power, the Holy Spirit will help us avoid the traps that threaten to snare us. As my friend Karin says, "Prevention is always easier than cleanup."

Staying on Guard

My friend, Leslie, and I stayed once at the Boardwalk Villas in Orlando, Florida. The hotel, located right outside Epcot in Disney World, is a lovely facility with great amenities and is situated on a picturesque boardwalk overlooking a beautiful lake.

It's an entertaining place—a perfect location to shop, take a stroll, view the Epcot fireworks, play boardwalk games and watch local entertainers. But the thing I enjoy most are the cute eateries scattered along the way.

On our trip Leslie and I stopped by one of my favorite locations, the Boardwalk Sweet Shop, to satisfy my craving for a tasty butter pecan ice cream cone before heading back to the hotel. We purchased our ice cream and began the short stroll back to the hotel, savoring every delicious moment.

We were deep in conversation, walking side by side with our ice cream cones in hand, when suddenly, out of nowhere, a vexatious and brazen seagull swooped in from behind Leslie, catching her freshly coiffed hair with his talons and brushing the top of her forehead with his wings. She let out a bloodcurdling scream as he nosedived toward her coveted ice cream cone. Quicker than you can say Mickey Mouse, the seagull snatched the cone from her hand and promptly deposited it a few feet ahead to the delight of a swarming group of his feathery friends and relatives. We stood in shock as the seagulls devour the pilfered delicacy.

We hadn't seen the sneak attack coming. Had we been watching more closely, we would have realized the massive flock of seagulls swarming overhead, and we would have guarded our ice cream more carefully. Had we been alert to what was happening, we would have eaten our ice cream under cover in the restaurant. But we were caught off guard.

The Enemy of our soul counts on our guard being down. He waits to catch us while we are unaware and distracted, and then he steals from us.

Plundering the Enemy's Camp

Second Corinthians 2:11 reminds us that we must not be "outwitted by Satan; for we are not ignorant of his designs." The devil is a pickpocket, longing to steal from us. He wants to rob us of the fullness of all we have in Christ, and sadly, too often we sit back idly and let him rob us blind and then find ourselves forced to restore that which we did not steal (see Ps. 69:4).

In Psalm 91:3 the word "deliver" also means "the taking of objects from another's power."[5] The word can also be translated "to recover." But my very favorite definition of "deliver" is "to spoil" or "to plunder."[6] The Enemy loves to plunder our camp. Some of us have been through some difficult things. Tragically, many of us have innocently had to endure painful situations and challenging circumstances. Several of us have been ripped off royally—the Enemy has taken what belongs to us.

Scripture says that the thief, the Enemy of our soul, comes to "steal and kill and destroy" (John 10:10). The word "thief" means "embezzler, pilferer."[7] It paints the image of a pickpocket who is deceitful and clever in his scheming. My friend Brandon was the victim of a pickpocket at the state fair a number of years ago. He didn't know that he had been ripped off until he got home hours later and reached for his wallet, only to realize it wasn't there. Pickpockets are slick; they are calculated, smooth operators. That is what the Enemy is like. He comes as a pickpocket with a desire to steal from us in such a way that we don't even realize that we've been taken.

The thief tries to steal our children. He lures them into his trap, baits them, and gets them addicted to drugs and alcohol—and some of us sit back and let him steal from us. Some of us let him pilfer our marriages.

But here's the good news: when we dwell in the shelter of the Most High, we no longer have to allow the Enemy to plunder our camp; instead, we have the power to plunder his camp!

We need to forget the divorce papers, forget the verbal battles between us and our spouse and begin fighting the battle where it needs to be fought: in the secret place of the Most High God. We need to start recovering what is ours in Jesus' name. It is time we stopped letting the thief steal from us and begin plundering his camp for all it's worth.

We see this word "plunder" over and over in the Bible. After an enemy was defeated in battle, the victor went into their camp and stripped them of all their goods and treasures and recovered anything that the defeated foe had stolen from them.

We have a defeated enemy, but instead of taking back what belongs to us and pilfering his camp, we sometimes allow a defeated foe to continue to steal from us and plunder our lives. He's stolen from us long enough; it's time that we begin to recover what's been stolen. We need to stop fighting against flesh and blood and begin to get angry with the right person and direct our battle toward him.

Old Testament law says that if someone steals and is caught, he has to pay back seven times what he stole (see Prov. 6:31). Seven is always the number of completion. It means perfection. This implies that you and I can have complete restitution for whatever has been stolen from us. We can take back everything that the Enemy has stolen and fully recover it all, because God doesn't just promise us deliverance, He promises to plunder the Enemy's camp. What the Enemy has meant for evil God will always use for good (see Gen. 50:20).

I got a hold of this truth in 2009, the hardest year of my entire life. Through it all, God trained "my hands for war, and my fingers for battle" (Ps. 144:1). I learned how to plunder the Enemy's camp.

One day I got a revelation of what was mine in Jesus' name and began walking in the authority of it. I got tired of the thief stealing from me. It took me a whole year to get there, but I got there. I started to realize who I was in Christ and the inheritance that was mine in Him. I made up my mind that I would be just like David, who used the very thing that his enemy had used against him to gain the final victory—Goliath's own sword. I decided that whatever the Enemy brought against me, I would turn around and use it against him. I planned to take what the Enemy intended to use to harm me and let God turn it around for good.

During that difficult year I read a quote that said, "Live your life so that every morning when you wake up the devil says, 'Oh no, she's awake again!'" That's how I wanted to live—a force to be reckoned with. No longer defeated but instead motivated by the understanding that I had the power to tread upon the tactics and schemes of the enemy and to overcome all his power in Jesus' name (see Luke 10:19).

The understanding that the only power the Enemy had in my life was what I surrendered to him became a reality to me, and I made up my mind that I was done surrendering to him. It was about plundering now, and I intended to take back what was mine in Jesus' name. I began to comprehend who I was in Christ, and I started walking in victory as a rule and defeat as the exception.

The Enemy doesn't want us to arrive at that place. The purpose of his traps is to keep us in bondage so that we are not effective for the kingdom of God. He understands that if we are free and truly understand the victory that we have in Jesus, we will do damage to the kingdom of darkness. He knows that if we let the peace of God umpire our mind, will and emotions, God's peace will make the final call in our thinking, and the Enemy's lies will be rendered powerless.

But our God has the power to deliver us from the snare of the fowler. Let's run to Him for cover and hide in His shelter and rejoice in our freedom from the Enemy's traps of offense and wrong thinking and of his attempts to plunder our camp.

SIX

Finding Refuge under His Wings

He will deliver you . . . from the deadly pestilence. He will cover you with
His pinions, and under His wings you will find refuge;
his faithfulness is a shield and buckler.

Psalm 91:3–4

I was born and raised in rural Pennsylvania, where farms blanketed the countryside. As a child, I discovered that there is nothing sweeter than watching a mother hen protect her chicks. If the hen senses danger, she will make a clucking sound, and her chicks will run for cover under the shelter of her wings. Under the hen's cover, the chicks are not at all visible. What a picture of being hidden in Christ under the protection of His wing!

We are as defenseless as newborn chicks. The Enemy will throw all kinds of things at us to confuse and scatter us—temptations, danger, sickness, loss, betrayal—and unless we run quickly to our Father in heaven, under whose wings we can find refuge, we will be vulnerable to the devil's schemes and to our own bewildered thoughts.

God's gracious invitation for security, safety, provision and protection is open to all, but sometimes the stubbornness of our heart and our ignorance of His provision keep us looking to other sources that will only disappoint. He calls us, like a mother hen signaling for her chicks, knowing that when we are overshadowed by Him, we are safe. The question remains, are we willing? If we want God's protection, we must be willing to run to Him, follow Him and live under His dominion.

Deliverance from Disease

We see a second device of the Enemy presented in Psalm 91:3: "the snare of the fowler *and* . . . the perilous pestilence." The New Living Translation translates this verse, "He will rescue you from every trap and protect you from deadly disease." God doesn't just want to deliver us from the Enemy's snare; He wants to deliver us from the perilous pestilence as well.

Matthew 8:16–17 reminds us that Christ didn't just die to heal our spiritual condition; He died for our physical condition as well: "That evening they brought to him many who were oppressed by demons, and he cast out the spirits with a word and healed all who were sick. This was to fulfill what was spoken by the prophet Isaiah: 'He took our illnesses and bore our diseases.'"

In September of 2013, I developed a small growth on the right side of my temple. It was very small but began bleeding with even the slightest touch. I visited my dermatologist, and after taking one look she knew it needed to be removed. She excised the area and sent the specimen to the lab for a biopsy. A few days later her nurse called with the results: the growth was squamous cell carcinoma.

The nurse set up an appointment for me to visit a MOHS surgeon to further excise the area and perform reconstruction if necessary. MOHS surgery is the gold standard for skin-cancer removal; it provides the highest cure rate for the skin cancer while preserving as much surrounding tissue as possible.It is highly successful and the best option when treating skin cancer on the face.

The day arrived for me to have the MOHS surgery, and as I was prepped for the procedure, the doctor inquired about another spot that had recently appeared on my forehead. "How long has that spot been there? She asked.

"Oh, just a few days. I think it's a blemish," I answered.

"That's not a blemish," she replied. She asked if I would object to her removing it and sending it to the lab for testing. I agreed, and with that she carried out the surgery, and I was on my way home.

I completely forgot about the second spot until I received a telephone call from the hospital a few days later. The lab results were back, and the specimen from my forehead was inconclusive.

They needed a larger sample in order to do further testing. Ironically, this all happened during the time I was teaching a series on Psalm 91 and at the exact time that I was studying about pestilence. Webster's defines "pestilence" as "something that is destructive or pernicious, a disease that is virulent and devastating."[1]

I'm pretty sure that cancer fits that category! The writer of Psalm 91 actually mentions pestilence twice—in verse 3 and in verse 6. I was especially drawn to verse 6, because it says that we will not fear "the pestilence that stalks in darkness." We *will not* fear it.

As long as we make the Lord Most High our dwelling place, we won't have any reason to fear pestilence, and we can trust that we will be delivered from it. It's not a magical formula—it's the truth, a promise that God wants us to stand on and believe by faith. The question was, did I have faith to own that truth and make it mine?

I made note of the promise and put it on the back burner of my life, filing it away with other promises to be pulled out the next time I had opportunity to pray for someone who was sick.

Little did I know that I would soon be given the opportunity—and the someone would be me!

If you have to have cancer, I thought, *skin cancer is the best kind to have. It rarely, if ever, spreads and is basically harmless.* Boy, was I deceived. When I went in to give a larger sample of the area around the second spot, the doctor removed the tissue and stitched up the wound, instructing me to return a week later to have the stitches removed. She said that her office would call me with the results and stressed that I would not see her at that next appointment but rather that her nurse would remove the stitches for me. She assured me I had nothing to worry about, and I left her office unconcerned and completely at peace.

I didn't hear anything from the office that week (no news is good news, I thought) but returned a week later to have the sutures removed by the nurse. After removing the stitches, the nurse informed me that the doctor wanted to see me. "No," I said, "you must be wrong. She explicitly told me she didn't need to see me during this visit."

"No," the nurse assured me. "Things have changed. She would like to talk with you."

Fear gripped me, and my heart began to pound—what could she possibly have to tell me that had to be said in person? She had always telephoned with results in the past. The doctor entered the room, and the look on her face told me all I needed to know. My heart sank as she pulled her stool up to my side and placed her hand gently on my leg. "Rhea, I'm sorry, but your pathology report is back, and it's not good."

Not good? Worst-case scenario, I had another spot of skin cancer, right? I'd had many spots removed prior to this one, and there had never been anything to worry about. How "not good" could it be?

This time was different. The pathology revealed squamous cell carcinoma with perineural invasion. The "blemish" that had been visible for only three days was malignant and had already invaded the space surrounding the nerve.

Squamous cell carcinoma is usually easily treatable, but perineural invasion is always associated with decreased survival rates and has a high rate of metastasis to other areas of the body. What did that mean in layman's terms? It meant that I was sunk. I knew it, the doctor knew it and now I had to go home and break the news to my family so that they would know it too!

The doctor scheduled me for immediate MOHS surgery and informed me that the surgery would need to be followed by a series of radiation treatments. Our family had plans for a much-needed vacation the following week; we had already made the final payment and would lose the money if we canceled now. Certainly this procedure and the treatments could wait a week. But the doctor was concerned about the aggressiveness of this cancer and strongly advised canceling the vacation so that I could begin treatment immediately.

My head was spinning when I left her office. What did all this mean? I spent the next twenty-four hours researching and delving into the meaning of the pathology report and the diagnosis I had received. I slept very little that night. I rose early the next morning and made my way to the kitchen table, where I opened my Bible to the familiar passage that I had been studying:

> Surely He shall deliver you from the snare of the fowler and from the perilous pestilence. He shall cover you with His feathers, and under His wings you shall take refuge; His truth shall be your shield and buckler. You shall not be afraid of the terror by night, nor of the arrow that flies by day, nor of the pestilence that walks in darkness, nor of the destruction that lays waste at noonday. A thousand may fall at your side, and ten thousand at your right hand; but it shall not come near you. (Ps. 91:3–7, NKJV)

I had read it at least a hundred times. I practically had it memorized. I had studied it, meditated on it, preached it and declared it boldly from the pulpit, but the question remained, did I believe it? Did I truly realize the safety in running for cover, the importance of abiding in God's presence and the refuge that He would provide for me there? Did I really believe that *surely* my God would deliver me from this "pestilence" and that I had nothing to fear?

It was about to be tested, and I intended to pass the test!

I decided not to go public with the pathology report and to trust God with the situation. I confided in my husband and a few other prayer warriors and spent the next couple days seeking second opinions and abiding in the secret place.

I refused to cancel the vacation and decided instead to believe that my God would deliver me. This is where the rubber would hit the road and I would find out what I really believed—not what I testified to but what I *believed*. I asked God to deliver me from this pestilence, and while I was not sure what that deliverance would look like, I had a firm confidence that He would take care of me.

The MOHS surgery was set for eight thirty on a Friday morning, and our flight left that afternoon at two. The MOHS surgeon who had performed my last surgery was on vacation, and I was scheduled with a new doctor. This doctor was foreign and came with very high recommendations.

When I arrived at the facility and was being prepped for surgery, the doctor came to talk with me about the radiation treatments. He was not pleased that I was delaying the treatments until after my vacation. "Doctor, my husband is a pastor, and I am a Christian, and I believe that God is going to heal me and that I won't need radiation treatments." He smirked and gave me a patronizing response before walking out of the room. I bowed my head and asked God to show

His power in the situation. I, like the doctor, was not convinced, but I had the faith of a mustard seed, and Scripture says that that's all it takes to move a mountain. I prayed that it was so.

The doctor return to the operating room and began the surgery. He started by measuring the tumor, which had regrown since its earlier removal and had increased in size daily. He gave the measurements to his nurse and began the excision. He informed me that he would remove the tumor and then examine it under the microscope and would continue to remove samples until the margins proved clear. A plastic surgeon on standby would close the wound if the incision became too deep. I tried to remain calm.

The doctor removed the first section and bandaged my head. He would return in twenty minutes to remove the next sample. As I waited, I ran for cover in prayer and felt a calm descend on my soul. The Lord's presence was tangible in the room. I was thankful. I was shocked when the doctor returned in only a few minutes. His face look puzzled, and he appeared a bit shaken.

"Mrs. Briscoe," he said, "I cannot find any evidence of nerve invasion."

Praise God! I thought.

"There is absolutely no sign of nerve invasion, not even in the smaller nerves. Not only that, but I can't even find evidence of a tumor." My husband, who was in the room with me, let out a sigh of relief. The doctor went on to tell us that he would have to take one more layer that he called an "insurance layer." Since what he had found did not align with the pathology report, a sample would need to be sent to an outside lab to confirm his findings. This second layer, he added, would be deep and, regrettably, would cut some facial nerves. I would lose feeling immediately upon his incision. He assured me that the loss of feeling would be permanent.

Sure enough, the second he cut, a wave of numbness went from my forehead back over my head to the back of my neck. It was the weirdest feeling. "Why would the Lord heal me of cancer but leave me with this annoying numbness?" I wondered. It didn't make sense to me.

Nonetheless, I was thankful not to have cancer. The doctor informed me that unless the lab report came back with an opposing report, I would have no need of follow-up radiation treatments. He closed the incision on my forehead, and we left the office with our hearts filled with joy.

We stopped by our church on our way to the airport so my husband could pick up some work to take along on vacation. As we made our way to his office, me with a massive bandage on my head, we were stopped by a fellow pastor inquiring about the surgery.

We told her the good news, and she celebrated with us. She lifted her hands and placed them on each side of my head and said, "Thank You, Lord, that You are healing this numbness now in Jesus' name." I thanked her for her prayer, and we continued to Dave's office to quickly gather his work before leaving for the airport.

Only when we were en route to the airport did I realize that the numbness had disappeared. I had complete feeling in my head. I was overwhelmed and undone. Let me say it once again: *surely* God will deliver His people from the fowler's snare and from the deadly pestilence.

Finding Refuge Under His Wings

God has promised to protect us from the deadly pestilence, but what happens when we believe God to heal someone, and He doesn't?

Some things we will never understand until we get to heaven. One of the scriptures that ministers to my heart so deeply is Psalm 115:3: "Our God is in heaven; He does whatever He pleases" (NKJV).

He is God, and we are not. But that doesn't mean that He isn't faithful. Our job is to run to Him for cover, shelter under His wings and stand believing in the One who has promised to heal and protect us. What He does and how He responds is up to Him, but as long as we are safely tucked away in His shelter, we can rest assured that we will win, no matter how things turn out in the natural.

We will be shaken by every difficult situation if we fight it in our own strength. We must learn to hide ourselves in the Lord and let the peace of God umpire our mind, will and emotions. He will be a place of security and safety for us. The storm may continue to rage around us, but we will be protected from the effects of it.

This doesn't mean we won't have trials or troubles, but it does mean that we can remain stable and fixed in the midst of them. No matter what is happening in our lives, no matter what we are facing, Psalm 91 testifies that we can put our trust and confidence in God, for He will bring us through.

Psalm 91 goes on to say, "He will cover you with his pinions, and under his wings you will find refuge" (Ps. 91:4). The mother hen does not run to her chicks, gathering them to herself; rather, there is in the chicks a natural instinct to run to their mother for protection. In Matthew 23:37 Jesus laments, "O Jerusalem, Jerusalem . . . how often would I have gathered your children together as a hen gathers her brood under her wings, and you were not willing!" Can you hear the grief in His voice? God longs for His people to come to Him, but like the chicks with the mother hen, we must be willing to run to Him for cover.

God's Word Can Be Trusted

The Enemy knows that God is faithful, but he works very hard to convince us that He is not. The enticement to distrust God's Word and His faithfulness, particularly when healing doesn't come as we expect it to or when our prayers aren't answered as we hope, is a very effective trap of the Enemy. It began in the Garden of Eden when the serpent tempted Eve to question God's Word by saying, "Did God really say . . . ?" With one simple statement he implanted doubt in Eve's mind, and the rest is history. He convinced her to question the faithfulness of God, and as a result, instead of running to Him, she hid from Him.

The fact is, God *is* faithful. Psalm 91:4 goes on to say, "His faithfulness is a shield and buckler." In other words, the fact that He is faithful actually shields us and keeps us safe from the devil's schemes. But the Enemy knows that if we really start to believe that God is faithful to His Word, we will use that belief like a shield to ward off the fiery darts of the Enemy's lies and deception. The Enemy can't afford that, so he entices us to analyze God's promises and question His faithfulness to them. He sows seeds of doubt and unbelief that make us hesitant to act on God's Word.

When this happens, we become people who say we believe *in* God but fail to *believe* God. We read and meditate on God's Word. We say that we believe it as truth, but we are afraid to act on the faithfulness that backs it. We need to not only read God's Word but really believe it and believe that God will be faithful to it.

Faithfulness is part of God's character. It's who He is, and Scripture says that He "cannot [and won't] deny who he is" (2 Tim. 2:13, NLT). He will *always* be faithful. Psalm 91:4 promises us that God's faithfulness will be a shield to those who dwell in the shelter of His presence. The knowledge of that faithfulness will drive us to take refuge in Him.

Hebrews 10:23 encourages us to "hold fast the confession of our hope without wavering, for he who promised is faithful." We can hold fast to the promises of God's protection found in Psalm 91. As long as we are dwelling and abiding in His shelter, running for cover under His shadow, He will be faithful to protect us. We can rest secure behind the shield of His faithfulness.

When we are tempted to question God's watchful protection of us, we need to refuse to waver, trusting that He will always be faithful. We cannot be moved by what we see in the natural but rather must continue to trust in the faithfulness of the One who is supernatural. We cannot afford to lose hope. In the secret place of the Most High, under the shelter of His wings, we are shielded and faithfully protected by the One who is able. No trap of the Enemy, no scheme of the schemer will avail when we are securely sheltered within the arms of the One who is faithful.

SEVEN

Fear Not!

You will not fear the terror of the night, nor the arrow that flies by day, nor
the pestilence that stalks in darkness, nor the destruction that wastes at
noonday. A thousand may fall at your side, ten thousand at your right hand,
but it will not come near you. You will only look with your eyes and see the
recompense of the wicked. Because you have made the lord your dwelling
place—the most high, who is my refuge—no evil shall be allowed to befall
you, no plague come near your tent.

Psalm 91:5–10

My sister, Robin, lives in a historic manor that dates back to
the 1700s. It's a beautiful home and resembles something
directly from an episode of HGTV's *Rehab Addict*—Nicole
Curtis would be proud! Robin's house has all the appeal of a historic
home: tall ceilings, stone exterior, stained-glass windows and of
course, bats in the attic!

Robin has two beautiful grandchildren—Henry, six, and his little
sister, Polly, four. On a recent visit to her house, Henry asked Robin
to take him up to her attic (a.k.a. Gotham City) to retrieve some costumes for his latest adventure. Robin readily agreed, but Polly wasn't
quite as enthusiastic. When Robin questioned why, flabbergasted
Polly retorted, "Gigi, there are *bats* up there!" she said. Trying to hide

her amusement, Robin confidently assured Polly that she would protect her and that there was nothing to fear.

After much persuading Polly eventually consented to join them
on the fieldtrip to the attic, but she followed tentatively at a distance
behind her fearless grandmother and courageous elder brother. At the
top of the creaky staircase, when Robin paused briefly to unlock the
attic door, she realized that Polly was quietly muttering something
under her breath. Listening in a little more closely, Robin's heart
melted as she overheard the valiant but cautious Polly exhorting herself to "be a *brave* little girl, be a *brave* little girl!"

I laughed as Robin shared that story with me, but I couldn't help
thinking about how easily fear paralyzes us, keeping us from the abundant life Christ died for us to possess, from stepping out and enjoying
life. It can cause us to live like little Polly, tenaciously trying to convince ourselves to be brave in the face of our fears.

Psalm 91:5 tells us that in God we do not need to "fear the terror of
the night, nor the arrow that flies by day." If we are hidden in Him,
we are protected from all that threatens to drain us of courage in life.

Scripture tells us that "God has not given us a spirit of fear" (2 Tim.
1:7, NLT). Pause and reflect on the fact that fear is a spirit, and take
note—it's not from God! In fact, it's quite the opposite, for Scripture
says that the Spirit we received from Christ is "the spirit of sonship"
(Rom. 8:15, RSV).

We are sons and daughters of the Most High God. Good fathers
don't want their children held captive by fear. We must learn to renew
our minds and realize that when we feel fear, it is never from Father
God; it is always a tool of the Enemy of our soul.

God has gone to great lengths in His Word to encourage us not to
be afraid. Lloyd Ogilvie, in *Facing the Future without Fear*, said, "There
are 366 'Fear nots' in the Bible, one for every day of the year, including

Leap Year!" Whether or not that's true, my Bible concordance confirms that fear is spoken of more than five hundred times in the King James Version.

Obviously God knew that fear would be an issue in our lives, and He wanted us to know we didn't need to live enslaved by it!

We have other options. Psalm 56:3 says, "When I am afraid, I put my trust in you." In other words, we have a choice. When we feel afraid, we can choose to be immobilized and paralyzed by fear or to put our trust in God. We can let fear dominate our lives, or we can choose to run for cover and dwell in the shelter of the Most High God by putting our trust in Him.

It is in the protection of His presence that we realize that we don't need to fear the terror by night nor the arrow that flies by day, for God is more than enough. We overcome our fears by trusting Him more than our feelings of fear. We must learn to fear God more than we fear our fears. Fearing God has nothing to do with being afraid of Him or feeling terror in His presence—rather, it is realizing His awesomeness and regarding Him with such reverence and respect that it impacts and affects the way we conduct our lives.

With the fear of God comes an understanding of the magnitude of His power to protect us and the beauty of His ability to deliver us. When we have a healthy fear of God, we realize that we don't need to live in terror or be dismayed, for He is our God, and He is with us.

Isaiah 41:10 says, "Fear not [there is nothing to fear], for I am with you; do not look around you in terror and be dismayed, for I am your God. I will strengthen and harden you to difficulties, yes, I will help you; yes, I will hold you up and retain you with My [victorious] right hand of and rightness and justice" (AMPC). It is the knowledge that God is with us that brings us courage and allows us to face our fears and walk victoriously in the midst of them. As we seek refuge in Him and run to Him for cover, He will prove He is bigger than any of our fears and that we can put our faith in Him.

Nothing we can face is more powerful or mightier than Him. He is the *Most High* God, as Psalm 91 continually reminds us, and He is with *us*! Therefore, we have nothing to fear. It is in that place of discovery and total trust that our fears will dissipate like dew in the morning sun and no longer dictate and dominate our lives.

Fear—A Lack of Faith

One of the things I love so much about the Bible is that we can find ourselves and our stories played out in the midst of its pages. As we read God's Word, we find that we are not the only ones who struggle with fear and a lack of courage. The Gospel writer Mark recounts a fascinating story about a time when Jesus' disciples dealt with those very things:

> On the same day, when evening had come, He said to them, "Let us cross over to the other side." Now when they had left the multitude, they took Him along in the boat as He was. And other little boats were also with Him. And a great windstorm arose, and the waves beat into the boat, so that it was already filling. But He was in the stern, asleep on a pillow. And they awoke Him and said to Him, "Teacher, do You not care that we are perishing?"

> Then He arose and rebuked the wind, and said to the sea, "Peace, be still!" And the wind ceased and there was a great calm. But He said to them, "Why are you so fearful? How is it that you have no faith?" And they feared exceedingly, and said to one another, "Who can this be, that even the wind and the sea obey Him!" (Mark 4:35–41, NKJV)

Everywhere Jesus went, crowds gathered. This day had been no different; in fact, the crowds had swelled to such great proportions that Jesus had to get into a boat and use it as a pulpit. Rumors had been circulating, and the crowds were curious about the things that people were saying about this captivating teacher from Galilee.

Mark tells us that Jesus and His disciples had been ministering to these masses all day, and now at the end of the day, tired as they were, Jesus suggested that they cross over the lake to the other side. Obediently, the disciples boarded the boat, and Jesus got in with them.

But suddenly a great windstorm arose, and the waves crashed into the boat, flooding it so that it was nearly swamped. Fear gripped the disciples, and they thought that they were going to drown. Overreacting, you think? Well, some of these panic-stricken disciples were experienced fishermen familiar with storms. The fact that they were fearful tells us that this was no ordinary storm but one of mass proportion. We can't dismiss the disciples' reaction as being overly dramatic or emotional; it was logical and substantiated by facts.

Maybe that's you! Perhaps you have a justifiable reason for allowing fear to motivate and dominate your life. But it doesn't change the fact that fear is slavery and that God wants us free from it.

Where Jesus was while all this was happening? Peacefully asleep on a pillow in the stern. What happens next is nothing short of amazing. Confident that they were going to die, the disciples woke Jesus and cried out to Him, "Teacher, do You not care that we are perishing?" (4:38, nkjv). That makes me smile, because isn't that what *we* do in the midst of our own terrifying storms? In our despair we accuse Jesus of not caring about us, and we charge Him with being asleep and unconcerned about our well-being.

Jesus arose, rebuked the wind and brought peace and calm to the storm. But after doing so, He said to the disciples, "Why are you so

afraid? Have you still no faith?" (Mark 4:40). Note that Jesus con-
nects fear with a lack of faith here. I especially like that verse in the
Amplified Bible, Classic Edition: "He said to them, Why are you so
timid and fearful? How is it that you have no faith (no firmly relying
trust)?" If we truly want to be free of fear, we must acknowledge the
same connection: our fear points to the fact that we do not fully trust
God.

Why is it so difficult for us to firmly rely on Jesus? Let's take the
disciples, for example. As I mentioned earlier, their fear seemed logical. If you or I had been in the same situation, we would probably
have responded the same way. Why then did Jesus rebuke them and
ask them why they were fearful?

After all, Jesus, wasn't the reason for their fear *obvious*? But that was
the point Jesus was making—the reason for their fear was obvious if
their situation was viewed in the natural, but they were dealing with
a *super*natural God who wanted them to firmly rely on Him.

Their fear was understandable only if we don't take into account
who was in their boat. There was nothing to fear—because Jesus was
with them.

God wants us to firmly rely on and trust in Him. We don't have to
live in terror or be dismayed, because He will strengthen and uphold
us with His mighty right hand. We can walk in victory and not be
defeated by fear, because the revelation of God's perfect love drives
away all fear (see 1 John 4:18).

The understanding that God is with us, that He will never leave us
or forsake us, should strengthen us and make us feel secure and free
of fear. The fact that He is a shield about us and like a mighty warrior
should bring us peace. But sadly, many of us live short of that place
of peace because we do not dwell in His presence, safely tucked away
in His refuge.

Be Strong and Courageous

I went into my daughter Kendal's bedroom the other night and found her studying the first chapter of Joshua. She was parked on the page where Joshua was about to lead the Israelites into the Promised Land. Joshua knew that it would be a daunting task, but God assured him that He would be with him.

Kendal was intrigued that in a span of four verses, God issued three commands to Joshua to "be strong and courageous" (Joshua 1:6, 7, 9). She was shocked that Joshua needed to be commanded to be strong and courageous. "Didn't Joshua *know* that God was with Him?" she wondered aloud to me. "Hadn't he seen His power as he journeyed with the Israelites in the wilderness? Why then did God need to *command* him not to be afraid?"

A command, after all, is different than a suggestion. God wasn't saying, "You might want to think about being courageous, Joshua," or, "Could I suggest that you try to be strong?" No, He issued a *command*, and He didn't just do it the three times listed in Joshua 1. He gave Joshua the same command through Moses several times in Deuteronomy as well (see Deut. 31:6, 7, 23).

As I studied the passage in the days following my conversation with Kendal, I saw that it went without saying that Joshua wouldn't need to be commanded to be strong and courageous unless there was an allure to do otherwise. Had a spirit of fear tried to creep in?

I'm sure that Joshua doubted his ability; after all, he had big shoes to fill. Moses had been a good leader and had shared deep intimacy with God. That alone must have been intimidating. Joshua had also heard the Israelites' whining and complaining, bickering and disputing. He had seen them rebel against God and grumble against Moses. And he had witnessed the massive walls around the Promised Land and knew all about the enemy who had lived behind those walls.

After all, he had been one of the twelve spies whom Moses had sent in to scout out the territory, and he was aware that massive giants lived in the land—giants who would not go down without a fight.

Now God was asking him to lead over two and a half million grumpy, rebellious whiners into that enemy territory and take possession of it—and people wonder why God had to command him to be courageous! Sometimes it takes a command to remind us that we have a choice when looking in the face of our fears.

After issuing this massive assignment, God promised Joshua that He would be with him wherever he went. That's important, because as I said earlier, it is the awareness of His presence that elicits courage. Courage arises when we understand that the Great I Am, the Most High God, the One in whom there is nothing impossible promises to be with us wherever we go.

It is the knowledge that He who is with us is greater than those who are against us that produces fearlessness. It's that same knowledge that makes us want to stay under cover, in the shelter of His protective presence. Joshua was about to realize that he had nothing to fear, for his assignment wasn't about *his* ability or power—it was all about the One who had promised to be with him wherever he went. Sometimes we make the same mistake; we make it about us.

We focus on what we can or cannot do, and in doing so we allow room for a spirit of fear to creep in. We actually think that we have something to bring to the table or that we have the ability to deliver ourselves. I find it interesting that Joshua's given name at birth was "Hoshea" (see Num. 13:8), which means "salvation," but in Numbers 13:16 we read that Moses started calling him "Joshua," which means "Jehovah is salvation." Do we know that Jehovah is our salvation? And by "salvation" I mean "deliverance, to set free or to be victorious."[1]

It might seem like a minor detail, but Moses was purposeful in this name change. He was sending Hoshea a message. He wanted him to be clear about the fact that the only One who had the ability to bring deliverance was Jehovah, and lest Joshua be quick to forget, Moses made sure that he was reminded every time he heard his name spoken.

We do not have the ability to deliver ourselves—only God does. We do not have the capability to bring ourselves life or overcome issues that have overcome us. We can't free ourselves from an addiction or change a thinking pattern that has been embedded in us. We can't break through the chains that bind us or shatter the strongholds that hold us captive. It's not about us. It never was. It's about the One in our boat whose power is made perfect in our weakness. It's about Jehovah who is salvation and who promises to deliver. We can't deliver ourselves. Only Jesus can, and the sooner we understand that truth, the more bold and courageous we will become!

I love my mother-in-law dearly. She is a mighty woman of God and a model of godliness to all who know her. She, however, confesses to occasionally struggling with fear. In fact, she will admit that at times in her life, fear has been a stronghold for her—paralyzing her and causing her to lose sleep. What is her secret to overcoming and facing her fear? She says that in those times she makes the decision to trust God and "do it afraid."

I think that Joshua learned the same lesson—he could make the choice to be strong and courageous in the face of legitimate fear because he knew that he wasn't in the boat alone. You and I must do the same. We must shut the door to the spirit of fear by realizing that the One living in us is greater than anything coming against us. We must be gripped with a fear of God that is greater than the fear trying to grip us.

We don't have to live afraid or be dismayed, because we have made the Most High our dwelling place, and we realize, as Psalm 91:4 tells us, that He will be our refuge in times of trouble and our shield and buckler in the midst of the battle. We do not need to be afraid of "the terror of the night, nor the arrow that flies by day" (Ps. 91:5), for God is with us.

God commanded Joshua to be strong and courageous. Joshua needed to be reminded that courage was a choice; it required an act of the will. Isn't that what four-year-old Polly demonstrated for us? She willed herself to face her fear with courage and strength. She made a decision to override her fear with courage—even when she didn't feel courageous. God reminded Joshua that he would need to do the same thing. God knew Joshua wouldn't be the only one who would need to remember this, so He made sure that the story was recorded. As First Corinthians 10:6 says, "These things took place as examples for us."

The writer of Psalm 91 knew the same thing, and so he reminded us that when we make the Lord Most High our dwelling place and live in His presence, we do not need to be afraid. "If God is for us, who can be against us?" (Rom. 8:31). Still, we must choose to "be strong in the Lord and in the strength of *his* might" (Eph. 6:10) and not rest in our own strength and ability.

The dictionary defines "courage" as "the state or quality of mind or spirit that enables one to face danger, fear, or vicissitudes with self-possession, confidence, and resolution; bravery."[2]

In other words, courage doesn't mean that we will never have to face "bats in the attic," storms in our life or giants in the land. It doesn't mean that we won't encounter things that make us fearful and afraid.

Courage simply means that we will confront them with confidence and boldness. We will meet them with resolution, knowing that we can be brave not because we've talked ourselves into it but because the Lord our God is with us wherever we go.

Seeing Things from God's Perspective

It was as Joshua was about to enter the Promised Land that God commanded him to be brave and courageous, but as we have noted, this was not Joshua's first excursion into this area. Forty years prior to this, God had told Moses to send spies into this territory to scout it out, and Joshua was one of those spies.

The twelve spies spent forty days doing reconnaissance work in the Promised Land, and they returned with a full report of what they had seen. Ten of the men said,

> We came to the land to which you sent us. It flows with milk and honey. . . . *However*, the people who dwell in the land are strong, and the cities are fortified and very large. And besides, we saw the descendants of Anak there. . . . We are not able to go up against the people, for they are stronger than we are. (Num. 13:27–28, 31)

Now keep in mind, God had already promised the Israelites that they were going to take possession of this land. He had given them His Word, and that should have been enough. It was a promise from the One who cannot lie.

God wanted the Israelites to trust Him to do what He had said He would do. He wants the same for us, but as with the Israelites, it's not always that easy for us. Fear of what we see grips us, and instead of acting in faith, we react in fear. The Israelites ended up spending forty years in the wilderness as a result!

Now on the surface their response to the giants in the land might seem reasonable. After all, the thought of fighting giants would be pretty scary! But God actually wants us to be confident in His Word. The Israelites just had trouble believing God in light of the frightening things they could see.

Why is it so difficult at times for us to take God at His Word? The Bible tells us that "without faith it is impossible to please him" (Heb. 11:6). Taking God at His Word and believing what He says is not radical Christianity or crazy over-the-top stuff; it's taking a promise-keeping, covenant-making God at His Word, and that pleases Him. I'm in full agreement with the person who coined the phrase, "God said it; I believe it; that settles it!" I wonder how our lives would change if we truly lived that way.

From the people's perspective taking the land looked impossible at best, but from God's perspective it was already a done deal. We must look at things from God's perspective, not our own.

The ten spies checked out the land, and it appeared to be all that God had said it would be. However, they added a "however" to their report, and it was that "however" that got them into trouble and led to their fear-based report. Theirs was not a report based on faith in what God had said but on what they could see with their natural eyes.

Isn't that what the Enemy tries to get us to do? He diverts us from the promises of God by getting us to focus on what we can see with our eyes and understand with our logic. We go on a fact-finding mission, and the Enemy blinds our faith by filling us with fear over the magnitude of what we've observed. He defeats us with "giants," paralyzes us with fear and then entices us to add a "however" to what God has said He will do.

But when God tells us something or makes us a promise, He wants us to take Him at His Word.

The promises of God are true. We need to get our eyes off what we can see in the natural and onto our *super*natural God. If God said it, He will do it. Despite what we see on our fact-finding missions, we can rest in the goodness of God. Yes, there might be giants in the land, but God is not limited to our reality. He knows our "however" and has already accounted for it. We must not let the Enemy entice us with a spirit of fear. We have a spirit of power and of might. We have a sound mind.

The ten spies added one more thing to their report. They said, "We even saw giants there. . . . Next to them we felt like grasshoppers!" (Num. 13:33, NLT). Can you relate? Are your problems so colossal that they tower over you like a giant, making you feel small and powerless against them? We need to get our eyes off ourselves and our own abilities and back onto the promises of God and His ability to deliver and bring us through victoriously. Our problems may be big, but our God is bigger. That's why Jesus could sleep soundly in the midst of a storm.

I find it so remarkable that during the forty years of wandering in the wilderness, the cloud by day and fire by night went before the Israelites. And when they crossed the Red Sea and, later, the Jordan River, and when they marched around Jericho, the ark of the covenant went before them.

These were reminders to Israel that the presence of God dwelt with them and was leading them. The people of Israel had every reason to keep their eyes on the Lord and their minds renewed with the knowledge that His presence was with them, fighting for them and leading them in victory.

They had nothing to fear, for God was with them. Of the twelve spies, there were two who had a different report. Joshua and Caleb had seen the same obstacles as the other ten, but they didn't let what they saw influence their report.

They saw the same giants but didn't walk away from the Promised Land feeling like grasshoppers; they walked away knowing that their

God was bigger than any giant. In their report they told the Israelites, "Let us go up at once and occupy it, for we are well able to overcome it" (Num. 13:30).

I love that the Bible calls Caleb a man with "a different spirit" (14:24). It was clearly demonstrated in his "different" report. Caleb and Joshua saw the same things that the other ten spies saw, but they viewed the obstacles through the eyes of the promise of God, and as a result, they wanted to face the situation in a different way. Even though the other spies gave a report of fear, Joshua and Caleb gave a report of faith, because they knew what God had said, and they believed it! They made a choice to trust God.

We don't know if these two felt fear, but it doesn't matter, because faith is not dependent on feelings. Faith makes a choice to trust even in the face of fear. Caleb and Joshua saw what the other spies saw, but they also heard what God had said and chose to believe God over what they could see in the natural.

They came at it with a different spirit, and God rewarded them for it. I wonder what our lives would be like if we began to confront situations with a different spirit.

A Different Spirit

We have talked about not fearing "the terror of the night, nor the arrow that flies by day" (Ps. 91:5). The term "terror of the night" may bring obvious fearful images to mind, but what is the "arrow that flies by day"?

In the original language, the word used for "arrow" in Psalm 91 means "calamities inflicted on men or a wound inflicted by an arrow."[3] The *Complete Word Study Dictionary* on the Old Testament says that "arrow" can mean "a fool's or demented person's words." This phrase is a picture of our life being damaged by nasty, unkind words, and we don't need to fear these kinds of attacks from the Enemy or from other people either.

Over and over in Scripture we see the mouth and our words being described as arrows. Have you ever been wounded by someone's harsh, unkind words or pierced by things spoken in anger or jealousy? Perhaps you've been hurt by lies told about you or hateful words spoken over you. They may have been spoken thirty years ago, but the memory of them still poisons your mind today.

Psalm 91:5 says that we don't need to be afraid of the arrows that fly by day. We can find a place in God where people's words no longer have power or potential to inflict pain or to wound our lives, a place where we are so secure in Him that we can be free to love those who are not kind to us.

One woman in my life has been absolutely hateful toward me. As far as I know, I've never done anything to her; in fact, I rarely even see her; but she has made it clear that she does not like me one bit.

A number of years ago, God said to me, "I want you to be like Caleb and respond to everything she does with a different spirit. If she's nasty, I want you to be super kind. If she speaks ill of you and fires her arrows at you, I want you to say something good about her."

Now that didn't seem fair to me. Quite frankly, I wanted to clobber her. Every New Year I ask God to show me what He wants to clean up in my life. I am intentional about seeking Him regarding one thing that He wants me to focus on and allow Him to change in me that year. This particular year I felt that my word for the year was "meekness."

I laughed when I heard it, because let me assure you, "meek" is not a word that describes Rhea Briscoe! In fact, I told the Lord that cultivating meekness in me was going to be His best miracle since He had parted the Red Sea. But He taught me meekness that year, and

He used that nasty, unkind person to do it. He used the arrows of her words to make me a woman of a different spirit.

Oh, trust me, I wanted to be the nastiest person in the world to her. I wanted to be twenty times nastier to her than she was to me, but God wouldn't let me. Our nature is to fight fire with fire, but the Word of God says that "a gentle answer turns away wrath" (Prov. 15:1, NIV).

Each time this woman said something nasty to me or about me, I heard God say, "Respond with a different spirit, Rhea. If she does you dirty, you do her kind. If she says something mean about you to somebody, you say something kind about her to somebody else."

I was not happy, but I'm telling you, it worked. That woman could be as nasty as long as she wanted and say the meanest, most horrible things possible to me, but I lived in a place of peace, because I chose to respond with a different spirit. Her words no longer had any power over me. Safe in the refuge of His protective Word, her sharp arrows couldn't penetrate me anymore. Her comments didn't elicit fear in me. She could react one way, and I would respond the other—in a different spirit.

Our Father Holds the Rope

When Joshua and Caleb brought back their report to the Israelites, they were confident that they could take the land and defeat the Enemy: "Do not rebel against the LORD. And do not fear the people of the land, for they are bread for us. *Their protection is removed from them, and the LORD is with us*" (Num. 14:9). The word used for "protection" here means "shadow," and yes, if you are wondering, it's the same word used in Psalm 91:1: "He who dwells in the shelter of the Most High shall abide in the *shadow* of the Almighty."

God was saying to the Israelites, "You can take this land. You don't have to fear the Enemy, because their protection has departed from them. They have gotten out from under My covering." How had they gotten out from under His covering? Through disobedience and rebellion.

There is no safer place than under the shelter of God's presence. We need to continually run to the Lord for cover and live under the shadow of His wing, for in that place we can be bold and courageous, confident even when surrounded by the worst threats and biggest enemies:

> You will not fear the terror of the night, nor the arrow that flies by day, nor the pestilence that stalks in darkness, nor the destruction that wastes at noonday. A thousand may fall at your side, ten thousand at your right hand, but it will not come near you. You will only look with your eyes and see the recompense of the wicked. Because you have made the Lord your dwelling place—the Most High, who is my refuge—no evil shall be allowed to befall you, no plague come near your tent. (Ps. 91:5–10)

A story in *Our Daily Bread* shows us a beautiful picture of the kind of confidence we can have when we trust our Father:

> A group of scientists and botanists were exploring remote regions of the Alps in search of new species of flowers. One day they noticed through binoculars a flower of such rarity and beauty that its value to science was incalculable. But it lay deep in a ravine with cliffs on both sides. To get the flower someone had to be lowered over the cliff on a rope. A curious young boy was watching nearby, and the scientists told him they would pay him well if he would agree to be lowered over the cliff to retrieve the flower below. The boy took one long look down the steep, dizzy depths and said, "I'll be back in a minute." A

short time later he returned, followed by a gray-haired man. Approaching the botanist, the boy said, "I'll go over that cliff and get that flower for you if this man holds the rope. He's my dad."[4]

Do we have faith like that? Are we unafraid because we know that our Father holds the rope? That's what faith is—total trust. May we walk bravely and courageously, knowing that the Lord our God is with us. We don't need to talk ourselves into being a brave little girl—we just need to rest in the knowledge of who holds the rope.

As we dwell in the secret place of the Most High and abide under the shadow of the Almighty, we will be able to say of the Lord, "My refuge and my fortress, my God, in whom I trust" (Ps. 91:2). As we trust in Him, we won't need to be afraid of the terror of the night nor of the arrow that flies by day, for our Father holds the rope, and He's not about to let us go!

EIGHT

Angels to Guard Us

He will command his angels concerning you to guard you in all your ways.
On their hands they will bear you up, lest you strike your foot against a stone.
Psalm 91:11–12

M any years ago my husband, Dave, went through an excru-
ciatingly painful time. Someone he loved dearly had hurt
him deeply, and he describes it as the worst pain he has
ever experienced. It was all he could do to get through those days.
He continued to go through the motions of life, but inside he was
devastated and overwhelmed with pain.

One day as he left the YMCA after a workout, he was accosted
by one of the people responsible for the pain he had been forced to
endure. The gentleman was irate. Fury burned in his eyes, and hatred
filled his words. The confrontation was loud and threatening.

This gentleman did not believe in the God we serve, so knowing
that Dave was a minister of the Word, he derided him relentlessly in
an attempt to get him to react. "What do you think of that, 'man of
God'?" he jeered.

"Why won't you respond to me, 'man of God'?" People began to
gather around. Dave maintained his composure, but he knew that
the situation was escalating.

Suddenly, out of nowhere, another gentleman approached. Dave had been a faithful member of the YMCA for many years and was familiar with almost everyone who attended there, but he did not recognize this gentleman, nor did he ever see him again after that day.

The stranger was tall with a strong physique and towered over my six-foot husband. He walked with an air of confidence and was not shaken at all by the situation. He was wearing a tank top, and his bulging muscles gave the appearance of a buff weightlifter. Even Mr. Olympia would have been dwarfed beside him. This three hundred-plus-pound man was intimidating.

This man got between Dave and his aggressor and, placing a gentle hand on Dave's shoulder, said, "Is everything okay here, Dave?" He knew my husband's name! Dave nodded, stunned. The gentleman turned to look Dave's assailant square in the eye before walking away as quickly as he had appeared. The encounter was enough to diffuse the situation, sending a clear message to everyone that Dave had help available if he needed it.

Psalm 103:20 declares, "Bless the LORD, you His angels, *mighty in strength*!" (NASB). To this day Dave insists that God sent an angel, mighty in strength, to help him that day, and that memory is still vivid in his mind twenty-odd years later.

Sometimes it's easy for us to feel alone when we are going through hard times. Who am I kidding—sometimes it's easy for us to feel alone even when we are surrounded by friends and family and life is going fine!

But no matter how we feel, we are not alone. Not only is Emmanuel, "God with us," always present in our lives, but He also has an invisible army assisting us and ready to serve us. We have angelic aid available to us as we walk through life. Angels are real. The Bible tells us that they are "ministering spirits sent out [by God] to serve (accompany, protect) those who will inherit salvation" (Heb. 1:14, AMP). Angels not only exist and are validated in God's Word, they are sent by God to assist you and me as believers.

Perhaps this is a bit over the top or out of the box for some when it comes to the things of God, but over and over in Scripture we see confirmation of the ministry of angels toward people. They are mentioned 283 times in the Old and New Testaments.

There are two realms in this world: the natural and the supernatural, or the seen and the unseen. So many of us are motivated and influenced only by what we can see and comprehend in the natural, but if God peeled back the veil that separates the natural from the supernatural realm, we would be amazed by the angels and demons battling and contending in the spirit realm. Ephesians 6:12 says,

> We are not wrestling with flesh and blood [contending only
> with physical opponents], but against the despotisms, against
> the powers, against [the master spirits who are] the world rulers
> of this present darkness, against the spirit forces of wickedness
> in the heavenly (supernatural) sphere. (AMPC)

References to the supernatural sometimes make people uncomfortable; nonetheless, Psalm 91 declares that God has given angels charge over us to guard us in all our ways, and Hebrews 13:2 reminds us to "show hospitality to strangers, for some who have done this have entertained angels without realizing it!" (NLT). Angels are among us—we need only to have our spiritual senses sharpened to the awareness of them.

Surrounded by Angel Armies

One of my favorite stories about angels can be found in Second Kings 6. In this story we see an example of God's angelic forces at work in the life of one of His servants—Elisha, a man who knew God as his refuge and his very present help in times of trouble:

> Once when the king of Syria was warring against Israel, he took counsel with his servants, saying, "At such and such a place shall be my camp." But the man of God sent word to the king of Israel, "Beware that you do not pass this place, for the Syrians are going down there." And the king of Israel sent to the place about which the man of God told him. Thus he used to warn him, so that he saved himself there more than once or twice.
>
> And the mind of the king of Syria was greatly troubled because of this thing, and he called his servants and said to them, "Will you not show me who of us is for the king of Israel?" And one of his servants said, "None, my lord, O king; but Elisha, the prophet who is in Israel, tells the king of Israel the words that you speak in your bedroom." And he said, "Go and see where he is, that I may send and seize him." It was told him, "Behold, he is in Dothan." So he sent there horses and chariots and a great army, and they came by night and surrounded the city.
>
> When the servant of the man of God rose early in the morning and went out, behold, an army with horses and chariots was all around the city. And the servant said, "Alas, my master! What shall we do?" He said, "Do not be afraid, for those who are with us are more than those who are with them." Then Elisha prayed and said, "O LORD, please open his eyes that he may see." So the LORD opened the eyes of the young man, and he saw, and behold, the mountain was full of horses and chariots of fire all around Elisha." (2 Kings 6:8–17)

Elisha's servant, Gehazi, was influenced strictly by what he saw in the natural, resulting in nothing but fear and defeat. He needed his spiritual senses sharpened. The horses and chariots of fire that Elisha prayed for Gehazi to be able to see were already present, but the servant had simply been unaware of their existence.

We are no different. So many of us are governed and ruled by the reality that surrounds us in the natural. We are moved by circumstances, dictated to by fear and dominated by strategies that the enemy employs against us. Too often we are oblivious to the battle taking place in the spiritual realm and ignorant of our ability to wage war and influence that realm through prayer. Let's look at the story a little more closely.

Syria was a formidable enemy of Israel. The king of Syria was "warring" against Israel, plotting to set up an ambush to take Israel by surprise. But every time Syria tried to attack Israel, their plans were foiled, thanks to Elisha, the prophet who walked in tune with God. Each time an attack was planned, Elisha received a revelation from God and alerted the king of Israel and gave him insight into the enemy's strategy.

Frustrated that his attacks were being outwitted, the king of Syria summoned his servants and demanded to know which of them was a spy for the Israelites.

Now clearly the king had his own spies in the Israelite camp, because someone was able to give him inside information about the man of God: "Elisha . . . tells the king of Israel the words that you speak in your bedroom" (2 Kings 6:12). We must wwnever be ignorant of the fact that the Enemy has spies in our camp. When God wants to bless us, He sends a person into our life; when the Enemy wants to defeat us, He too sends a person.

We need to learn to discern the difference between the people God sends and the one the Enemy sends. Then, as Pastor T.D. Jakes says, "we need to get the gift of good-bye."[1] So often we try to hold onto people in our lives who are simply tools that the enemy is using to mess us up and bring us down.

First John 2:19 says, "They went out from us, but they were not of us; for if they had been of us, they would have continued with us. But they went out, that it might become plain that they all are not of us." If these kinds of people had been God's will for us, they would have continued with us.

We need to get the gift of good-bye and stop trying to make people love us, stop trying to force them to accept us and, by all means, stop trying to bend over backwards to gain their approval. Learn to identify those who are with you who are pawns in the hand of the Enemy.

Having heard from his spy that Elisha was a threat to him—and all threats must be dealt with—the king of Syria sent "a great army" to get Elisha. I love that. A great army to apprehend *one* man. Really? This shows the threat that Elisha really was to them.

Don't miss the fact that Elisha was not unknown in Syria. The servant simply said his name and gave no further details about who he was, because no explanation was necessary. Elisha's reputation had obviously preceded him. Israel's army didn't intimidate the Syrians, but Elisha, a faithful man of God, was a threat to them.

Don't you want a life like that? A life that is so known to others that when people hear your name, they've already heard about you and your God? A life that is so significant for the kingdom that your reputation precedes you? I do.

During the time of Moses and the plagues in Egypt, God told Moses over and over that He was going to use him to do something so great that it would cause the people to know that the Lord was in their midst and that there was no God like Him. Oh, may God demonstrate His power in our lives so that by watching us, the world will know that there is none like Him.

But remember, a person living that kind of life can be a threat to some—and especially to the Enemy of our soul. And all threats must be dealt with. We have an enemy who doesn't want us walking in the power and authority of God. He doesn't want us demonstrating the power of God in our lives. He doesn't want the power of the Spirit to be evident in us. We cannot be unaware of his schemes.

My mother used to tell me that if Satan isn't on our tail, we are doing something wrong. He will let us alone if we are not a threat to his kingdom. Elisha was a threat, and the king of Syria sent a strong force to bring him down: "He sent there horses and chariots and a great army, and they came by night and surrounded the city" (2 Kings 6:14).

Not only did the king send a whole army to apprehend one man, his soldiers came by night and surrounded the whole city. Overkill or not, the king went to great lengths to be sure that he had a surefire plan this time.

This attack was strategic and would not be foiled. That's the way our Enemy works. His attack is planned and calculated, and it comes at a time when we are most vulnerable and unprepared.

But like Elisha, we are not alone. Those who are with us are greater than those who are against us. Elisha's servant woke early, and when he went out, he realized that an army with horses and chariots had surrounded the city. If ever a situation looked hopeless, this was it! Terrified, Gehazi called for his master. "Alas, my master!" he said. "What shall we do?" (2 Kings 6:15). Elisha saw the same thing his servant saw, but he was unmoved by it. He calmly replied, "Do not be afraid, for those who are with us are more than those who are with them" (2 Kings 6:16). Elisha could see what his servant could not—that they were surrounded by fiery armies of the heavenly host.

Lord, Open Our Eyes

There was no tone of panic in Elisha's voice. He was confident in the God he served. He knew that God is the Great I Am and that He would be faithful to be all that Elisha needed Him to be.

One can't help but notice the contrast in this passage—one of fear and one of faith. Elisha didn't fear, because he that knew he served a supernatural God, and his eyes were not fixed on what he could see but rather on what he could not see—and what he knew by faith was there (see 2 Cor. 4:18). Gehazi feared, because his eyes were fixed on what he saw in the natural, and his mind, will and emotions were controlled by it. It appeared hopeless, therefore it must be.

That's what unbelief does; it fools us into thinking that the natural is the reality. It is influenced greatly by what is happening around us and what we see in the natural. Faith, however, refuses fear. It refuses to be moved and influenced by the natural because it has its hope in the One who promises that He will never leave us or forsake us (see Deut. 31:6). Faith says, "This may be what's happening in the natural, but my God is *super*natural."

When Elisha told Gehazi that there were more with them than with the Syrians, I'm sure that the servant thought the prophet was crazy. *What does he mean, "Do not be afraid"?* the servant must have thought. *Is he oblivious to the chariots and horses filling the horizon?* But Elisha prayed and said, "O LORD, please open his eyes that he may see" (2 Kings 6:17).

God answered Elisha's prayer, and the servant's eyes were opened. The veil that separates the seen from the unseen was peeled back, and Gehazi could clearly see the angel army that surrounded him.

Our eyes may never be opened the way Gehazi's were that day, yet that doesn't change the fact that angel armies are protecting and defending us. Those who have made the Most High their dwelling place can by faith believe that those who are with us are greater than those who are against us. That's what Psalm 91:11 tells us: our God has commanded His angels concerning us to guard us in all our ways! Oh, Lord, open our eyes so that we can see!

Paul's prayer for the Ephesians petitioned God for the same thing:

> [I always pray] that the God of our Lord Jesus Christ, the Father of glory, may grant you a spirit of wisdom and of revelation [that gives you a deep and personal and intimate insight] into the true knowledge of Him [for we know the Father through the Son]. And [I pray] that the eyes of your heart [the very center and core of your being] may be enlightened [flooded with light by the Holy Spirit], so that you will know and cherish the hope [the divine guarantee, the confident expectation] to which He has called you, the riches of His glorious inheritance in the saints (God's people). (Eph. 1:17–18, AMP)

The God of Angel Armies

Have you ever been in a situation like Elisha and his servant were? In a place where you felt surrounded on every side and there didn't seem to be a way out? Have you ever been overwhelmed by an attack that the Enemy launched against you and felt that everything was hopeless? Maybe you are in that place now. Psalm 91:11 assures us that we are never alone: "He will command his angels concerning you to guard you in all your ways. On their hands they will bear you up, lest you strike your foot against a stone."

One of the names of God is "Jehovah Sabaoth." It means "Lord of Hosts" or, as Eugene Peterson translates it in The Message, "GOD-of-the-Angel-Armies": "GOD, King of Israel, your Redeemer, GOD-of-the-Angel-Armies, says: 'I'm first, I'm last, and everything in between. I'm the only God there is. Who compares with me?'"

(Isa. 44:6). No one compares with Him. He is the commander of the heavenly host.

First John 4:4 promises that whatever we are facing, no matter how hopeless it appears or how helpless we feel, the One who is in us is greater than anything we can come up against in our life, and He dispatches his army of angels to protect us and guard us as we walk through life. The eyes of our hearts need to be opened and enlightened so that we can know and understand the hope that we have in Him (see Eph. 1:18).

The question is, will we trust God's plan when we can't see Him? Will we put faith in His promise that He has given an invisible force charge over us? Do we believe that all around us are ministering servants who are invisible to the natural eye but ready to assist those who are to inherit salvation and that the God we serve is the God of those angel armies?

My friend Leslie and I were shopping in Chicago. At the time, I had just finished a study on the names of God and had been struck by the name "Emmanuel," which describes the God who is always with us.

Leslie and I spent the entire two-hour drive to Chicago talking about how thankful we were to serve a God who will never leave us or forsake us, a God who promises to be with us wherever we go. We conversed about how we can trust him, rely on Him and count on Him never to relax His hold on us. We prayed and asked Him to make us more aware of His presence with us and to give us a sensitivity to Him being our Emmanuel, the One who is always with us.

When we arrived in Chicago, we parked in a massive parking garage just shy of Michigan Avenue—the same garage we always use when we are in Chicago. We like this garage because, after parking the car and before entering the elevator that takes us to street level, we get a reminder card to take with us to help us recall where we parked.

Needless to say, in a city the size of Chicago, those cards are helpful.

Now perhaps I was overly excited to get shopping, or maybe I just assumed that Leslie had picked up a card, but it was only after a full day of shopping, when we returned to the parking garage, that we realized that neither of us had the remotest idea where we had parked.

Trust me when I tell you that this was not a small parking garage, and while I could easily tolerate the frigid Windy City temperatures while shopping, it felt as if the thermometer dropped twenty degrees as we stood in that garage looking for our lost car!

We must have looked comical as we navigated up one level and down the next, checking every space on every level. I can't even begin to tell you how much time we spent trying to find our car or how cold we became while doing it.

We activated the remote, tried setting off the car alarm, and even tried calling security—to no avail. At that point I started to panic, thinking that perhaps someone had stolen our car or that maybe we were in the wrong parking garage! Exasperated, we breathed a quick prayer to Emmanuel and thanked Him for being the God who is always with us, and we asked Him to please help us find our car.

Leslie was making her way back up a ramp and I was standing alone when suddenly a kind gentleman appeared out of nowhere. He asked if we were okay. I laughed and told him that we couldn't find our car. He said, "That's not a problem at all. Can you give me your keys?"

I am not sure what came over me, but I handed this complete stranger my car keys! This man wasn't a security officer or wearing the uniform of someone employed by the parking company, but I gave him my keys without a second thought. Leslie had reached my side by that time, and I turned to her dumbfounded and said, "I just gave that man my car keys!" Desperate times require desperate measures,

I suppose. Thankfully, the man appeared only seconds later, driving our car and waving in delight. We thanked him profusely and offered to tip him. He refused our money, but as he was leaving, something caused me to ask him his name. He smiled and said, "Oh, my name? It's Emmanuel."

The story still makes us laugh with pure delight—we can't recount it without absolute joy. Hebrews 13:2 tells us that sometimes we "entertain angels unaware." I believe God commanded an angel charge over us that day (see Ps. 91:11, NASB). We had spent the entire trip to Chicago talking about Emmanuel, the God who is always with us, asking Him to grant us a deeper understanding of that name. And sure enough, living up to His character, He did immeasurably more than we could have asked or imagined (see Eph. 3:20, NIV).

No matter what we encounter today or what we are going through in our lives, the God-of-the-Angel-Armies is with us:

> I lift up my eyes to the hills. From where does my help come? My help comes from the Lord, who made heaven and earth.
>
> He will not let your foot be moved; he who keeps you will not slumber. Behold, he who keeps Israel will neither slumber nor sleep.
>
> The Lord is your keeper; the Lord is your shade on your right hand. The sun shall not strike you by day, nor the moon by night.
>
> The Lord will keep you from all evil; he will keep your life. The Lord will keep your going out and your coming in from this time forth and forevermore. (Ps. 121)

We do not need to be afraid. We can confidently face whatever situation we find ourselves in, knowing that because we have made the

Lord our dwelling place and the Most High our refuge, no evil shall be allowed to befall us, for He will command his angels concerning us to guard us in all our ways.

NINE

Made for Authority

*You will tread on the lion and the adder; the young lion and
the serpent you will trample underfoot.*

Psalm 91:13

A duckling was once hatched under the watchful eye of a motherly collie dog. The baby duck took one look at the collie and decided that the dog was its mother. It followed the collie around, ran to it for protection, and slept with it at night. It spent the hot part of the day under the front porch with the collie. When a car pulled into the driveway, the duck, along with the dog, would run out from under the front porch quacking viciously, trying to peck the tires.

"This is known as imprinting—an animal attaching itself to the first thing it sees after it is born, thinking that it is that thing. Some things cannot be changed, however. In the case of the duck, it still quacked, enjoyed the water, and flapped its wings. Sometimes it acted like a duck, and sometimes it acted like a dog."[1]

We as Christians often do the same thing. We act like what we think we are instead of becoming who we were created to be. We take on behavior that we have seen modeled around us instead of realizing the true beauty of all that God created us to manifest. Sometimes we act like a Christian; sometimes we act like the world. It's because, like the duck, we are confused about our identity.

When we are born again, "hatched" into this world as Christians, many of us remain attached to the world around us and take our cues from it instead of becoming imprinted with the truth of who we are in Christ. Like the duck, we learn our behavior from what we see around us and the messages that others convey to us, never realizing that we are settling for so much less than the awesomeness of who we can be in Christ.

In this state we are oblivious to the magnificent creation that God made us to be, unmindful of the fact that we have been uniquely designed with a plan and a purpose, filled with power from on high and made to be coheirs with Christ. Because of this, we continue to be content with so much less than what is available to us in Christ. We continue to act like a "dog" instead of the "duck" that we truly are.

Created for Authority in Christ

So what *is* available to us in Christ? What kind of people are we created to be that we might be missing out on? We were made to walk in power and authority, in victory over the Enemy and his schemes in our lives, but so often we imprint to the world and end up weak and defeated in the face of difficulties or temptations.

Our authority doesn't come from our own power or ability, however. It comes from Christ, who lives inside us. We see the source of His authority in Ephesians 1:20–23:

> [God] raised [Jesus] from the dead and seated him at his right hand in the heavenly places, far above all rule and authority and power and dominion, and above every name that is named, not only in this age but also in the one to come. And he put all

things under his feet and gave him as head over all things to the
church, which is his body, the fullness of him who fills all in all.

Christ is seated at the right hand of the Father, and the right hand
is symbolic of victory or of power and authority. This passage also says
that God has put all things under Jesus' feet. In Bible times, when a
king conquered an enemy, the defeated enemy was brought before the
king in chains. He prostrated himself before the throne of the conquering king, and the king placed his feet on the back of the enemy as
a sign of victory and complete subjection. Since God has put all things
under Christ's feet, all things are in subjection to Him.

"All" indicates that *everything* is in subjection to Him. Not just
powers and principalities; not just rulers and authorities. It means
anything we could encounter, anything we could come up against,
anything that tries to have dominion over us.

The things that you and I think we cannot get control over in
our own lives, the things that enslave us and threaten to overpower
us—drug addiction, alcoholism, gossip, heartache and pain, rage and
anger, despair, hopelessness, gluttony, hatred, gambling, fear, pornography—all these are under Christ's subjection. Isn't it comforting to
know that these things are under Jesus' feet? Everything we encounter
must bend its knee to Christ.

Not only did God put all things under His feet in subjection to
Him, He made Jesus head over all things. The word translated "head"
is a "metaphor for anything supreme, chief, prominent. It means
Master Lord."[2] In other words, Jesus is supreme, prominent above
all things and Lord of all.

It gets even better, because it goes on to show how Christ's authority plays out in our own lives. The passage says that we, as believers,
are the fullness of Him who fills all in all. "Fullness" here means "that
which is filled with the presence, power, agency, riches of God and of

Christ."[3] Do you know that as believers we are filled with the *fullness* of the One who is supreme over all things and the One to whom all things are in subjection?

There is no thing or no one more powerful or more mighty; no name above His name; no ruler, authority or power greater than Christ—and you and I are the fullness of Him! Filled with His presence, filled with His power, filled with the riches of God—and filled with Christ's authority.

Think about that the next time you have to face something difficult or when it appears that the enemy is winning or when you feel overcome by problems. We are the fullness of the One in whom all things are in subjection. If our difficulties are in subjection to Him and we are the fullness of Him—then guess what? Our problems are in subjection to us! In Christ we have authority over the Enemy and over the circumstances that threaten to overwhelm us. This is who we were made to be.

Staying Connected to Our Power Source

In this passage in Ephesians 1, Paul calls the church the body of Christ. We are the body, and Christ is the Head. But just as in our natural life the head must be connected to the body or life ceases, so it is spiritually.

When we disconnect from the Head (Christ), we disconnect from our power source and, consequently, become detached from our source of power and authority. That's why it's so vital that we maintain intimate connection with Him.

I have a beautiful lamp in my den that I found at a local interior designer's warehouse. It is a captivating myriad of colors and truly adds to and brings out the beauty of its surroundings. It sits on a side table in my den, accenting the furniture adjacent to it.

Although the lamp is lovely, I bought it to serve a purpose: the room was dark and needed additional lighting. Now what if that beautiful lamp sat on my side table and was never plugged into an outlet? It would give an appearance of usefulness and even add to the beauty of the room, but it would not fulfill its true purpose.

In order to fulfill its purpose, it needs to be connected to the power source. Without that connection it would be powerless and not much use. This is the way many of us live the Christian life. We go through the motions, look good on the outside, blend in with the world around us. We were purchased at great cost, we are saved and going to heaven—but we live powerless and ineffective lives.

Like my lamp, we can't expect to walk in authority if we are disconnected from the power source—detached from our Head. Psalm 91:13 tells us that we "will tread on the lion and the adder; the young lion and the serpent [we] will trample underfoot," but Psalm 91:1-2 reminds us of this psalm's conditional promise: it is only when we abide in the secret place of the Most High that we will have the authority to trample on snakes and scorpions and overcome all the power of the enemy.

God created us with a purpose and put us here on the Earth to be a vessel for Him to flow through and to show forth His power. He wants us to shine for Him and illuminate the world as we walk in victory over the Enemy, but we need to be connected to our power source in order to do so.

Jesus Has Finished His Work—and That Means Victory for Us

In this Ephesians 1 passage, Paul reminds us that Jesus is seated at the right hand of the Father—a place of honor and authority, in a position to rule and reign.

In Bible times the priests in the tabernacle never sat, because their work was never done. They stood daily, offering the same sacrifice over and over: "Every priest stands daily at his service, offering repeatedly the same sacrifices, which can never take away sins" (Heb. 10:11).

But Jesus, who is our High Priest, conquered hell, death and the grave on the cross of Calvary, ascended to the right hand of the Father and sat down: "But when Christ had offered for all time a single sacrifice for sins, he sat down at the right hand of God" (10:12). He's not repeatedly offering the same sacrifice over and over—He offered it once and for all, and it was done. Forever finished. Then He sat down. There was nothing left for Him to do.

Jesus is not up in heaven pacing because He is worried about our situation or concerned because we have messed things up too severely. No, He's seated, in a position of rest, because He knows what many of us have not yet realized: His work is finished, the Enemy has been defeated and death has lost its sting.

He has ransomed us from all that we think is stronger than us and delivered us from the power that seems to be defeating us. He gave a deathblow to the Enemy and his strategies. He stripped the devil of the final say, and as a result, He leads us in triumph and has made us more than conquerors in Christ Jesus.

The last words He uttered on the cross were, "It is finished." He was making a declaration—one that so many of us have not yet applied to our lives. Our sin debt was satisfied, the punishment that brought us peace was upon Him and we now have salvation and new life through Jesus Christ.

But too often we fail to realize that salvation is so much more than just the forgiveness of sins. We have been rescued, delivered, set free and given power over the Enemy! Christ secured the victory on the cross of Calvary; every foe was defeated, conquered and rendered powerless. He redeemed us from the curse of the law and from the dominion and power of the Enemy—and He has given us His victory.

Colossians 2:15 says that Jesus "disarmed the powers and authorities" and "made a public spectacle of them, triumphing over them by the cross" (NIV).

The picture is that of the triumph of a Roman general. William Barclay, in his *Daily Study Bible* series, writes, "When a Roman general had won a really notable victory, he was allowed to march his victorious armies through the streets of Rome, and behind him followed the kings and the leaders and the peoples he had defeated.

"They were openly branded as his spoils. Paul thinks of Jesus as a conqueror enjoying a kind of cosmic triumph, and in His triumphal procession are the powers of evil, beaten forever, for everyone to see."[4] Christ neutralized the Enemy and put him to open shame by what He accomplished through His death and resurrection. It's a finished work; God can do no more than He has already done. He overcame the Enemy and paraded him as a defeated foe so that all could see.

We, however, must continue, by faith, to appropriate all that was accomplished for us on that cross and manifest it in our daily walk with Christ. We must enforce the victory that Christ accomplished for us on the cross of Calvary and never lose sight of the fullness of the authority that we walk in.

As we have seen over and over, the only power the Enemy has is what we surrender to him. We empower him by believing his lies or partaking in his deception.

It cost Christ so much for us to walk in victory and not defeat, and yet often we are satisfied for so much less.

But close your eyes and picture Jesus dying that brutal death on the cross for us. Imagine the strength that it took for Him to utter those dying words from his parched lips as He proclaimed something that

He knew you and I would need to be reminded of—"It is finished, done, over and accomplished."

Hanging on a wall in my den is a stunning picture of a maned lion head. My friend, Mailey, sketched it for her mother, Lisa, to give to me as a gift. The picture is breathtaking and a topic of conversation with everyone who enters my home. Mailey is a talented artist, and I feel privileged to own one of her designs. In my mind, she's as gifted as Picasso. I, however, have trouble drawing stick men!

Now imagine if I began to add to the picture, scribbling my own touch on the canvas. Would I ever dream of doing that? Absolutely not. It's perfect the way Mailey drew it for me. I couldn't add to it—I would only take away from it. My job is to simply enjoy it and display it for all to see.

The same is true of the finished work of Christ on the cross of Calvary. We cannot add to it with our works or our performance. We cannot earn it or perfect it. It's a finished work. Our job is to simply enjoy and benefit from the gift of grace given to us and display it for others to see.

His finished work includes salvation and the forgiveness of sins, but it also includes the knowledge that the Enemy of our soul has been defeated. Victory is ours. We don't fight *for* victory; we fight *from* victory. We, however, cannot remain passive in this truth.

First Peter 5:8 says, "Be sober, be vigilant; because your adversary the devil walks about like a roaring lion, seeking whom he may devour" (NKJV). Notice that it says "seeking whom he *may* devour." The Enemy knows that he's defeated and has no power in our lives. He knows that the only power he has is when we come into agreement with his lies and deception. So he aggressively prowls, seeking. The word translated "seeking" means "to seek in order to find out, to enquire into."[5]

Our Enemy is on a fact-finding mission, seeking to find out whom he *may* devour. He's inquiring to see whose guard is down and who is vulnerable enough to *let* him devour. He's looking for the duck who is confused about who it is and helplessly will follow his lead instead of becoming all it was created to be.

We must be alert. The Enemy needs our permission—our agreement. We are powerful in Christ and do not have to sit back idly and allow the Enemy of our soul to assault and rob us blindly. We have authority in Christ. Let's use it!

Enforcing God's Authority

Hebrews 10:13 goes on to say that once Christ was seated at the right hand of the Father, he then waited "until his enemies should be made a footstool for his feet." Wait, didn't Colossians 2:15 say that Christ has already "disarmed the powers and authorities" and "made a public spectacle of them, triumphing over them by the cross" (NIV)? Yes. Didn't Ephesians 1:22 tell us that everything is "under his feet"? Yes. Isn't Christ's victory past tense and already accomplished? Why then does Hebrews 10:13 say that He's *waiting* till His enemies are made His footstool?

Jesus is waiting for man to participate with Him in what He has already accomplished. When the Enemy comes to steal, kill and destroy, he operates illegally, and it's up to the church, God's delegated authority, to manifest the power and authority of God in this world.

Early one Saturday morning when I was ministering God's Word in Alabama, my friend, Leslie, drove me from the hotel to the conference center.

A worship CD blared in the background, and we zealously praised the Lord, belting out worship at the top of our lungs. In the passenger seat, I extended my hands upward, pressing them against the roof of the SUV. I even considered opening the sunroof so that I could be even more expressive—after all, we didn't know anyone, so what did we have to lose?

Leslie confessed later that she was so lost in worship that she doesn't remember many of the landmarks we passed. I'm pretty sure that the windows vibrated from the joyful noise we made, and we were overwhelmed with an awareness of the powerful presence of the Holy Spirit filling the car.

Apparently Leslie's foot on the accelerator felt the weight of His presence as well, because suddenly she glanced in the rearview mirror and realized that a policeman was following us—lights on, sirens blaring. Her eyes immediately dropped to the speedometer that now registered eighty.

Apparently, much to our humiliation, the policemen had been following us for miles. I'm sure that he enjoyed our concert from afar. The loud music that filled our car had drowned out the sound of his siren, and although I had felt like we were in the throne room of God, we obviously were still on the rural highway in Alabama, well exceeding the speed limit.

We pulled over. Leslie apologized profusely, telling the officer that we had been deep in praise and worship—and for good measure, conscious that we were in the Bible Belt, she added that I was a preacher and that we were on our way to speak at a local church retreat. The officer wasn't impressed!

As the man stood by the car window, I thought that for a police officer he wasn't very intimidating. He was short, scrawny, and bone thin. He had a kind and gentle demeanor. So kind, in fact, that he compromised and issued us a $61 seatbelt citation (even though we were wearing our seatbelts) and not the $350 fine we deserved. He teased us a bit, and we shared a laugh with him.

We talked with the officer about Jesus and invited him to attend the conference. After tentatively issuing the ticket, he dutifully pulled away in his squad car, lights no longer flashing and with the Alabama state seal in full view on the hood of his car. As I watched him drive away, God spoke to my heart profoundly about the importance of authority and what it means to truly walk in power. That kind policeman had authority, no doubt about it. It didn't matter how harmless or mild mannered he appeared to be, how timid or kind he was.

It didn't matter that I probably weighed more than he did or that with Leslie at the wheel, we could easily have outrun his squad car. No, none of that mattered when he flashed his badge—a badge that said he was operating under the authority of the government. He had the legal backing of the state of Alabama.

I might not have been intimidated by his stature or his appearance, but I certainly was intimidated by his authority. The marked car he drove and the flashing lights in our rearview mirror were all it took to get us to pull over. Even if it was five miles after we should have! The officer had exercised his authority, and our concert was over. Yes, authority is a powerful thing.

The Enemy recognizes a believer who is walking in authority. If we are not enforcing the victory that Christ accomplished on the cross of Calvary, the Enemy will never yield ground. He will continue to operate illegally and take full advantage of our ignorance and failure to manifest all that God created us to be and to do.

We must apprehend him in the name of Jesus and remind him of his position as a footstool for the Most High God. This is what those who dwell in the shelter of the Most High are meant to do: "You will tread on the lion and the adder; the young lion and the serpent you will trample underfoot" (Ps. 91:13). Jesus said it again in Luke 10:19: "Behold, I have given you authority to tread on serpents and scorpions, and over all the power of the enemy, and nothing shall hurt you."

Authority is only as good as the force that stands behind it. Leslie and I could have ignored the flashing red lights that followed us that day in Alabama, but because we understood the weight of the authority that the driver of that squad car carried, we thought it might be a good idea to submit and comply immediately.

After all, the officer was operating under the authority of the state of Alabama and ultimately the president of the United States—who were we to mess with him?!

We have been given authority from the One who is Head, supreme, Lord of all, the One who has *all* dominion, all power and is above all names. The authority that we have been granted is backed by the very powers of heaven. God above has chosen to partner with man to bring about His victory on Earth. The authority we carry and are called to enforce is not a wimpy authority; it's a supreme power to which all things bow in subjection.

Using Our Authority under *the* Authority

If we are going to walk in authority, we need to keep an important truth in mind: our authority is *in* Christ—not outside Him. We cannot walk outside the protection of His Word and hope to walk in authority. We cannot usurp His lordship over us and then expect to tap into His power.

Even Jesus Himself said, "Truly, truly, I say to you, the Son can do nothing of Himself, unless it is something He sees the Father doing; for whatever the Father does, these things the Son also does in like manner" (John 5:19, NASB). That's how we should live our lives.

Jesus said, "He who sent me is with me. He has not left me alone, for I always do the things that are pleasing to him" (8:29). My mother-in-law, Jill, often tells a story that illustrates this principle. When she was in her teenage years, a good friend of hers tried to entice her to make a choice that would not please her father. When Jill refused to participate, her friend retorted, "You are just afraid of what your father will do to you!"

Jill replied, "No, I'm afraid of what *I* will do to my father." Do we conduct our lives doing only what the Father would do, making choices that will please Him? Matthew 18:18 gives us further insight on this matter. I love this verse in the Amplified Bible's classic edition: "Truly I tell you, whatever you forbid and declare to be improper and unlawful on earth *must be* what is already forbidden in heaven, and whatever you permit and declare proper and lawful on earth must be what is already permitted in heaven."

Do we declare anything "proper and lawful" in our lives that God would not allow in heaven? Do we excuse and justify away anything that, if truth be told, we know that God would never permit? This scripture is clear—whatever we permit in our lives, whatever we declare "proper and lawful" for ourselves, *must be* what is already permitted in heaven. Our actions and our words ought only to be tolerated if they're things that God would permit in heaven. The stubborn mind-set or harsh attitude that we declare "proper" and permit in our lives must be measured against what heaven calls proper and lawful.

There is no room in heaven for grudges or unforgiveness. We must be sure that the words that come out of our mouth and the actions we exhibit toward people are things that heaven allows. If they're not things that we would see the Father doing, then we should not do them either. We may feel that our situation is different and that we have a right to hold something against someone. But in John 5:30 Jesus says,

I am able to do nothing from Myself [independently, of My
own accord—but only as I am taught by God and as I get His
orders]. Even as I hear, I judge [I decide as I am bidden to
decide. As the voice comes to Me, so I give a decision], and My
judgment is right (just, righteous), because I do not seek or
consult My own will [I have no desire to do what is pleasing to
Myself, My own aim, My own purpose] but only the will and
pleasure of the Father Who sent Me. (AMPC)

We must not seek or consult our own will. We must not desire to
please ourselves and selfishly serve our own purposes. Our goal should
be to do the will and good pleasure of the Father and nothing else.
We must function as a soldier under orders who desires to please his
commander. We cannot walk in authority unless we live and conduct
our lives in submission to *the* authority.

Disobedience Forfeits Authority

When God created Adam and Eve, He created them in His image,
in His likeness, and He granted them dominion and authority over
all the Earth. But Satan cunningly deceived them, spurred them on
to rebel against God's Word and robbed them of their God-given
authority.

You know the story. When God created Adam and Eve, He planted
a beautiful garden and placed them in it, and He gave them clear
instructions: "You are free to eat from any tree in the garden, but
you must not eat from the tree of the knowledge of good and evil"
(Gen. 2:16–17, NIV). Yet Adam and Eve, with enticement from Satan,
chose to act outside God's rule, rebel against His Word and choose for
themselves what they thought was right and pleasing to the eye. In
doing so, they stepped outside God's government, and it resulted in
their authority being forfeited. It was the work of the deceiver, the

Enemy of our soul, and he hasn't changed his tactics since—he's still after our authority.

First John 3:8 says, "The reason the Son of God appeared was to destroy the works of the devil." The first Adam lost the authority given to him; the second Adam, Jesus, came to take it back! Christ came, in the flesh, to defeat the Enemy and take back all that Adam and Eve surrendered to him at the fall.

As a result, as Luke 10:19 reminds us, we have authority "over all the power of the enemy," but in our ignorance, like Adam and Eve we often allow Satan to deceive us and rob us of that God-given authority.

Each time we choose for ourselves what we think is right (that is, when we eat of the tree of good and evil) rather than listening to what God has said, we step outside God's rule, and by not submitting to the authority of His Word, we get outside the shelter of His protection. As a result, we forfeit authority and become vulnerable to the attacks of the Enemy.

Each time we rebel against God's Word and attempt to live independently of the protection of God's government and rule, we surrender power. For authority to work, it must function in keeping with the government that backs it. That's why it's so important that we stay under the shelter of the Most High, in submission to His authority.

Obedience Leads to Victory

Staying under the protection of God's commands, however, is not a popular message. Somehow the message of obedience has become lost by many in the church today.

Don't get me wrong; I'm so thankful for the message of grace—the message found in Ephesians 2:8–9 that we are saved by grace, through faith and not by works so that no man can boast. With my tainted past, no one is more thankful for grace than I am.

However, Romans 1:5 tells us that we have received grace *for* obedience—in order to *be* obedient. Grace is not defined simply as getting what we don't deserve; rather, it is God's enabling power. We have been saved by grace and kept by grace, and that same grace now enables us to obey God's Word.

Hebrews 5:9 tells us that Jesus "became the source of eternal salvation to all who *obey* him." Titus 2:11–12 says, "The grace of God has appeared that offers salvation to all people. *It teaches us to say 'No' to ungodliness* and worldly passions, and to live self-controlled, upright and godly lives in this present age" (NIV).

Grace provides us with power to do what God has called us to do—it's not just God's amazing grace, it's God's *empowering* grace. Grace is not just God lavishing on us what we don't deserve and then letting us continue the way we were; grace comes with an enabling power to change, with the power to say no to ungodliness and walk in obedience to His Word.

This has nothing to do with works; even our obedience is an act of grace. But the overflow of God's grace will transform and change our lives. It will not leave us as we are. We can't do our own thing and live like hell and then expect to walk in authority. I once heard Bishop T. D. Jakes say, "It's very difficult to defeat a devil you just got done sleeping with—you can't hang with the devil for two weeks and then try to rebuke him in the third."

It sounds obvious enough, and yet often we live as if we don't know this truth. Our choice to eat of the tree of good and evil (following our own will) and not of the tree of life (obeying God's will for our lives) will always affect the authority we carry and the power we walk in.

Many Christians belong to God but make blatant choices to disobey, and then they wonder why their life stinks. People come to me all the time and complain about how horrible and unproductive their lives are, and yet they are not spending time in God's presence, they are not living under the protection of His Word, they are not running for cover and exercising their God-given authority when the Enemy assaults.

The reality is, what we do and how we live affects our quality of life. It doesn't affect whether or not we will go to heaven, but it does affect our ability to bring heaven to Earth. Grace is amazing, but righteousness matters.

Christ modeled the importance of obedience with His own life when He walked on this Earth. He said, "Behold, I have come to do your will, O God" (Heb. 10:7). He recognized the authority of His Father and placed Himself under it. Even as Jesus was about to face the agony of the cross, He prayed to His Father, "Father, if you are willing, remove this cup from me. Nevertheless, *not my will, but yours, be done*" (Luke 22:42). He knew that His purpose on Earth was to do the will of the Father.

One day His disciples were concerned because they had brought Him some food and urged Him to eat, and He didn't want any. Jesus replied to them, "My food is to do the will of him who sent me and to accomplish his work" (John 4:34). He knew His purpose and intended to fulfill it: "I have come down from heaven, not to do my own will but the will of him who sent me" (6:38).

Nothing would divert Him, and neither should anything divert us. Jesus not only modeled obedience to the Father's will in His life, He instructed His disciples to pray for it in their own lives: "When you pray, say: Our Father in heaven, hallowed be Your name. Your kingdom come. *Your will be done*" (Luke 11:2, NKJV).

We read God's Word, attend church and pray to Him occasionally, but that's not enough. If we want to walk in authority and be

who we were created to be in Christ, we need to honor God's authority and accomplish His will by obeying what He tells us to do.

We need to live in submission to His Word, lining up our will
with His and from that place expect to see His kingdom come. We
cannot violate His authority and expect to be a part of bringing His
kingdom to this Earth and manifesting His power in it.

The Bible says, "Submit yourselves therefore to God. Resist the
devil, and he will flee from you" (James 4:7). Part of resisting the
devil is submitting to the authority and rule of God.

The Greek word for "submit" means "to arrange under, to sub-
ordinate, to put in subjection, to subject one's self, obey, to submit
to one's control."[6] This word was a Greek military term meaning to
arrange troop divisions in a military fashion under the command
of a leader. Many of us try to resist the Enemy, but we fail, because
we fail to submit to God.

As we walk in submission to God's will, obeying His Word and
living in subjection to Him, we can effectively oppose and resist
the tactics of the Enemy.

When we run for cover under the shelter of the Most High and
are safely tucked away in the stronghold of His truth, we will recognize who we truly are and live as God meant us to—not defeated
along with the world but as victorious Christians exercising our
God-given authority.

TEN

Stomping on Serpents

You will tread on the lion and the adder; the young lion and the serpent you will trample underfoot.

Psalm 91:13

We were planning the wedding of my middle daughter, Brooke. As much as I loved planning this big day with my daughter, I was limited in what I could do, because Brooke lived in Georgia, and I lived in Wisconsin. I could, however, foot the bill for the wedding!

One day as I visited with Brooke on the phone, she asked for a check so that she could make the final payment to the florist. She didn't know the exact cost, so I told her that I would give her a signed blank check and that she could fill in the amount later.

Once she received that check, Brooke had unlimited access to my bank account. The funds were available for her to utilize when she needed them—but it would be up to her to take advantage of the resources that I had made available to her.

Let's say that Brooke came back to me a month later, holding the blank check in her hand and saying, "Mom, could I have money to pay the florist?" Would I write another check? No. I would reply, "Brooke, I already gave you a signed check. That's all you need. Use the check!"

Imagine if, after the wedding was over, Brooke still hadn't utilized the check, and her florist bill was still unpaid. Would I be at fault? No. Brooke would have failed to appropriate what I had given her. She had in her possession what she needed, the resources were available—she could blame no one else if she failed to appropriate those resources.

We have been given a signed check by the Creator of the universe—the One whose resources are unlimited and whose power no foe can withstand. We have been granted authority to use the name of Jesus—to conduct business on this Earth in His name and in His power. His resources are boundless and unmatched.

If we fail to appropriate the authority that we have been given, the fault lies with us. All authority has been given to us to trample on snakes and scorpions and to overcome all the power of the Enemy, but we must begin to utilize it and walk in the fullness of it.

Utilizing Our Authority

There is a big difference between authority and power. Jesus said "I have given you *authority* . . . over all the *power* of the enemy" (Luke 10:19). The word "power" here means "strength, power, ability."[1] A person can be strong and powerful but not have authority. Now the devil has power, but Jesus has given us authority over the Enemy's power. We fool ourselves when we say there is no Enemy or that he doesn't have any power.

But we do not need to fear him, because we as believers have the power of the Holy Spirit and the authority of the One whose dominion cannot be matched or surpassed. But we must choose to utilize it. Christ has indeed granted us authority, but He leaves it up to us to *enforce* it. What if my friendly Alabamian police officer from the previous chapter didn't enforce the law? What if he just sat in his squad car and waved cheerily at motorists speeding illegally by but did nothing to stop them? Without someone walking in authority and enforcing the government, lawbreakers would be free to do whatever they pleased.

You and I have been given a badge of authority by Christ. We have the legal backing of the government of heaven. Yet countless Christians, myself included, fail to utilize the authority we carry. We sit back idly as our families and friends are robbed blind, plundered and stripped naked.

Meanwhile, all that Christ secured for us is not manifested in this world. If we as the body of Christ never enforce the authority that we have been given, Satan doesn't have any reason to yield ground. He'll push the limits and take advantage of our failure to walk in authority.

We were made to have dominion. Psalm 8:4–6 says,

> What is man that You are mindful of him, and the son of man that You visit him? For You have made him a little lower than the angels, and You have crowned him with glory and honor. *You have made him to have dominion* over the works of Your hands; You have put all things under his feet. (NKJV)

We are God's chosen vessels to govern the Earth—we are partnering with Him to bring heaven to Earth. He has delegated His authority to us, but so many in the church today have little or no victory.

We might be saved and going to heaven, but by failing to take the authority that God has given us, we live tormented by the Enemy, walking in victory only as the exception and in defeat as the norm.

We must learn to say with Jesus, "The ruler of the world (Satan) is coming. And he has no claim on Me [no power over Me nor anything that he can use against Me]" (John 14:30, AMP).

Treading Underfoot

Let's visit Psalm 91:13 again: "You will tread on the lion and the adder; the young lion and the serpent you will trample underfoot." In order to tread on something, it has to be under our feet. We have already established that Christ is seated in the heavenly realms and that all things are under His feet, and we have also seen that we are filled with His fullness. If that is the case, then all things are under our feet as well.

In the vision I shared at the beginning of this book, one of the things that was so profound to me was the deep understanding of my position with God. I had such an awareness that I was hidden with Christ in God, seated spiritually in the heavenly places with Him, even though bodily I was walking and talking here on Earth. What I saw in that vision was a clear picture of Ephesians 2:4-7:

> God, being rich in mercy, because of the great love with which he loved us, even when we were dead in our trespasses, made us alive together with Christ—by grace you have been saved—and raised us up with him and seated us with him in the heavenly places in Christ Jesus, so that in the coming ages he might show the immeasurable riches of his grace in kindness toward us in Christ Jesus.

As we saw earlier, the metaphor of treading underfoot is a picture of a conquering king placing his feet upon the backs of defeated enemies as a sign of subjection. So when Psalm 91:13 declares that we "will tread on the lion and the adder; the young lion and the serpent," it reminds us of the position of power that we occupy with Him—that these things are under our feet and have no power over us. Let's look a little closer at things that we can trample and tread upon. *Lions* are territorial, and they roar to establish their domain. They are mainly nocturnal and work in teams to stalk and ambush their prey.[2] They prowl and pounce on their unsuspecting victim. This phrase in Psalm 91, "You will tread on the lion," refers to things that ambush us, that pounce on us out of nowhere—the sudden attack. Perhaps it's an unexpected layoff, a sudden illness or a bad report. It might be coming home and finding your spouse in bed with your best friend or the unexpected passing of a loved one. The "lion" refers to things that we aren't prepared for and don't see coming.

The *adder* is any venomous serpent, perhaps a cobra. The word "adder" comes from the Hebrew root meaning "to twist."[3] It's a picture of venomous words—gossip, slander, malice, unkindnesses, untruths. Many of us have been wounded by twisted, hurtful words that have deposited poison and toxic venom into our minds and have deeply penetrated our hearts. Some of us still deal with the side effects of venom that was inserted in our system years ago. Romans 3:13 refers to an adder or asp to describe a mouth filled with venomous, deceitful words: "The venom of asps is under their lips."

One of the most dangerous things about an adder is how well it blends in with its environment. It's not easy to see, so we fall victim to its venom as we casually pass by it.

Third, we will trample on *young lions*. Mentioning the word "lion" twice in this verse might seem a bit redundant. After all, isn't it the same word with the addition of "young"?

The writer is trying to make a point: young lions need to be trampled before they grow into big lions. Solomon wrote about "little foxes" that spoil the vine (Song of Sol. 2:15), implying that we build fences to protect against the big foxes but don't protect our vineyard from the little ones that can wreak all sorts of damage. The young lions paint a picture of the "little" sins that we allow to creep into our lives—little things that we tolerate but that can cause a lot of destruction and grow into big issues. Things like jealousy, bitterness, critical and negative attitudes, idle words.

The word *serpent* is translated "dragon" in the original language.[4] You and I know that there is no such thing as a dragon. Dragons are make believe, fantasy, a figment of our imagination. Yet these are the very things that we need to trample on in our minds—those things that we invent in our imagination and that occupy way too much space in our thinking. These are the things that the Enemy whispers to us to get us to take on a spirit of fear, to torment us or to make us worry—and they usually don't even materialize. "Serpents" are the products of over-thinking and over-analyzing—concerns that we obsessively replay in our minds until they become bigger than the God we serve.

I have to be honest—even if dragons are make believe, they still elicit fear in me. Irrational thoughts do the same thing to us—they make us slaves to fear. Joyce Meyer often refers to F.E.A.R. as False Evidence Appearing Real. That's what the Enemy can do in our mind; he takes false evidence and makes it appear real, causing us to meditate on it and lose our peace.

Not Immunity but Authority

Many people believe that being able to trample on snakes and scorpions and overcome all the power of the Enemy means that we will never have to go through hard times. But Christians are not immune to problems. People will hurt us, trials will come and storms will arise.

Jesus walked in authority, but He still had to go to the cross. Why would we expect any less for ourselves? Scripture is clear on this:

Jesus told his disciples, "If anyone would come after me, let him deny himself and *take up his cross* and follow me." (Matt. 16:24)

Through many tribulations we must enter the kingdom of God. (Acts 14:22)

To this you have been called, because Christ also suffered for you, leaving you an example, so that *you might follow* in his steps. (1 Pet. 2:21)

Since therefore Christ suffered in the flesh, arm yourselves with the same way of thinking, for whoever has *suffered in the flesh* has ceased from sin. (4:1)

Rejoice insofar as you *share Christ's sufferings*, that you may also rejoice and be glad when his glory is revealed. (4:13)

Psalm 91:13 never promises immunity—it promises authority. The Greek word for "authority," *exousia*, means not only "power, delegated authority, the power of rule and government" but also "power of choice, right to decide."[5] Having authority over the devil does not mean that we will be protected from trouble, but it does mean that we have the right to decide how we will respond to the hard things in our lives.

Will we allow trouble to defeat and define us, or will we rest securely in Christ and trust that He will redeem all things and turn what the Enemy has meant for evil into good? Will we choose, when trouble comes, to run for the place of refuge, where we can take cover and ride out the storm and be empowered to walk in victory and not in defeat?

Psalm 91:13 doesn't promise us a life free from heartache and trouble; it promises us the power of God's presence and assures us of triumph. It promises us that we can rise from the ashes, more than conquerors. Christ told us, "In this world you will have trouble. But take heart! I have overcome the world" (John 16:33, NIV). The Amplified Bible's classic edition of this verse sums up what Psalm 91:13 promises: "Be of good cheer [take courage; be confident, certain, undaunted]! For I have overcome the world. [I have deprived it of power to harm you and have conquered it for you.]." Christ has deprived trouble and trials, tribulation and distress, frustration and the Enemy of the power to harm us, because He conquered them for us.

Choose Life

If we are living in defeat, it's because we have chosen it. We are empowering the lion, the adder, the young lion and the serpent instead of using our authority to drain them of power and trample them underfoot. We can live victoriously in the middle of heartache and pain, hurt and disappointment.

When we are in the shelter of the Most High, we don't have to walk through life as Debbie Downer or Pity-Me Paul. The things that have happened to us may have been devastating or heartbreaking, but they do not have to define us, nor do we have to spend the rest of our lives defeated by them. We have the power to trample these things, to tread them underfoot.

God has set before us the choice of life or death—and we must *choose* life. In God's presence we will find assurance, power from on high, and freedom from the things that try to enslave us. We are more than conquerors in Christ Jesus.

We can't conquer what we haven't had to confront; we can't overcome what we have never come up against. We learn to walk in authority only as we go through difficult things. In this world we will have trouble, but we have the advantage of knowing who wins. No matter what we encounter, no matter how hot the furnace becomes, we can be confident that God will bring us through triumphantly.

We have no reason to be terrified of the assaults of the enemy, because Jesus "has delivered us from the domain of darkness and transferred us to the kingdom of his beloved Son" (Col. 1:13). Darkness doesn't have power over us any longer. We have nothing to fear, as Christ has disarmed Satan forever. Heaven knows that, and hell knows that, but we must know that deep in our hearts.

The Enemy is a defeated foe, and we should face every battle with him in the knowledge that he is conquered and that in Christ we have authority over him.

Sometimes we wait for God to show up in our circumstances, but He waits for us to run for cover to the stronghold of His presence, the rock of His refuge, and to utilize His authority and enforce the victory that He has obtained for us.

Our Weapon Against the Enemy: The Word of God

When Jesus was on Earth, He faced the Enemy and defeated him. But it's important to note that Jesus didn't defeat the Enemy as God but as a *man* functioning with God's authority. He demonstrated how one who is surrendered to the Spirit, submitted to the authority of God's Word and set on doing God's will has authority over the devil.

Jesus defeated Satan using the same resource that is available to you and me—the authority of the Word of God:

> Jesus was led up by the Spirit into the wilderness to be tempted by the devil. And after fasting forty days and forty nights, he was hungry. And the tempter came and said to him, "If you are the Son of God, command these stones to become loaves of bread." But he answered, "It is written, 'Man shall not live by bread alone, but by every word that comes from the mouth of God.'"

Then the devil took him to the holy city and set him on the
pinnacle of the temple and said to him, "If you are the Son of
God, throw yourself down, for it is written, 'He will command
his angels concerning you,' and 'On their hands they will bear
you up, lest you strike your foot against a stone.'"

Jesus said to him, "Again it is written, 'You shall not put the
Lord your God to the test.'" Again, the devil took him to a very
high mountain and showed him all the kingdoms of the world
and their glory. And he said to him, "All these I will give you,
if you will fall down and worship me." Then Jesus said to him,
"Be gone, Satan! For it is written, 'You shall worship the Lord
your God and him only shall you serve.'"

Then the devil left him, and behold, angels came and were
ministering to him. (Matt. 4:1–11)

Over and over the tempter came at Jesus, and over and over He
defeated the Enemy with the same offensive weapon that we have
available to us as believers: "the sword of the Spirit, which is the word
of God" (Eph. 6:17). At no point did Jesus waver or compromise the
truth. He wielded the Word with utmost accuracy, defeating and
overcoming the tempter until, as it says in Luke, the Enemy "left him
until an opportune time" (4:13, NIV).

Note as well that Jesus had been fasting for forty days and nights.
Fasting is an important tool in learning how to overcome the devil.
When we fast, we learn to say no to fleshly appetites and instead
submit to God's will and ways.

If we can't discipline ourselves to say no to our flesh when it
screams for chocolate cake or a cheeseburger and fries, we will never
learn that we can say no when we want to have a temper tantrum or
to indulge in sex outside of marriage. The more we deny our flesh,
the stronger our spirit will be.

Because Jesus was in every way human like you and me, He was hungry. When the Enemy comes to tempt us, he looks for an area of weakness or vulnerability, and since Jesus was hungry, he tempted Jesus with food! But Jesus resisted—not in his flesh but by submitting His flesh to the authority of the Word of God. As a result, He trampled on the Enemy.

The Enemy not only tempted Jesus with bread, but he tried to strike a blow to Jesus' identity as God's Son as well. "*If* you are the Son of God," he said. *If?* Of course Jesus was the Son of God. But the Enemy knew that—that's why he had come to tempt Him. He knows who we are as well—he just hopes that we don't realize it! By introducing the "if," the devil hoped to get Jesus to forget who He was and to doubt His position as the Son.

Scripture tells us, "The Spirit himself bears witness with our spirit that we are children of God, and if children, then heirs—heirs of God and fellow heirs with Christ" (Rom. 8:16–17). John 1:12 tells us, "To all who did receive him, who believed in his name, he gave the right to become children of God." If we know Jesus Christ as our Lord and Savior, we are children of God, joint heirs with Jesus. We have an inheritance in Him, but the Enemy hopes that we lose sight of that fact.

Jesus was deeply rooted and secure in who He was as the Son of God. The question is, do we know who we are? Will we allow the Enemy to sow seeds of doubt and get us to question our position in the family of God and forfeit our authority?

Just as the duck imprinted as a dog, if the Enemy can get us to doubt that we are sons and daughters of God, he can imprint us with a false identity and lead us astray from our position of authority in Christ. Don't give him the power to do it.

The Enemy finally left Jesus, but it was not because he was tired or had run out of schemes. No, he left because his deception was not working. Jesus had resisted him, so he had no choice but to leave and wait for the next opportune time. Pastor Jesse Duplantis says that the Enemy left because "he had experienced resistance instead of assistance!"[6] I love that! We must stop assisting the Enemy and begin resisting him!

Speaking God's Word Aloud

When Jesus overcame the Enemy with the power of God's Word, He did it by speaking the Word out loud. There is power in speaking God's Word. When God created the world, "the earth was without form and void, and darkness was over the face of the deep. And the Spirit of God was hovering over the face of the waters. And God *said*, 'Let there be light,' and there was light" (Gen. 1:2-3). He said it! God's Word is powerful. His words have the force of heaven behind them.

We see the importance of speaking out loud in Romans 10:8-10:

> "The word is near you, in your mouth and in your heart" (that is, the word of faith that we proclaim); because, if you confess with your mouth that Jesus is Lord and believe in your heart that God raised him from the dead, you will be saved. For with the heart one believes and is justified, and with the mouth one confesses and is saved.

Over and over in Scripture we see the significance of confessing with the mouth what we believe in our heart. In Mark 11 we read a story about the disciples being amazed at the power of Jesus' words. They overheard Him speaking to a fig tree and were amazed when they found out later that the tree had withered in response to Jesus' words. When they questioned Him about it, Jesus answered them, saying,

> Have faith in God. Truly, I say to you, whoever *says* to this
> mountain, "Be taken up and thrown into the sea," and does
> not doubt in his heart, but believes that *what he says* will come
> to pass, it will be done for him. Therefore I tell you, whatever
> you ask in prayer, believe that you have received it, and it will
> be yours. (Mark 11:22–24)

Jesus told them to speak to the mountain. The mountain here is
symbolic of the obstacles in our lives—things that seem overwhelming and too powerful for us to move. Jesus said that if we speak to
the mountain and believe in our heart that what we say will come
to pass, it will! But look at the prerequisite attached to this verse: we
must "have faith in God." Jesus wanted His disciples—and us!—to
have such confidence in God that we know that when we speak His
Word, no matter how great the obstacle in front of us, something is
going to change.

It's so important that we come to the place in our faith walk that
we have absolute confidence that God means what He says and that
He'll do what He promises. Then we need to speak forth His Word in
faith—trusting it to accomplish what He says it will do. Speaking God's
Word unleashes His power into a situation. Our challenge is to look
our obstacles in the eye and not back down—to be more convinced of
the power of God's Word than in what we see in the natural.

My husband and I have seven children, all of them at different
places in their walk with God. However, I have scriptures that I speak
over their lives and believe regardless of what I see them doing in the
natural—scriptures that look at the mountain and command it to be
removed.

Almost daily I confess, "All my children will be taught by the Lord,
and great shall be the peace of my children" (see Isa. 54:13). I speak
out loud in agreement with God's Word that "the offspring of the

righteous are blessed and will be mighty in the land" (see Ps. 112:2), and I agree that "no weapon formed against me or my children can prosper, because that is my inheritance from Him" (see Isa. 54:17).

I confess these things because I believe them, and I refuse to be moved by what I can see with my eyes.

Second Timothy 3:16 says, "All Scripture is breathed out by God." That means that the Bible contains the very words of God. They may be words on a page in a book, but they originated from the mouth of God and were written under the inspiration of the Holy Spirit.

They are His life-giving words speaking to us today. They have the creative power of God behind them, and they are authoritative and life changing. God's words are so powerful that they never return to Him void but always accomplish that which He purposes and succeed in the thing for which He sent them (see Isa. 55:11). That's something worth speaking about!

Using Our Double-Edged Sword

Hebrews 4:12 calls the Word of God a "double-edged sword" (NIV). In the original language the word "double-edged" is *distomos*. It is a compound word made up of *di*, which means "twice," and *stomos*, which means "mouth,"[7] so it literally means a "twice-mouthed" sword.

That tells us that God's Word is intended to be mouthed twice and used as a weapon! It's mouthed first from God into our Spirit when He uses it to pierce our hearts and then, second, from our mouths into the atmosphere in agreement over our circumstances, our lives, our families, our finances. It's a sword—a powerful weapon that is often underutilized by believers today.

Ephesians 6:17 includes the Word of God in the list of armor that is available to believers: "the sword of the Spirit, which is the word of God." It is the only piece of armor that is both an offensive and defensive weapon.

It is a strategic weapon in our spiritual arsenal that we need to be intentional about wielding against the Enemy of our soul.

The power behind a double-edged sword is deadly and can quickly incapacitate an assailant. It does damage in two directions when it is inserted, as it cuts on either side of the sword. That's what God's Word does to the Enemy when we, like Christ, wield the sword of the Spirit. It incapacitates him.

That's why its so important for us to store up God's Word in our heart so that when the Enemy tries to assail us, we can easily retrieve the sword and add the second edge to it as it comes out of our mouth in agreement with God's initial declaration. Jesus didn't need to grab a Bible when He was facing the Enemy in the wilderness; He had hidden it in His heart.

It's vital that we keep our sword sharp. We do this by spending time in the Word, hiding it in our heart and meditating on it. When my children were growing up, each week in their Sunday school class they had "sword drills."

Each child would have a Bible in hand, and the teacher would call out a specific verse. When she said "Charge!" the children would race to find the verse, and the first one who stood and correctly read it got a point or a piece of candy.

My children loved it. It was a fun game for them, but it also taught them the importance of storing up God's Word in their hearts and of knowing how to retrieve it when needed.

One of the most valuable weapons we have available to us as Christians is the Word of God. It is a powerful offensive weapon. If Jesus needed it to defeat the devil, how much more do you and I?

In the Name of Jesus!

A number of years ago, on the way home from a Christian conference in Chicago, my friend, Denise, and I stopped by a local outlet
mall to do some shopping. Denise and I are avid shoppers (I like to call
it retail therapy), and it didn't take us long to find our favorite store,
load up on the latest fashions, and scurry off to the dressing room. I
found an adorable sweater set, on clearance of course, and made my
way to the counter to pay.

As I reached for my wallet, I realized that my purse was missing.
Panic set in. I sprinted back to the dressing room, hoping that in my
excitement to purchase the sweater I had absentmindedly left my
purse there. Unfortunately I had not. By this time Denise and the
store manager had joined the frantic search—all to no avail. I sent up a
quick prayer of desperation, reminding the Lord that He knew exactly
where my purse was and asking Him to help me find it.

Our search was futile, and eventually we returned to the car empty
handed. Reluctantly I called my husband and conveyed the bad news.
My wallet contained every credit card we had ever owned! Dave gra-
ciously agreed to call the credit-card companies and report the cards
stolen, but he did not have the contact information for one of the
cards. Fortunately, because I had recently used that number, I knew
it by heart and agreed to call that company myself.

I immediately dialed the number and was greeted by a friendly
customer service representative. As she accessed my account, she
informed me that the card was currently being used at a nearby store
in that same outlet center. The thief had wasted no time running from
store to store accumulating a large balance on my card!

Determined to get my wallet back, I slammed my car into reverse
and went looking for the one who was getting a new wardrobe at my
expense, praying all the while!

As I drove, I stayed on the phone, and the customer service clerk continued to inform me of each purchase as it was being made. As I stepped on the gas, a van driven by an elderly man pulled out directly in front of me. Did he not know that I was in hot pursuit? The customer service representative, who was enjoying her part in the investigation far too much, advised me that the purse snatcher had now purchased several hundred dollars worth of items at a children's store in that same mall.

Deeply saddened, I headed toward that store. As we passed it, Denise pointed out a couple that she recognized from the store where my purse had first come up missing. Not waiting for confirmation, I impulsively took her at her word and jumped out of my car (I don't even remember putting it in park!). With my car sitting in the middle of the street, doors ajar, and a crowd now accumulating, I approached the couple with complete confidence. I was angry.

Anyone who knows me would tell you that I would give you the shirt off my back, but please don't steal it from me! A righteous anger mounted within me. The gentleman was about seven feet tall—the largest man I had ever seen—quite muscular and very intimidating. His wife was a petite woman with a dainty frame and a not so dainty mouth. Needless to say, Denise immediately called 911.

I, however, took matters into my own hands. Perhaps it was the shock of knowing that someone could be so callous and coldhearted, or perhaps it was the fear of having to pay back all the debt that they had accumulated. As I approached the couple, fear vanished, and confidence took over. Not even certain that these people were the thieves, without another thought I demanded that they give me back my wallet.

Both the man (who seemed to grow taller with every passing minute) and the woman (who I noted was carrying bags from all the stores the customer service representative had mentioned) were not quite sure what to do with this irrational woman who had so boldly approached them. As the large crowd grew larger, the woman exclaimed, "You are crazy, lady," and with that she turned and walked toward her car. Quite honestly, I was beginning to wonder if she could be right!

The man, however, did not move. I tried again, this time with even more confidence, "Satan, in the name of Jesus, I command you to give me back my wallet!"

He replied, shocked, "Are you calling me Satan?"

"No," I said, "but I'm telling you that you are under the influence of Satan, and in the name of Jesus, I command you to give me back my wallet!"

In all the excitement, I had never thought to put my phone down. My friendly little customer service representative had placed my call on speakerphone so that everyone in her office could enjoy this episode of *Starskey and Hutch*. I could hear the people in her office laughing hysterically. I was bound and determined to get my wallet back. Again, with my finger pointed directly at the man, I said, "In the name of Jesus, I command you to give me back my wallet." The man stood still. Time seemed frozen.

That is, until I was distracted for a brief moment by a shuffle behind me. I dropped my pointed finger and turned around, and when I did, the gentleman ran toward his car.

As I watched him run, I could not help adding one more comment. "You might have my wallet, but I've got Jesus, and I would not want to be you for anything in this world. You are messing with my Jesus!" Those were the last words he heard before he and his wife raced from the parking lot, bumped over the curb and headed to the highway for their escape.

Denise and I jumped into our car and followed. I was still on the phone with the credit card company, and Denise was talking with the police dispatcher. At one point the police dispatcher told Denise to tell me to pull over.

"I'm not pulling over until I see squad cars," I replied.

"Rhea, there are four squad cars behind you. *Now pull over!*" Denise ordered. Reluctantly I agreed, and four squad cars streamed by me at breathtaking speed. "I'm not missing this for anything in the world," I excitedly exclaimed as I maneuvered my car back onto the highway. As I did, a car coming in the opposite direction did a U-turn in front of me, nearly colliding with me. I would find out later that this was an off-duty police officer who had been shopping at the mall that day and had witnessed the man throw my purse out the window. He was going back to retrieve the missing purse with the stolen credit cards still intact (remember my prayer, "Lord, You know exactly where my purse is, and I'm asking You to lead me to it").

Further up the street, the police pulled the couple over and arrested them. We later found out that the authorities had been looking for this couple for seven weeks. Apparently their little escapade had become a weekly ritual that was put to a stop by the powerful name of Jesus and a stubborn little woman who was silly enough to believe that she had authority.

As Denise and I sat in my car waiting for the men in blue to finish their reports, they occasionally glanced our way and laughed. Obviously the couple had told them about my temporary loss of sanity. Eventually an officer approached my car and told me that I would need to write a report. With a confident look of satisfaction, I smiled and kindly asked him if he'd like me to include the "Satan in the name of Jesus" command in the report or not. At that he lost his composure, and we both had a good chuckle.

God has given us authority over the power of the Enemy. Our part is to recognize that authority and, in the name of Jesus and from the secret place of the Most High, use it to tread the Enemy underfoot.

ELEVEN

Holding Fast to God and Giving Place Only to Him

Because he holds fast to me in love, I will deliver him; I will protect him, because he knows my name.

Psalm 91:14

God wants our hearts. He desires deep relationship with us—deeper than the most personal, one-on-one relationship we have with our closest friend. The problem is, we have an Enemy who wants to crowd into our party of two and take over the affections of our hearts. A humorous Arab proverb pictures this well:

> One cold night, as an Arab sat in his tent, a camel gently thrust his nose under the flap and looked in. "Master" he said, "let me put my nose in your tent. It's cold and stormy out here."

> "By all means," said the Arab, "and welcome," as he turned over and went to sleep.

> A little later the Arab awoke to find that the camel had not only put his nose in the tent but his head and neck also. The camel, who had been turning his head from side to side, said, "I will take but little more room if I place my forelegs within the tent.

It is difficult standing out here."

"Yes, you may put your forelegs within," said the Arab, moving a little to make room, for the tent was small.

Finally the camel said, "May I not stand wholly inside? I keep the tent open by standing as I do."

"Yes, yes," said the Arab. "Come wholly inside. Perhaps it will be better for both of us." So the camel crowded in. The Arab with difficulty in the crowded quarters again went to sleep. When he woke up the next time, he was outside in the cold, and the camel had the tent to himself.[1]

We have an enemy who wants to get "a nose into our tent," and like the camel in this story, if we give him even the smallest bit of access, before we know it, he will infiltrate our entire life.

The only One who should be in our tent is God! When we fulfill the conditional promise to dwell in the shadow of the Almighty and in the secret place of the Most High, we will be people, as Psalm 91:14 tells us, who hold fast to God in love. The psalmist also tells us that we will know His name—in other words, He will fill our thoughts and our lives. The problem comes in when the Enemy tries to nose his way into our personal relationship with the Lord and take over our thoughts and emotions. All too often we let him do this.

My mother used to tell me, "If you give the Enemy an inch, he'll take a foot. If you crack the door for him, he'll push the entire door in." That is so true. That's why, in his letter to the Ephesians, Paul encouraged his readers not to "give place to the devil" (Eph. 4:27, KJV).

Don't Give Place to the Devil

Paul exhorts us to be aware of the access we give the devil in our lives. Our Enemy is on the prowl, waiting to capitalize upon any area of weakness or opportunity that we present to him. The word Paul uses for "give" means "to give of one's *own accord* and with good will; to give, grant, permit, yield; to put into the hands, power, or possession of anyone; to commit or trust to the charge or care of anyone; to give oneself, deliver oneself."[2] Are we giving Satan, of our own accord, opportunity to act in our lives?

The tense that Paul uses for "don't give" is present imperative with the negative—it means to stop something that is already in progress. In other words, he is calling us to stop giving the devil a place to operate in our lives. We might be doing it, but we can stop.

The word Paul uses for "place" refers to "the place which a person or thing occupies or *has a right to*, a place or spot where one can settle, abide, dwell."[3] Figuratively the word means "opportunity" or "occasion."

One "place" the devil likes to get hold of is our mind. He surveys our lives, looking for a negative thought pattern, a bent toward sin or a false belief, and he capitalizes on it. He's looking for a breach where he can gain access to our minds, because he knows that where the mind goes, the man will follow. Then he fires his lies at us repeatedly until he gets penetration and we come into agreement with him. His goal is to get us to accept his lies as truth so that they will become embedded in our life as beliefs.

Do we give the devil a place in our lives from which operate? Are we, through bad habits or ungodly thought patterns, giving him an opportunity or occasion to function in our relationships and day-to-day routines? On the cross of Calvary, Jesus stripped the Enemy of his rights, and the only "right" he has to function in our lives is the opportunity that we provide for him.

The word Paul uses for "devil" is *diabolos*, and it means "prone to slander, slanderous, accusing falsely."[4] *Diabolos* is derived from two greek words—*dia* and *ballos*. Greek scholar Rick Renner tells us, "The first part of the word is the prefix *dia*, which means 'through' and often carries the idea of penetration. Because *dia* is used at the first part of this word, it tells us that the devil wants to make some kind of penetration."

The second part of the word is *ballos*, which means "to throw." Renner adds, "When these two words are put together to form the word *diabolos*, it paints a vivid picture of the devil as one who repetitiously throws accusations at the mind striking again and again until he ultimately penetrates the mind with his slanderous lies and relationship destroying insinuations."[5]

Paul tells us, "Don't give place to the devil; don't give him an opportunity or occasion to get a foothold in your life."

Jesus told his disciples, "The ruler of this world is coming, and he has nothing in Me" (John 14:30, NASB). When Satan came to tempt Jesus, absolutely nothing in Jesus was enticed by what Satan had to offer. The Enemy, try as he might, could not find anything in Jesus that would allow him to gain a foothold.

Don't miss the fact in this verse that Jesus called Satan the ruler of this world. He didn't minimize the devil's ability or influence, and neither should we. Satan has influence in this world—in the media, the world's philosophies, the government, the educational system, the world's lack of morals. First John 5:19 confirms to us that "the whole world lies in the power of the evil one."

While this is true and he is indeed the "god of this world" (2 Cor. 4:4), as born-again believers, we do not lie in his power. We serve the one true God, who is the King of Kings and the Lord of Lords. He is "the King eternal, immortal, invisible" (1 Tim. 1:17, NIV), who has all authority and all power, and it is to Him that we must hold fast in love.

Who Has Our Devotion?

When we accepted Jesus Christ as our Lord and Savior, Scripture says that God "delivered us from the domain of darkness and transferred us to the kingdom of his beloved Son" (Col. 1:13). However, a clash between kingdoms is going on in this world.

We are delegates of the kingdom of light, ambassadors of Christ in a lost and dying world. Satan may be the prince of this world, but we are not of this world, and we need to keep in mind that the One who is in us "is greater than he who is in the world" (1 John 4:4).

The kingdom that we represent is radically different from the world around us. Jesus prayed to the Father regarding His followers, "I do not ask that you take them out of the world, but that you keep them from the evil one" (John 17:15).

We live in this world, but we should not behave as though we were of it. The ruler of this world should have nothing in us—like Jesus, we need to holding fast to God in love and purposefully set on doing His will if we want to shut off the Enemy's access to our lives.

Jesus walked so closely with the Father in obedience that He committed to doing only what the Father told him to do, and that's why He could confidently say, "The ruler of this world . . . has *nothing in Me*" (14:30, NKJV).

When we "hold fast to [God] in love," we live like Jesus, set on doing His will. Jesus was intentional about not giving the devil an occasion to act—the only One who had access to His life was the Father.

Like Jesus, we must settle it in our heart that God's Word will have the final authority in our life—that our hearts are set on Him. We must be committed to doing only what the Father tells us to do, recognizing that it is for our good and not our harm. No matter how enticing the Enemy's offers may seem, no matter how strong the draw from the world may be, we must learn to say with the psalmist, "You are my Lord; I have no good apart from you" (Ps. 16:2).

Giving Place to the Devil—It's a Choice

Years ago a popular motel chain began a brilliant advertising campaign with the tagline "We'll leave the light on for you." It conveyed the message that people were always welcome and could stop by any time—the door would always be open. But have some of us "left the light on" for Satan? Have we been open to his strategizing and invited him to put a nose into our tent?

Biblical scholar Skip Moen says that when Paul told us not to give place to the devil, he used the verb *didomi* for "give," and it means "to give of one's own accord with good will. You don't use *didomi* for something *taken* from you. You don't use it to describe something you gave up under duress. This is a verb used for *bestowing* something, granting permission or delivering something for personal advantage."[6] So many of us want to blame the devil for stealing from us and wreaking havoc in our lives, but the reality is that we grant him permission to do these things.

Flip Wilson was a successful comedian who made the world laugh with his persona of a preacher's wife, Geraldine Jones. Any time Mrs. Jones did something wrong or inappropriate, instead of accepting responsibility, she was quick to dismiss her actions with the retort, "The devil made me do it." Flip Wilson won a Grammy award for his performance and made Americans double over with laughter watching his weekly television show, but Geraldine's theology couldn't be more wrong. The devil *can't* make us do anything—we willfully give him place in our lives. He is powerless to do anything without our consent and cooperation.

Why we would intentionally choose to give the Enemy place in our life? Who would be silly enough to do that? That's simple—we'd do it if we believed that we had something to gain in the process, if what he was offering appealed to our desires and made us feel that we couldn't live without it. The apostle James makes it clear that it is our own desires, the lusts of our flesh that open the door to the Enemy:

> Each one is tempted when he is dragged away, enticed and *baited* [to commit sin] by his own [worldly] desire (lust, passion). Then when the illicit desire has conceived, it gives birth to sin; and when sin has run its course, it gives birth to death. Do not be misled, my beloved brothers and sisters. (James 1:14–16, AMP)

A number of other scriptures support this, showing several ways that we as believers allow the Enemy access to our lives:

> Peter said, "Ananias, why have you *let* Satan fill your heart? You lied to the Holy Spirit, and you kept some of the money for yourself." (Acts 5:3, NLT)

> Be sober, be vigilant; because your adversary the devil walks about like a roaring lion, seeking whom he *may* devour. Resist him. (1 Pet. 5:8–9, NKJV)

Notice, "whom he *may* devour." He's searching for someone who will *let* him have an opportunity, or a place, from which to function.

> The devil had already *put it into the heart of Judas Iscariot*, Simon's son, to betray [Jesus]. (John 13:2)

> Some have already *turned aside after Satan*. (1 Tim. 5:15, NKJV)

> The Spirit clearly says that in later times some will *abandon the faith* and *follow deceiving spirits* and things taught by demons. (4:1, NIV)

> Satan stood up against Israel and *moved* David to number Israel. (1 Chron. 21:1, NASB)

Before reading further, do some self-examination, and ask the Father to reveal to you any places where you have given the Enemy an occasion to act in your life. Is there some place where you have failed to hold fast to God and instead allowed the Enemy to stir up in you a divided heart, mixed loyalties or devotion to the world and the things in it? Take a moment and slam the door to him now before continuing on.

Access by Deception

I once read an article about the large blue butterfly. In its adult form this creature is a strikingly beautiful insect with speckled black dots scattered throughout its dazzling blue wings. It is a parasitic insect that preys on a certain species of ants and fools the ants into allowing it to invade their home.

The female large blue butterfly strategically lays her eggs in the path of the vulnerable ant species so that when the caterpillar hatches, the ants will stumble upon it. The clever caterpillar deceitfully draws the ants to itself by emitting chemicals similar to what ant larvae produce. Thinking that the caterpillar is one of their own, the ants are deceived into believing that the young insect is not a threat.

The ants are further enticed when the scheming caterpillar secretes a sweet tasting glandular substance that allure them and causes them to become quickly addicted to it. In their craving for more of the tasty substance, the ants escort the caterpillar back to their nest, completely unaware that they have allowed an enemy to infiltrate their home. All they know is that their lusts are being fulfilled and their longings temporarily satisfied.

As the caterpillar makes its way to the ants' nest, it mimics the sounds of the queen ant in order to disguise its true identity and further deceive the ants. After slyly gaining access to their home, the caterpillar begins destroying the ant larvae and robbing the ants of the food source they need for their survival. Naive to the danger that they have placed themselves in, the ants protect the invading caterpillar because of their desire for more of the enticing succulence that the caterpillar offers.[7]

What a picture of what happens to us when we give way to what seem to be irresistible lusts of our flesh. We have a parasitic enemy who works just like that caterpillar.

He comes disguised as something we think we can't resist, offering a tasty indulgence that we can't seem to turn away from. Cunningly he works his way into our lives and from that place strategically connives until he brings destruction upon us.

Some of us have been tricked into taking the Enemy of our soul to our "nests" and letting him infiltrate our home simply because we fail to hold fast to God and come to a place at which we can't resist the lure of the tasty sin he offers.

Because of this, homes are destroyed by adultery, wives are crushed by their husbands' pornography addictions, children are broken by an alcoholic or abusive parent. We need to wake up. We are willing to surrender our convictions and dismiss our beliefs simply because of the appeal of a tasty morsel of sin.

Satan does not come to us dressed in a red suit with horns and a pitchfork. Like the clever caterpillar, he comes disguised, offering us something that we think we can't resist—a look at pornography, a rage that rises up and doesn't feel as if it can be contained, a sexual relationship that seems right, a reason not to forgive, a desire for one more drink or one more indulgence, an occasion to be offended or a compelling motivation to cheat or lie or hate. We cannot be unaware. He will appeal to our desires, and if we are not careful, we will give him place, thinking that we will actually gain in the transaction.

Sealing Off the Access Point

Let's look more deeply at the definition for the word "place" in Ephesians 4:27 (KJV). The Greek word is *topos*. It is where we get our word "topography," and it refers to refers to "a specific, marked-off, geographical location. It carries the idea of a territory, province, region, zone, or geographical position."[8] It's a picture of the Enemy wanting to gain ground in every place of our lives—to cover the map of our lives, so to speak. He wants access to our minds, marriages, children, finances, jobs, friendships and ministries. We must stay alert, loving God deliberately with all our heart and not giving the Enemy place to infiltrate our tent.

Every night before we go to bed, my husband, Dave, and I check the doors in our house to be sure that our house is secure. We would never dream of going to bed with the doors unlocked or the garage door wide open. To do so would give thieves and intruders an open invitation.

Just as Dave and I are intentional about fortifying our house from intruders, we need to be intentional about safeguarding our lives against the spiritual intruder as well. We would never invite an escaped convict to dinner or give a murderer the code to our garage door, yet too often we roll out the red carpet for the Enemy of our soul, inviting him to inhabit an area of our thinking, our actions and yes, even our beliefs.

Scripture calls Satan a thief, and thieves are masters at gaining entrance into our territory in order to rip us off. We must recognize this and keep him from accessing areas of our lives.

My in-laws recently had trouble with mice infiltrating their home. They set traps, hired a pest-control service, and went to great lengths to rid their home of these intruders—all to no avail. They were at a loss as to how these pesky varmints were gaining entrance to their home.

One day I stopped by to visit them and entered their house through the garage. As the electric garage door settled back into its closed position, I couldn't help but notice the light of day peeking through a corner of the darkened garage. *Aha*, I thought. *I found the access point!*

Sure enough, the devious little creatures had nibbled their way through the seal of the garage door, allowing them free access not only to the garage but also the house.

It didn't take a rocket scientist to realize that no matter how many mice my in-laws got rid of, until they sealed up the access point, the mice would still be able to gain entry to their home. Not surprisingly, once they closed up the hole, the mice issue took care of itself.

We need to seal up the access points in our life. We try to rid ourselves of the pesky behaviors that come as a result of that breach, and it never seems to last. It's because we haven't dealt with the access points.

When I was a little girl, my mother suffered with a mental illness that caused her to become self-absorbed and to display narcissistic tendencies.

Although she told me often that she loved me, her actions and lack of attention toward me conveyed another message. Despite her mental illness, my mother was a wonderful woman, but sadly, as a little girl, I had not yet learned to separate my mother from her illness, and as a result, I felt alienated, unloved and rejected.

My father was a gentle man. But because his family owned and operated a trucking company, much of his time and emotional energies went to his job. As a long-haul truck driver, he was often on the road for lengthy periods of time—making him unavailable to me, which further fed my sense of rejection and isolation.

Open wounds—emotional ones included—are always breeding grounds for infection. For this reason all wounds need to be dealt with so that they can be healed thoroughly. Mine was not, and infection set in and plagued me for many years as an adult.

You see, as a little girl, my deep wound of rejection and deep-seated feelings of unworthiness gave the devil place in my life and provided fertile ground for him to deposit his lies and then fortify his territory with false beliefs. My feelings of unworthiness and the deep-rooted belief that I was not good enough to be loved resulted in a stronghold of self-rejection, which opened the door to an environment that fed perfectionism, a sense of abandonment, anger and an intense self-hatred.

Although I tried to sweep my house clean and rid myself of the secondary issues of anger and self-hatred, like the mice in my in-laws' house, the behaviors always came back, because the access point was not sealed up. I learned that to truly become free, I had to deal with the place I had given to the devil and seal it up, knowing that once the access point was dealt with, the other issues would take care of themselves.

Ways We Give Place to the Devil

We can give the devil an access point in our lives in many ways. When we look at the context of Ephesians 4:27, where we are told not to "give place to the devil" (KJV), we can see a number of them. This passage in Ephesians 4 clearly points to the fact that one of the ways we provide an opportunity for the devil to work is by having an angry spirit:

> Be angry and do not sin; do not let the sun go down on your anger, and *give no opportunity [or place] to the devil*. Let the thief no longer steal, but rather let him labor, doing honest work with his own hands, so that he may have something to share with anyone in need. Let no corrupting talk come out of your

mouths, but only such as is good for building up, as fits the occasion, that it may give grace to those who hear. And do not grieve the Holy Spirit of God, by whom you were sealed for the day of redemption. Let all bitterness and wrath and anger and clamor and slander be put away from you, along with all malice. Be kind to one another, tenderhearted, forgiving one another, as God in Christ forgave you. (Eph. 4:26–32)

Famous nineteenth-century preacher Charles Spurgeon said, "Anger is temporary insanity. I have no more right as a Christian to allow a bad temper to dwell in me than I have to allow the devil himself to dwell there."[9] When we indulge in anger and rage, we give place to the devil and provide an environment conducive for him to act.

The rest of the passage points to other areas in which we give access to the devil. Look at the list immediately following verse 27:

- Stealing
- Corrupt talk—criticism, gossip, lies, swearing, foul joking, a judgmental spirit, etc.
- Bitterness
- Wrath, or bad temper
- Resentment and animosity
- Clamor and quarrelling
- Slander
- Malice, spite and ill will
- Lack of kindness and love
- Hatred and a critical spirit
- Unforgiveness

Bad attitudes, a quickness to take offense, rebellion, unkindness and irritability are all breeding grounds for the devil to strip us of authority and take us captive to do his will. Don't give him advantage through behaviors that do not bring God glory. He wants to dethrone truth in our lives and get us to function in a fleshly manner dictated by our emotions so that we will express his character rather than the character of Christ.

We must determine deep within that God's way is best and that we will hold fast to Him and His ways with all our heart, no matter how enticing the Enemy's schemes may be. The Enemy tried to convince Eve in the garden of Eden that God was holding something back from her and didn't have her best interests at heart. He does the same to us today. It's a deception and a snare, and we must be alert to it.

I once heard someone describe the mark of the beast, 666, like this: six is the prophetic number of man, so triple sixes translates as "man, man, man" or "me, myself and I." Rebellion makes things all about us, as if we know better than God. Everything we do that we know we should not do is plainly and simply *rebellion* against God and His Word—and it always offers the Enemy an invitation to have place in our lives.

Eve made the mistake of listening to the serpent's lies and reasoning with the devil, which led to man's rebellion and spiritual downfall. Don't listen to the Enemy's lies or attempt to reason with him—we must set our love instead on the One who is able to deliver and satisfy us in ways that we have never dreamed.

But What About Our Pesky Emotions and Mixed-Up Thoughts?

Refusing the Enemy access into our lives isn't always easy. Even when we want to give him no place, we find that he has a way of getting to us through our own fluctuating thoughts and emotions. The apostle John gives us an antidote for that: "Beloved, do not believe every spirit, but test the spirits to see whether they are from God, for many false prophets have gone out into the world. By this you know the Spirit of God: every spirit that confesses that Jesus Christ has come in the flesh is from God" (1 John 4:1-2).

Note that John is writing to believers in this passage—we know that because he calls them "beloved"—and he tells them not to believe every spirit. The word "spirit" here is "the disposition or influence which fills and governs the soul of any one." Keep in mind that the soul is our mind, will, emotions. "Spirit" can also mean "the efficient source of any power, affection, emotion, desire."[10] John is saying, "Do not legitimize every emotion you have nor empower every thought that runs through your mind; rather, scrutinize your thoughts and feelings, examine them and see if they are from God.

The word "believe" in this passage means "to think to be true, to be persuaded of, to credit, place confidence in."[11] We must not think to be true or be persuaded by every thought we have. We must not place confidence in the emotions that rise up within us or the lies that the Enemy whispers to us. We are not to credit every thought we have as from the Lord but rather to test each thought. The word "test" means "to scrutinize and to examine."[12]

John goes on to say, "By this you know the Spirit of God: Every spirit that confesses that Jesus Christ has come in the flesh is of God." The word "confess" means to "say the same thing as another, to agree with."[13]

In other words, if the voice we are listening to doesn't say the same thing as Jesus or agree with His Word, *don't believe it*! If a thought we have doesn't agree with the truth of God's Word or isn't something that the voice of love would say, we need to get another thought.

While we can't trust our thoughts and emotions, we *can* trust the Lord. Proverbs 3:5-6 says, "Trust in the LORD with all your heart, and do not lean on your own understanding. In all your ways acknowledge him, and he will make straight your paths." The Lord is the only

One worthy of our trust. Putting our hope in anything else will disappoint, but the Bible says that those who hope in the Lord will not be disappointed (see Isa. 49:23).

The Hebrew word translated "trust" in Proverbs 3:5 means "to confide in anyone, to set one's hope and confidence upon any one." It further means "to trust, to have confidence, to be bold, and to be secure."[14]

The word is in the imperfect tense, which means that the action is continuous and is never completed. In other words, the decision to totally trust God is a choice that we need to intentionally make day in and day out, minute by minute, at every turn and in every situation. It's choosing to confidently put our trust in the One who promises not to disappoint us.

Proverbs 3:5 urges us to completely trust God with all our "heart." The word for "heart" means "inner man, mind, will, understanding, thinking, reflection, memory, and the seat of emotions, passions and appetites."[15] I love that! We need to weigh our every thought, emotion and desire against the Word of God. If our thoughts or the emotions and actions they trigger do not say the same thing that Jesus would say, we need to reject them, refuse to put our trust in them and refuse them place in our lives. We need to train our mind, will and emotions to totally trust in the Lord and His desires for our lives, and we must not lean on our own understanding. That takes intentionality.

I don't know about you, but I can be very emotional at times. It's easy to let my emotions drive my understanding of situations or to let my memory and the constant replaying of an offense taint my understanding as well. If we rely on our own understanding of situations and circumstances, we will always be misled and deceived, because the Bible says that our heart (same word used for heart in Proverbs 3:4–5) "is the most deceitful of all things, and desperately wicked"

(Jer. 17:9, NLT). That means that *nothing* is more deceitful than our fleshly thoughts, will, emotions, passions and appetites.

Think about that! If we put our trust in these things, they will mislead us, cause us to stumble and give place for the devil to act. They will cause us to arrive at conclusions that are driven by the intensity of the moment and based on feelings, not fact. By relying on our emotions and limited thinking, we manufacture unfair opinions, fleshly reactions and mistaken judgments about people and situations. Our deceitful heart will always taint our perception of things. Our understanding will be influenced by our brokenness and skewed by our illogical deductions.

We need to defer to the Lord. We need to set our whole heart upon trusting in Him. Our understanding is finite and limited, but God's is not. It is when we process and filter things through our own understanding that we give place to the devil, are gripped with fear, overcome by anger, feel cheated or dismayed and lose our sense of peace and well-being, but when we practice total trust and complete reliance on Him, the peace of God floods our soul, and we are at rest.

Preaching to Ourselves

A number of years ago, I met up with my friend, Andrea, to minister with her at an event in California. Andrea is a dynamic worship leader whose love for the Lord and heart for worship catapults people into His presence. Worship for Andrea is not a performance or a gig to provide financial means for her; she worships because she knows that God alone is worthy, and it shows in her life and overflows into her ministry.

This particular day, however, I couldn't help but notice that Andrea was not her jovial self. Normally full of joy and laden with charisma, Andrea appeared burdened and disheartened.

I inquired as to how she was doing, and she shared with me numerous life-shattering events that she was encountering—any one of which would have rendered a normal person down for the count.

But not Andrea. She went on to assure me that she would be fine because she had done some "soul talking" on the way to the event. The puzzled look on my face led her to explain.

"Rhea, sometimes we just need to talk to our soul."

She told me about her drive to the conference and how difficult it had been for her to get there. Burdened and heavy laden, the pressure of all she was facing weighed heavily on her, and she knew that she had given place to the devil to begin sowing hopelessness and helplessness into her life. She felt distraught and defeated and wondered how she would even have the strength to minister.

Emotionally she was a mess, and she allowed her emotions and what she was facing in the natural to influence her thinking process and her well-being. But Andrea knew better—God had proven Himself faithful to her time and time again, and she was confident that He would once again carry her through victoriously.

As she drove, she began meditating on God's faithfulness, and suddenly a scripture verse came to her mind. It was a *rhema* word—a personal word from the Lord—that went deep into her spirit. She pulled the car over to the side of the road, mustered up every bit of authority she could and began to declare Psalm 42:11 to her soul: "Why are you cast down, O my soul? . . . Hope in God."

Sometimes we give place to the Enemy in our tangled emotions and distraught thinking. We need to instead set our love on the One who is able to bring us through triumphantly and seal up the access door that has given the Enemy an occasion to act in our lives.

So many of us give the Enemy an opportunity to act simply because we are ignorant of his devices. Scripture exposes his devices. As long as we are ignorant of Scripture, we will be ignorant of the Enemy's schemes. We must study the Word of God, spend time meditating on it and store it up in our heart. The sword of the Spirit, the Word of God, is our only offensive weapon. It's the weapon that Christ used to fend off the devil, and it should be our weapon of choice as well. When we walk in the truth, in the light, there is no room for the darkness to gain ground.

The devil is a defeated foe. He has no power or authority in our lives. He has no "legal" right to access our life and wreak havoc—he is only allowed what we willfully surrender to him. We need to be alert to his devices so that we do not permit him access to our lives.

In Job 1 we read that the angels came to present themselves to God, and Satan was with them. God asked Satan where he was coming from, and the devil replied, "I have been patrolling the earth, watching everything that's going on" (Job 1:7, NLT). It's what he does best! Satan is on a spy mission, surveying our lives, looking for weaknesses and vulnerabilities that he can play on and use to gain an advantage over us.

We need to set our love on the One who promises to deliver and under whose feet the Enemy resides. Like Jesus, when we are completely consumed with the Father, holding fast to Him and stubbornly set on doing His will, the ruler of this world will have nothing in us and no power over us. "Because he holds fast to me in love, I will deliver him," says the writer of Psalm 91. "I will protect him, because he knows my name" (91:14). Let us hold fast to God and be intentional about giving no place to the devil.

TWELVE

God's Conditional Promises

Because he holds fast to me in love, I will deliver him; I will protect him,
because he knows my name. When he calls to me, I will answer him; I will be
with him in trouble; I will rescue him and honor him.

Psalm 91:14–15

In the last three verses of Psalm 91, we discover a change of speakers. No longer is the psalmist orating; it is the Lord speaking now. In these verses we find eight promises, or "I wills," being proclaimed by the Most High, the Almighty, the One who is our refuge, our fortress and the God in whom we trust. He is identifying the benefits of dwelling in the secret place with Him.

Making God our all in all is what Psalm 91 is all about. It is about drawing near to God, as we saw in verses 1 and 2, and then realizing the benefits that we will reap in doing so. The eight "I will's" in these last three verses are just a few of the benefits we reap in drawing near to God in the secret place and making Him our priority. Let's look at them:

- I will deliver him.
- I will protect him.
- I will answer him.
- I will be with him in trouble.

- I will rescue him.
- I will honor him.
- I will satisfy him with long life.
- I will show him My salvation.

But again, it's important that we remember that these "I wills," although promises of God, are not given to all people—they are given only to those who dwell in His presence.

We may know Him as our Lord and Savior, but there is a huge difference between confessing Jesus Christ as our Lord and Savior and actually abiding in His presence. These eight promises are for those who share intimate fellowship with Him—those who know His name and have put their trust in Him. They are for those who hold fast to Him in love and have learned to run to Him for cover. Let's look at the first six promises (we will cover the last two in the final chapter of this book) in the context of the conditions that God attaches to them.

"Because He Holds Fast to Me in Love"

The first condition connected to these eight "I will's" is that we hold fast to God in love. The Lord doesn't say, "Because he never messes up or disobeys Me, I will deliver him." Nor does He say, "Because he is super spiritual and never misses church, I will protect him." He doesn't say, "Because he has a lot of Scripture memorized and listens to Christian radio in his car, I will answer him and show him My salvation." No, He says, "Because he holds fast to me in love, I will deliver him" (Ps. 91:14).

Holding fast to God in love isn't the same thing as holding fast to Him out of fear or obligation. It isn't about holding fast to Him out of duty or because we know it's the right thing to do. It isn't about serving in the church or giving money to the poor. Holding fast to God in love is about experiencing a depth of relationship with Him and making Him the priority in our lives. It's about positioning ourselves under His lordship at all times.

One of the teachers of the law once came to Jesus and asked, "Which is the great commandment in the Law?" Jesus answered him, "You shall love the Lord your God with all your heart and with all your soul and with all your mind. This is the great and first commandment" (Matt. 22:36–38). Do we love the Lord with all our heart, soul and mind? Do we love Him with every ounce of our being?

Jesus not only gave this religious leader the "great commandment" that he had asked for but also told him that it was the "first commandment." Interestingly, the word Jesus used for "first" in this verse was *protos*, from which we get the English word "priority."

Jesus was making a point that loving the Lord our God with all our heart, soul and mind is not only an important commandment to keep but needs to be the priority in our lives.

If we get that straight, everything else in our lives will fall into place. But sadly, so many of us have other loves that compete for that place of priority in our lives. Too often we commit spiritual adultery by placing other things before God, completely unaware that our actions deny Him while our lips hypocritically confess His lordship.

As we saw in chapter 1 of this book, Jesus condemned lip service: "These people . . . honor Me with their lips, but their heart is far from Me" (Matt. 15:8, NKJV). He was talking about people who go through religious motions, those who talk the talk but fail to walk the walk. People who claim to believe in Him but whose lives bear no fruit for God's kingdom.

How often are we guilty of honoring God with our lips and saying all the right things while our hearts are far from Him? Making God the priority of our lives begins with loving Him with all our heart and refusing to hypocritically confess His lordship.

One of the ways that we can be sure we are not walking in hypocrisy is to examine our lives and see if they are producing the fruits of righteousness. Jesus said in John 14:15, "If you love me, you will keep my commandments." Obedience is God's love language. It's one way that we communicate our love to Him and declare His primacy in our lives. When we truly love God and walk in deep intimacy with Him, a heart of obedience will be the natural overflow of our lives.

Obedience isn't burdensome. It is not a chore or a religious obligation. When we refuse to give Him lip service and make Him *the* priority of our lives, we automatically want to walk as He walks and talk as He talks, and our commitment to obedience will begin to manifest at a deeper level in our lives. This is what it means to hold fast to God in love.

The Hebrew word translated "holds fast to" means "to be attached to, to long for, to be joined together, adhere, to cleave to."[1] This is the prerequisite for experiencing God's delivering power. As we hold fast to Him and make Him the object of our focus, He promises to deliver us and set us free.

The King James Version translates Psalm 91:14 this way: "Because he hath set his love upon me, therefore will I deliver him." What does it mean to set our love upon someone? I get a small glimpse of that daily in the way my husband loves me.

Men are commanded in the Word of God to love their wives as Christ loved the church. Ideally, earthly marriages are meant to give us a glimpse of Christ's covenant love relationship with us. My husband does that well. Now he's not perfect, but I know that he loves me. I might even be willing to admit that he adores me.

I have no doubt about the fact that my husband has set his love upon me. I don't worry that another woman could entice him; I'm not at all concerned that he might decide to walk out on me; the thought of him growing distant and cold toward me never enters my mind. He is committed to me and holds fast to me in love. I am a blessed woman, and I know it.

When someone holds fast to us in love and cleaves to us, it creates a safe place for us and provides a breeding ground for intimacy. This is what God wants from His followers. He is looking for loyal, devoted people who have set their love on Him. He wants our undivided heart, not a heart that holds fast to the things of this world. It's why He created us; we were designed to love Him.

But we cannot experience intimacy with the Lord unless we are willing to draw near to Him. James 4:8 says that God wants us to draw near to Him, and when we do, He promises to draw near to us. He is not a far-off God who is unapproachable and disconnected; He desires relationship and longs for us to come close to Him.

Intimacy takes intentionality. We can't just wish it into being. Trust and intimacy are developed with the Father in much the same way we develop it with a spouse—by spending time with Him, getting to know Him, learning to love the things He loves.

Intimacy requires being honest and open and gives us a freedom to be ourselves without fear of rejection and ridicule. It requires vulnerability, and it cannot be found when we are hiding behind masks or living in false pretenses.

God provides an atmosphere conducive to those things—an atmosphere filled with unconditional love and complete acceptance. As intimacy is developed and we spend more time with God, we begin to know and understand His character in deeper ways and learn we can trust Him and rely on Him. We can have confidence in Him. Who wouldn't want to hold fast and cling to a God like that? Intimacy is essential in our relationship with God and will only happen when loving Him becomes the number-one priority in our lives.

The culture in which we live today suffers in the area of intimacy. It is laden with technology—people are more comfortable communicating via e-mail or text message than sharing deeply and conversing face-to-face. Online pornography and social networking offer the thrill of fraudulent intimacy at the expense of deep, meaningful relationships. This is sad. God created us to be known. He created us for intimacy—first and foremost with Him but also with each other.

Trust is the incubator for intimacy. Scripture tells us this in Hebrews 11: "Without faith it is impossible to please him, for whoever would draw near to God must believe that he exists and that he rewards those who seek him" (Heb. 11:6). If you've ever had someone question your integrity or not trust you, you will understand why it's impossible to please God without faith. If we don't have absolute faith in God, we imply that He is not trustworthy.

Faith is not this mystical thing that we need to conjure up in our mind. It is an intentional decision to put our trust in and rely on the truth of God's Word and the faithfulness of the One who spoke it into being. Faith is acting on the promises of God, knowing that the Lord is a promise keeper and cannot lie. We might say that we believe God, but the true test of that belief is acting on it. That's why James says, "Faith by itself, if it does not have works, is dead" (James 2:17).

If we want to live a life that is pleasing to God, we must put our faith totally in His Word. We must draw near to Him and believe that He exists and will reward us with the fulfillment of His promises. As we draw near to Him in the secret place, holding fast to Him in love, faith will come more easily for us as we begin to learn that He is a faithful God and that He indeed rewards those who seek Him.

God waits for our approach. Scottish minister James Hastings says, "For every advance on man's part, there is an immediate and corresponding advance on God's part. When man goes out to seek God,

God meets him more than halfway. When he calls upon God, God will answer him. Loving faith on man's part will be met by faithful love on the part of God."[2] That is the beauty of Psalm 91—when we draw near to God in faith, we will realize that God, in His faithfulness, has already drawn near to us.

Those who know Jesus Christ as our Lord and Savior have been saved by grace. God was merciful to us; we deserved hell, and we got heaven instead. But there is so much more to the Christian walk then being saved from a burning hell. God wants to bring us into a place of intimacy with Him. He wants us to have intimacy with Him and to know and experience His powerful presence in our life.

He wants us to know Him personally, to recognize His voice, to live close enough to Him to hear His heartbeat and to know and love what pleases Him. He desires us to walk in the power of His Holy Spirit and to know that our flesh has been crucified with Christ. He wants to surround us with favor as a shield and empower us to change the world for Him. He longs for us to know that we've been set free and no longer need to be bound by a yoke of slavery. He desires to lead us in triumph and enable us to walk in victory. He wants to be our bondage breaker and to heal and deliver and redeem us. He longs for us to truly know Him as our all in all. All these things will be ours when we hold fast to God in love.

"I Will Deliver Him"

When we honor the condition of Psalm 91:14 to hold fast to God in love, God then promises to deliver us.

Second Corinthians 1:10 similarly tells us, "He delivered us from such a deadly peril, and he will deliver us. On him we have set our hope that he will deliver us again." This verse is interesting, however, because three verb tenses are presented in it—past, present and future.

It's a picture of the absolute willingness of God to deliver. Just as He delivered the Israelites out of slavery into the Promised Land, we can trust Him to deliver us from all that tries to limit us or hold us back from what He has for us—we simply need to hold fast to Him in love.

Psalm 34:17 says, "When the righteous cry for help, the LORD hears and delivers them out of all their troubles." The Lord wants us to cry out for Him to deliver us.

The word "deliver" is used three times in Psalm 91. Each time the writer uses a different Hebrew word for it.

In verse 3 we read that God will deliver us from the snare of the fowler and from the perilous pestilence. The word for "deliver" used here and also in Psalm 34:17 is *natsal*. It means "to snatch away, to be torn out or away, to be plucked out."[3] No matter what trap we may have stumbled upon or what trouble is plaguing us, God promises to snatch us and pluck us out.

In verse 14 God promises to deliver us because we have set our love on Him. The Hebrew word for "deliver" used here is *palat* and means "to escape, save, to deliver from danger, slip away, to being into security, bring to safety."[4]

And in verse 15 the word for "deliver" is *chalats*, and it means "to remove, draw out, draw off, take off, withdraw, equip (for war), arm for war, rescue, be rescued."[5]

It's one of my favorite definitions of "deliver"—to equip for war! Sometimes God doesn't deliver us by removing us from the situation but instead by equipping us for the battle we are facing: "Blessed be the LORD, my rock, who trains my hands for war, and my fingers for battle; he is my steadfast love and my fortress, my stronghold and my deliverer, my shield and he in whom I take refuge, who subdues peoples under me" (Ps. 144:1-2).

God does want to rescue us from snares of the enemy and the things that plague us, but He also wants to use those things to teach us to war and to equip us for the battle. Jeremiah 20:11 says that the Lord is with us "like a mighty warrior" (NIV), and Isaiah 42:13 declares, "The LORD goes out like a mighty man, like a man of war he stirs up his zeal; he cries out, he shouts aloud, he shows himself mighty against his foes." Even when it doesn't feel as if the Lord is delivering us out of trouble, He is warring for us and with us in the midst of it.

"I Will Protect Him"

Another blessing of Psalm 91:14 is that God promises to protect those who know His name: "I will protect him, because he knows my name." Proverbs 18:10 says, "The name of the LORD is a strong tower; the righteous man runs into it and is *safe*." "Safe" in this verse is the same word as "protect" in Psalm 91:14.

Knowing the name, reputation, character and attributes of God guarantees us God's protection. In Proverbs 18:10 the name of the Lord is described as a "strong tower"—like a fortress that is secure from all that threatens to assault and attack those within. That place of protection is available to us as believers, but as Proverbs 18:10 further tells us, we must choose to run into it in order to be safe. God will never force us to run for cover.

I mentioned in chapter 3 of this book the importance of a city being protected by fortified walls. In Old Testament times a tower of defense was usually built on the corner of each city wall from which a watchman could look for an invading enemy army. From that tower the city had great defensive advantage.

The name and character traits of God in which we put our trust become like that tower for us. When we run to God and put our faith in all that He is and promises to be, we find ourselves in a place of safety and security in the midst of life's battles and the lurking danger of enemy attacks.

If you are in a battle for provision, run to the strong tower of Jehovah Jireh, the Lord our provider, and take refuge in the One who owns the cattle on a thousand hills and in His promise to provide and meet your needs according to His riches in glory. He will live up to His name.

Perhaps your battle is against illness and disease. Run for cover to Jehovah Rapha, the Lord our healer, and take refuge in His promise to be the great physician, the balm in Gilead and the One by whose stripes we are healed.

The Lord's name, character and attributes must be our only defense. We must not run to any other source. God will be for us like a fortress standing strong and secure in the midst of a battlefield. The battle can be raging around it, but the people dwelling behind the fortified walls, securely and safely hidden in the fortress, will be unaffected and untouched by the battle raging around them.

When we understand God's name and take refuge in it, we become more intimately familiar with God's character and nature. The deeper our revelation of who He is, the more we will want to call on Him, because we will have tasted of His proven faithfulness to be all that He promises to be.

"Because He Knows My Name"

The Lord has promised to protect us if we know His name, but what does it mean to know the name of God?

Prior to each of our children's births, my husband and I spent months debating the perfect name for our perfect child. My husband liked one name, I liked another; the in-laws had their opinion, and friends offered theirs. I didn't want to choose a name that I might regret later, as I had firsthand experience living with a name that I did not like, and I didn't want to make that mistake with my own children.

My parents named me Rhea after a woman who had babysat my mother when my mother was a little girl. My mother was particularly fond of this woman and thought it would be honoring for me to be her namesake. What was she thinking? I have been called everything from diarrhea to gonorrhea. I can laugh about it now, but it wasn't funny as a teenager growing up with that name. I cringe when I remember one particular story.

I like to talk—a lot! When I was in high school, one of my teachers offhandedly told me that it was a fitting that my mother had named me Rhea, because I had "diarrhea of the mouth." My mother paid an office visit to the school, and I'm pretty confident that after his encounter with my mother, that teacher chose his words a little more carefully.

My point is, names are important. They shouldn't be randomly assigned. The Bible says, "A good name is to be chosen rather than great riches" (Prov. 22:1). During Bible times names were carefully chosen to denote character and express the nature of the person named.

The word "name" in Psalm 91:14 refers not only to what a person is called, but it also means "reputation, fame, glory" and "memorial or monument."[6]

Throughout the Bible God reveals Himself to us through His names, and each of those names describes a specific aspect of His character—a different attribute or quality. God's names are not arbitrarily assigned; each of them gives us, His followers, insight and understanding into who He promises to be for us. Through a knowledge of His names, the Lord invites us to know Him more deeply and to understand His abilities and character at increasing levels of faith. When God reveals Himself by one of His names, that name is chock full of power and potential for our lives.

When we really *know* God's name, we become deeply and intimately acquainted with who He is and who He promises to be, and we learn to trust Him at a deeper level. Psalm 9:10 tells us this: "Those who know your name put their trust in you, for you, O Lord, have not forsaken those who seek you."

When we know who He is, we will run to Him for all He promises to be. For example, if we know and are intimately acquainted with the fact that God is Jehovah Jireh, the Lord our provider—if we have learned through experience that He will be faithful to provide—we will not hesitate to run to Him the next time we are in need instead of seeking provision from another source. The name Jehovah Jireh will become a memorial to us—a name that we can call to remembrance to remind us of God's faithfulness.

"When He Calls to Me, I Will Answer Him"

Psalm 91:15 goes on to tell us of another condition and subsequent promise: when we call to God, He will answer us.

Caller ID and voicemail allow us the privilege today of knowing who is calling and the luxury of deciding if we are going to answer the person's call or not. I get so frustrated when I call someone and they do not answer or they fail to return my call, but to be honest, I've done it myself.

I also dislike telemarketers; I have my telephone number on every "do not call" list available, but they still call me! Most of us have been the recipient of calls from scam artists who try to trick us into giving them our bank account information or social security numbers—I end those calls abruptly and wish I had never answered!

God declares in Psalm 91:15 that when we call, He will answer. In Jeremiah 33:3 He says, "Call to me and I will answer you, and will tell you great and hidden things that you have not known." Aren't you glad that we have a God who wants to answer when we call? He will never ignore our call or let it go to voicemail. We are never on His "do not call" list, and He doesn't begrudgingly accept our calls, tolerating us like we do an annoying telemarketer. He actually invites us to call Him, and then He promises to answer us. Hebrews 4:16 even reminds us that because of all that Christ has done for us, we can approach Him boldly and confidently and find grace to receive help from Him in our time of need.

Most of us end our prayers by saying "in Jesus name." This is not just a religious way to pray, it's scriptural. John 14:13–14 tells us, "Whatever you ask in my name, this I will do, that the Father may be glorified in the Son. If you ask me anything in my name, I will do it." What exactly does this mean?

To pray in Jesus' name is to pray as Jesus would pray. It is praying according to His will and asking for what He would ask for. One way to do this is to pray Scripture and not try to come up with our own fine-sounding words. Why? Because our human words are empty and powerless, but God's words are powerful and operable.

When we pray Scripture, we pray as Jesus would pray, but when we step outside the bounds of Scripture and use words according to our own will, our prayers tend to be selfish and birthed by the wrong heart motivation.

That's why Scripture says, "When you pray for things, you don't get them because you want them for the wrong reason—for your own pleasure" (James 4:3, GW). When we ask according to God's will, however, He will always hear and respond, because we are asking for His desires, not for our own pleasures.

When we know God's name, His nature, His character, we will not ask amiss, because we will pray according to His nature and ask for what He would ask for. First John 5:14–15 confirms this: "This is the confidence that we have toward him, that if we ask anything according to his will he hears us. And if we know that he hears us in whatever we ask, we know that we have the requests that we have asked of him."

We can pray with confidence when we pray according to His will. When we know who God is and are intimately acquainted with His name, we will want to call on Him, and we will do it with confidence because we realize that He is trustworthy and will not forsake those who seek Him. This kind of knowledge will make us bold and confident in our approach.

James 5:16 says, "The prayer of a righteous person is powerful and effective" (NIV). I want to pray powerful and effective prayers, don't you? I want to shake the world for God when I pray and to see those I am praying for be shaken by His power and His faithfulness to answer when we call.

When we abide in His presence, we will pray effectively and powerfully, because we have set our love upon Him, long to do His will and always ask according to it. We will not pray self-centered prayers that are powerless and ineffective, but rather we will ask boldly according to God's will and then have confidence that we will receive what we ask for because we have asked with the right heart motivations.

Those of us who have learned the secret of abiding and resting in God's presence have come to know we can trust in His love and rely on Him to be all that He promises to be.

In the midst of trouble and trials, we can choose to put our trust in Him and not fret and fear. We do not need to dispute or resist the things that come at us in life, because we can confidently rest in the fact that all God's dealings with us are good, that God is working all things together for our good and His glory and that in due time surely our God shall deliver us.

"I Will Be with Him in Trouble; I Will Rescue Him and Honor Him"

Here we see further promises given to the one who calls on God. Psalm 91:15 goes on to tell us that when we call on God, He will be with us in trouble, and He will rescue and even honor us.

One of the most favored stories in the Bible can be found in the sixth chapter of Daniel: the story of Daniel in the lions' den. Daniel, as many readers will know, held a high position on the king's cabinet during the reign of King Darius. Daniel was so successful, in fact, that the king planned to set him over the entire kingdom.

The other leaders in the kingdom, however, were jealous of Daniel. They wanted to bring him down, but because he was such faithful young man they could not find any fault in him.

So they decided to set him up. Knowing that Daniel was faithful to pray to his God, they convinced the king to issue an ordinance forbidding anyone to petition any god or man, except the king, of course, for thirty days. Those who failed to obey would be thrown into the lion's den.

This did not stop Daniel. He continued to pray three times a day and to give thanks before his God. All went according to plan for his schemers, and they caught Daniel petitioning his God.

The king was deeply distressed and tried to deliver Daniel himself, but to no avail. The men reminded the king that "no injunction or ordinance that the king establishes can be changed" (Dan. 6:15). No exceptions!

Grieved, the king commanded that Daniel be cast into the den of lions. Before he was thrown into the den, the king said to him, "May your God, whom you serve continually, deliver you!" (6:16). The king recognized what we too easily forget: Daniel could do nothing to rescue himself from this decree; unless the Lord intervened, he had no hope of deliverance.

Let's read the rest of the story directly from Scripture:

> At break of day, the king arose and went in haste to the den of lions. As he came near to the den where Daniel was, he cried out in a tone of anguish. The king declared to Daniel, "O Daniel, servant of the living God, has your God, whom you serve continually, been able to deliver you from the lions?" Then Daniel said to the king, "O king, live forever! My God sent his angel and shut the lions' mouths, and they have not harmed me, because I was found blameless before him; and also before you, O king, I have done no harm."
>
> Then the king was exceedingly glad, and commanded that Daniel be taken up out of the den. So Daniel was taken up out of the den, and no kind of harm was found on him, *because he had trusted in his God*. And the king commanded, and those men who had maliciously accused Daniel were brought and cast into the den of lions—they, their children, and their wives. And before they reached the bottom of the den, the lions overpowered them and broke all their bones in pieces. (Dan. 6:19–24)

Daniel, the Scripture says, was rescued and delivered "because he had trusted in his God." Daniel had total trust that God was his deliverer and that his life was in God's hands. He had absolute confidence that God would protect him, because He knew God's name and held fast to Him in love. Daniel acted on his faith, even when faced with a den of fierce lions. Take careful notice that God didn't stop Daniel from being thrown into the lions' den—rather He delivered him out of it. Psalm 91:15 proved true for Daniel: when he called on God for help, the Lord was "with him in trouble," and He rescued and honored him.

Psalm 34:4 says, "I sought the LORD, and he answered me and delivered me from all my fears."

Are you facing something that seems insurmountable? Something that, unless you have supernatural intervention, leaves you with no hope? Does fear plague your life and rob you of courage? Cry out to God, and watch His delivering power. If God can protect Daniel in the lions' den and then rescue him from it, He can certainly answer our prayers and deliver us from whatever is trying to destroy and devour us.

God is the "same yesterday and today and forever" (Heb. 13:8), and the same faithful God who delivered Daniel can be trusted to deliver, protect, answer, honor and rescue you and me. But we must remember that these promises, as great as they are, depend on us fulfilling God's conditions to hold fast to Him in love, to know His name and to call on Him in our time of need.

No matter how difficult or insurmountable our circumstances seem, as we run to our God for cover and make Him our trust, He will deliver us, protect us, answer us, rescue us and honor us.

THIRTEEN

He Will Deliver Us from Trouble

When he calls to me, I will answer him; I will be with him in trouble; I will rescue him and honor him.

Psalm 91:15

Not too long ago someone unfairly wronged me. This person deeply hurt me with unkind words, made me feel ostracized by cruel behavior and wounded me with unfair judgments. This situation weighed heavily upon me, cutting me to the core.

I cried out to God, asking Him where He was and why He wasn't taking up my cause. I wailed exclamations of "Unfair!" and accused God of not defending me and of failing to uphold His promise to "perfect that which concerns me" (Ps. 138:8, NKJV). I'm certain that none of you has ever felt this way (insert cynicism).

Quite frankly, though, I'm not sure why we allow ourselves to entertain feelings of injustice, because it only causes us to end up wandering in a wilderness of self-centeredness and self-pity, all the while spiraling downhill as we question God's faithfulness. There is no quicker route to the desert than in failing to let God defend us against injustice and relying instead on our own strength.

A Gentle and Quiet Spirit

One morning during this season of injustice in my life, I awoke early, still deeply troubled by all that was happening to me. Thinking about how I had been done dirty, I wondered where God was in the midst of my pain. I sat down at my desk with a strong cup of coffee and my dog-eared Bible and opened to a passage that I had been studying in First Peter:

> Do not let your adornment be merely outward—arranging the hair, wearing gold, or putting on fine apparel—rather let it be the hidden person of the heart, with the incorruptible beauty of a gentle and quiet spirit, which is very precious in the sight of God. (3:3–4, NKJV)

I was moved as I read about the beauty of a gentle and quiet spirit. Feeling neither gentle nor quiet at that moment, I dug a little deeper into the original meaning of the words "gentle" and "quiet." I was shocked by the first definition I found.

When we think of the word "gentle," we might think of a grandmother or a loving caretaker with a gentle disposition; perhaps a soothing melody comes to mind, or we might picture a soft sprinkling of rain on a hot summer day. We no doubt think of a nature that is not harsh or violent in any way. But in First Peter 3:4 the word "gentle" takes on a nuance all its own.

It does indeed refer to meekness or a mild disposition, but it also means "that disposition of spirit in which we accept His [God's] dealings with us as good, and therefore without disputing or resisting." In the Old Testament it means "those wholly relying on God rather than their own strength *to defend against injustice*."

Further, we are to understand that "God is permitting the injuries [that people] inflict, . . . He is using them to purify His elect, and . . .

He will deliver His elect in His time. [Gentleness] stems from trust in God's goodness and control over the situation."[1]

When Peter used the word "gentle," he was not talking about a bent toward kindness or tenderness. He was not referring to a calm personality with which some people are naturally born; he was describing a spirit at rest, subdued by the Holy Spirit, and restrained by a deep trust in God's goodness and control over all situations.

Let's be honest, sometimes it's hard to let go of injustice and trust a God whom we can't see to defend us. But is the alternative any easier? Bitterness? Anger? Hatred? Self-pity? Who wants to deal with those?! Why then is it so difficult for us to give our grievances to God and rest in His ability to take care of us?

The problem boils down to trust—at least it does for me. If we were gut-wrenchingly honest, could we truly say that we rest in God's ability and desire to defend us, or do we sometimes feel that He is indifferent to our pain? Do we possess a deep-rooted trust in His goodness and control over the troubles in our lives, or do we believe that the situations around us are more powerful and mightier than God is?

Unless we truly settle it in our hearts that God is always good and can be relied on to bring us through victoriously, we will tend to view situations through human wisdom and will question whether or not God has our best interests at heart.

Instead of being shaken and moved by hardship and troubles, we must get to the place where our trust in God manifests itself in a gentle and quiet spirit as we wait for and rely on God. Believe it or not, it is possible for us to be men and women who are undaunted and unaffected by trials and tribulations because of our deep-rooted trust in God and our knowledge of the secret place.

Manifesting a gentle and quiet spirit is not achieved by happenstance. Rather, we must choose it and cultivate it as we become more intimately acquainted with the dependable character and steadfast goodness of God. That happens in the shelter of the Most High. It is in that place of close fellowship with God that we develop a deeper understanding of His nature and begin to discover that all His dealings with us are truly good, even when in the natural it may appear otherwise.

As we begin to live a life of complete reliance on God to defend us against injustice and to be with us in trouble, we no longer need to keep a record of wrongs or to aimlessly pursue revenge and retaliation.

We no longer have to live with the fruits of unforgiveness flowing through our lives. We don't need to be filled with anxiety, wondering where God is and why He isn't coming to our rescue. Nor do we have to try to manipulate and control other people's lives and the situations in which we find ourselves.

We can rest in all that Psalm 91 promises and know that God will be with us in trouble and will deliver us, honor us and sustain us with life abundant.

Conquerors in Trouble

Let's face it: nobody likes troubles. While I love that God promises to be with me in trouble, I'd prefer that He promise to keep trouble *away* from me instead! Quite frankly, I'd prefer a life free from heartache and pain, disappointment and loss, and I'd rather not need to be delivered from anything. Unfortunately, we all know that's not realistic.

God's promise of protection, as we saw in Daniel's situation, does not exclude the presence of trouble: "When he calls to me, I will answer him; I will be with him *in* trouble" (Ps. 91:15). The Lord doesn't deny that we will have trials and tribulations; the fact is, we are going to have challenges in life.

Sometimes as believers we misrepresent Christianity to the world. It's easy to portray it as being all about blessings and favor and a life exempt from pain and heartache, but that's not the way Jesus portrays it. In fact, as we saw in chapter 10 of this book, Jesus Himself pronounced, "In this world you will have trouble. But take heart! I have overcome the world" (John 16:33, NIV). The "you" in John 16:33 is plural; it references us, Jesus' followers. It appears that none of us is exempt! Jesus is making it clear that tribulation—meaning "oppression, affliction, distress, pressure, anxieties, burden of heart"[2]—is inevitable for those who love Him.

Quite frankly, I don't like His pronouncement. I feel as if I've had more than my fair share of troubles, and I'm not overly elated at Jesus' promise that those troubles will continue all the while I'm in this world. Maybe you feel the same way. But isn't it reassuring to know that if trouble is going to come, Jesus promises to be with us in the midst of it?

Don't miss the conjunction that follows Jesus' warning: "But *take heart*! I have overcome the world." The Greek word translated "overcome" is *nikaō*—it comes from the root word *nikē*, which means "victory." Does a running shoe with a swoosh come to mind when you read that? *Nikaō* means "to conquer, to carry off the victory, to come off victorious."[3] By using this word, Jesus is making quite a statement. He's assuring us that although life will be hard and that trouble will certainly come, the good news is that He has already obtained the victory. Christ has overcome, and as a result, we are "more than conquerors through him" (Rom. 8:37).

It's as First John 5:4 says: "Everyone who has been born of God overcomes the world. And this is the victory that has overcome the world—our faith." We get the victory by activating our faith and walking in it. We do not need to fear or be discouraged by trouble and tribulation, we don't need to be defeated and rendered helpless; we can rest and maintain a gentle and quiet spirit, because God has already obtained the victory for us and promises to be with us as we encounter all that life brings our way. In every situation we face, in every hard place in which we find ourselves, we can undergo the challenge, because we fight *from* victory, not *for* victory.

The question is, do we believe that? We must cling to the promises of God and rest in the knowledge that He knows what He's doing and will indeed deliver us from trouble. If we are going to begin to be more than conquerors in Christ Jesus, we must have total trust that we walk in victory and not defeat and that God's promises are always good. We must believe that He always leads us in triumph and that every battle we face, every mountain we encounter, every trial and tribulation that looms on the horizon of our life comes with the promise that He has already overcome it. That's good news indeed!

Victory is ours in Christ Jesus. That's why Scripture tells us that the battle belongs to the Lord (see 1 Sam. 17:47). It was never ours to fight anyway. The Father has put all things under Christ's feet, and since we are seated with Christ in heavenly places, therefore all things are under our feet as well (see 1 Cor. 15:27; Eph. 2:6). That's what Psalm 91 is promising to those who dwell in the secret place, who make the Most High their refuge—not freedom from troubles but deliverance and victory in the midst of them.

Total Trust in God

As we have seen, Psalm 91 is chock full of God's promises. But here's the thing: we can look at those promises over and over, but until we come to a place of total trust with God, the promises of Psalm 91 will seem distant and unsubstantiated to us. Until we reach a place of unadulterated trust in God, we will always be suspicious regarding

His goodness, tempted to accuse Him of being unfair and apathetic or a myriad of other indictments. God's promises are trustworthy, and He is worthy of our trust. We must let that truth govern and direct our lives. To do anything less would be to accuse God of being a liar and to deride His faithfulness.

Martin Luther said on this subject,

> What greater rebellion, impiety, or insult to God can there be, than not to believe His promises? What else is this, than either to make God a liar, or to doubt His truth—that is, to attribute truth to ourselves, but to God falsehood and levity? In doing this, is not a man denying God and setting himself up as an idol in his own heart?[4]

Read that again slowly, and let it penetrate your heart. Oh, how it convicts me. How it spurs me on to a deeper faith in the One who cannot lie and whose Word is forever settled in heaven (see Ps. 119:89). Why do we question Him?

May we truly apprehend this truth today: to doubt God is to question the trustworthiness of the One in whom there is nothing false. Our unbelief implies that God is a liar and suggests that our finite minds have a greater understanding of truth than the God with infinite wisdom and boundless knowledge does. When we in stubbornness of heart ignore God's truth and yield to our own understanding and our own will, we are in essence attributing "truth to ourselves, but to God falsehood and levity." This should not be.

Guarded by God

So the Christian life is not without problems—Christians are not exempt from challenges and difficulties. In addition, we live in a hedonistic world, surrounded by a culture that does not encourage or promote godly behavior and Christian living. On top of that, Scripture proves that we have an enemy who comes to steal, kill and destroy and that we battle against powers and principalities who want to render us useless and hijack the destiny and purpose of God in our lives.

Nonetheless, we have clearly established that we have a Father who loves us, a God who empowers us and the promise in His Word that He will protect and preserve us in the midst of all the challenges that life may throw at us. We don't have to fear danger, attack, persecution, disease, peril or sword. The Enemy's traps are rendered useless by God's power, and God's light overcomes the darkness that threatens to overcome this world. We are safe in Him. This is why we must truly believe God and cast ourselves unreservedly upon Him in times of trouble.

Psalm 91 is not the only place where we see the proof of God's protection outlined; 1 Peter 1:3–5 also alludes to that protection:

> Blessed be the God and Father of our Lord Jesus Christ! According to his great mercy, he has caused us to be born again to a living hope through the resurrection of Jesus Christ from the dead, to an inheritance that is imperishable, undefiled, and unfading, kept in heaven for you, who by God's power are being guarded through faith for a salvation ready to be revealed in the last time.

Notice the two things working together in this verse: God's power and our faith. Until we fully inherit the final salvation of our souls, as believers, we are being guarded by God's power. However, it requires an act of faith to believe that and live securely in it. Do we have faith to believe that we are being kept and guarded by God's power?

The word "guard" in this verse means "to guard, protect by a military guard, either to prevent hostile invasion, or to keep the inhabitants of a besieged city from flight."[5] This word is in the present tense, meaning that it's an ongoing or continuous action, and it's in the passive voice, which means that the subject is the recipient of the action, not the performer of it. You and I are continuously being guarded and watched over by God. We are recipients of His protection, not the performers of it. We cannot protect ourselves; we are being kept by a force greater than us—the very power of God.

We Are Not Alone

One of the promises of God that we need to truly believe and apprehend by faith is that the Lord is with us. This is what Psalm 91:15 is telling us: "I will be with him." We do not journey through our difficulties and trials alone. God is with us, and He is for us.

As I worked on this portion of this book, my daughter Kendal was sitting beside me working on her schoolwork, and I couldn't help but notice that playing quietly in the background on her computer was Kari Jobe's song "I Am Not Alone":

> When I walk through deep waters,
> I know that You will be with me;
> When I'm standing in the fire,
> I will not be overcome;
> Through the valley of the shadow,
> Oh, I will not fear.
>
> I am not alone,
> I am not alone;
> You will go before me,
> You will never leave me.

In the midst of deep sorrow,
I see Your light is breaking through;
The dark night will not over take me;
I am pressing into You.
Lord, You fight my every battle,
And I will not fear.

You amaze me,
Redeem me,
You call me as Your own;
You're my strength,
You're my defender,
You're my refuge in the storm.
Through these trials
You have always been faithful;
You bring healing to my soul.

God is always with us, going before us, walking beside us and following after us. We do not need to fear, for we are His, and He takes care of those who are His own.

Scripture says that Jesus did not leave us as orphans (see John 14:18), but sadly, so many of us live as spiritual orphans. Romans 8:16-17 says, "The Spirit himself bears witness with our spirit that we are children of God, and if children, then heirs—heirs of God and fellow heirs with Christ."

We are children of God. He has adopted us as His own. We are loved and valued, not abandoned and rejected. As we stay by our Father's side, He promises to deliver us, set us on high, answer us, be with us in trouble, honor us and show us His salvation.

In the third chapter of Daniel, we read the account of Shadrach, Meshach and Abednego. These three Hebrew boys defied Nebuchadnezzar, the king of Babylon, and refused to bow down and worship any god but the God of Israel. This infuriated Nebuchadnezzar, and he commanded that Shadrach, Meshach and Abednego be brought to him. When the three Hebrew boys appeared before him, Nebuchadnezzar said to them,

> Is it true, O Shadrach, Meshach, and Abednego, that you do not serve my gods or worship the golden image that I have set up? Now if you are ready when you hear the sound of the horn, pipe, lyre, trigon, harp, bagpipe, and every kind of music, to fall down and worship the image that I have made, well and good. But if you do not worship, you shall immediately be cast into a burning fiery furnace. And who is the god who will deliver you out of my hands? (Dan. 3:14-15)

Undaunted by this very real threat, they maintained a gentle and quiet spirit and answered the king,

> O Nebuchadnezzar, we have no need to answer you in this matter. If this be so, *our God whom we serve is able to deliver us* from the burning fiery furnace, and he will deliver us out of your hand, O king. But if not, be it known to you, O king, that we will not serve your gods or worship the golden image that you have set up. (Dan. 3:16-18)

These men had faith in all that God had promised to be, and they would not be moved by the crisis before them. They were confident in God and unswerving in their belief that no matter what, He would deliver them, honor them and be with them in trouble.

We may confess that we believe God is able, but do our actions convey that belief when we are up against a wall of trouble and uncertainty? Do we fear and become dismayed when trouble comes, or do we rest, unmovable, upon the faithfulness of God?

Matthew 10:28 exhorts us, "Do not fear those who kill the body but cannot kill the soul. Rather fear him who can destroy both soul and body in hell."

Shadrach, Meshach and Abednego feared God more than they feared the edict of man. They had faith in their God, and God rewarded that faith. He didn't allow the three Hebrew boys to go to the fiery furnace alone; He was with them in the midst of it, and He delivered them out of it unscathed.

Scripture identifies a fourth man in the fire: Emmanuel, God with us, was in the furnace with these three young men, and as a result, the fire did not consume them. In fact, they were not even singed, nor did they emerge from the fire smelling like smoke. God will provide the same kind of victory for you and me.

When we go through searing trouble, we are not alone: "When you pass through the waters, I will be with you; and through the rivers, they shall not overwhelm you; when you walk through fire you shall not be burned, and the flame shall not consume you" (Isa. 43:2).

God will never leave us or forsake us, even when the fire is turned up a notch or we find ourselves in deep waters. God is with us, guarding and protecting us by His great power. He is fighting our every battle and healing our every pain. We are not abandoned as orphans left to fend for ourselves.

I love Hebrews 13:5–6 in the Amplified Bible, Classic Edition—it has always ministered deeply to me when I have felt alone or faced fires in my life:

> [God] Himself has said, I will not in any way fail you nor give you up nor leave you without support. [I will] not, [I will] not, [I will] not in any degree leave you helpless nor forsake nor let [you] down (relax My hold on you)! [Assuredly not!] So we

take comfort and are encouraged and confidently and boldly say, The Lord is my Helper; I will not be seized with alarm [I will not fear or dread or be terrified]. What can man do to me?

Any time a word is repeated in Scripture, it is always for emphasis or intensity. Notice that in this text "I will not" is repeated three times. God is stressing something that He doesn't want us to miss: He means it when He says that He will not in any degree leave us helpless or forsake us or let us down. He will not in any way fail us or leave us without support, and He will not relax His hold on us as we hold fast to Him in love. He overemphasizes this truth, because so often we underemphasize it in our unbelief.

We are safe with God, and His power not only guards and protects us through faith for a physical and spiritual salvation or deliverance, it also guards and protects us emotionally as well. Paul tells us this in Philippians 4:5-7:

> The Lord is at hand; do not be anxious about anything, but in everything by prayer and supplication with thanksgiving let your requests be made known to God. And the peace of God, which surpasses all understanding, will *guard* your hearts and your minds in Christ Jesus.

The word "guard" in this passage means "to keep with a garrison or to keep in custody."[6] These verses give us a picture of God guarding and protecting not just our physical bodies but our hearts and minds as well. It depicts a garrison of soldiers shielding our hearts and minds with peace as we purposefully reject anxious thoughts and instead cast our cares on the Lord in prayer.

Think about that—as we refuse anxiety and turn to God instead, He promises us that the peace that passes all understanding will take our minds into custody, protecting them from the hostile assaults of anxiety, worry and tormenting thoughts. Isn't it reassuring to know that God doesn't just deliver us from dangers and troubles; He delivers us from troublesome thoughts and anxieties?

Nowhere in Psalm 91 are we told to deliver ourselves; that is God's job. Deliverance is His promise to us. Our job is simply to run to Him for cover, calling on His name and exercising total trust in His ability to deliver us. As we saw in Second Corinthians 1:10, our God *has* delivered, *is* delivering and *will continue to* deliver us as we call on His name and trust that He will be with us and rescue us in times of trouble.

FOURTEEN

Satisfied with Long Life

With long life I will satisfy him and show him my salvation.

Psalm 91:16

I am writing this chapter alone in a hotel room in Orlando, Florida. It's lonely being here without my family, as usually my husband or my friend Leslie travels with me. Some people prefer to be alone; I, however, prefer to be surrounded with family and friends. Nevertheless, this is a quiet, peaceful place of rest and a perfect atmosphere in which to write, so the silence is welcoming and the undisturbed solitude inviting.

I went out late one evening to grab a quick bite to eat and walked to a restaurant in close proximity to the hotel. The parking lot was dark and a bit ominous. As I strolled quickly along the sidewalk bordering the busy Floridian thoroughfare, the thought occurred to me that it was probably not very sensible for me to be out that late at night by myself. I sped up my pace and reached into my purse to retrieve my cell phone, thinking that it would be wise to have it easily accessible.

At that moment I realized that I had left my phone at the hotel. Fear threatened to grip me, and the dark night appeared even darker and more ominous. The awareness that I was alone was foremost in my mind, and a sense of dread fell upon me like a two-ton boulder.

What if something happened to me? It would be days before anyone realized it. No one would even know that I had left the hotel. I was seized with regret and silently berated myself for being so careless.

But as quickly as the negative thought came, another canceled it out. It was the voice of the One I love reminding me of the scripture I had been studying earlier that day: "With long life I will satisfy him and show him my salvation" (Ps. 91:16).

The comforting realization that nothing could happen to me outside God's perfect will for my life settled upon me. A reminder of the truth that my days were numbered by God overrode my anxiety.

He had a perfect plan and an ordained destiny for my life, and nothing could short circuit it or end my life one day before He ordained it. I was safe in the Lord, hidden securely in Christ.

Peace came upon me like a flood, and with the renewed consciousness that I was safely protected by Him, I reduced my breakneck pace to a slow saunter and began to enjoy the beautiful Florida night for all it was worth.

Our lives were planned out by God before we were ever even conceived? He has a purpose and a plan for each of us, a destiny that only we ourselves can fulfill.

You and I were put on this Earth to bring God glory and to be a conduit through which He could bring heaven to Earth and manifest His glory to a lost and dying world. It's the chief end of man.

We will not die one moment sooner or live one second longer than what has been ordained for us.

Knowing that, we can be at peace. However, we do need to consider the fact that even though we are safe until our appointed time, our days here on Earth are limited at best.

In light of this fact, it's important how we use the time that we have here on Earth.

How Then Should We Live?

James 4:14 makes it clear that in the grand scheme of things, our lives on this Earth are brief: "You do not know [the least thing] about what may happen tomorrow. What is the nature of your life? You are [really] but a wisp of vapor (a puff of smoke, a mist) that is visible for a little while and then disappears [into thin air]" (AMPC). We are not guaranteed tomorrow, let alone next week or next year.

Life is a vapor—a puff of smoke! Here one minute, gone the next. We have no guarantees, no promises of another day; we must just live each moment fully grasping all that God has for us. Ecclesiastes 7:2 confirms this: "Death is the destiny of every person, and the living should take this to heart" (NET).

Playwright George Bernard Shaw in his observation of death said, "The statistics on death are quite impressive. One out of one people die." With statistics that high, it's important we be about the task of living.

I used to have a sign on my refrigerator that said, "Never forget the brevity of life, the certainty of death and the length of eternity." We must constantly be aware that life is short at best, that death awaits each one of us and that eternity is forever. When God says that our ordained days are over, where will we spend the forever of eternity?

My brother-in-law, Archie, was a selfless and deeply considerate man who lived every day fully, loved everyone deeply and truly knew what it meant to be satisfied with life.

He didn't know a stranger, was never too busy for anyone and was dearly loved and admired by most everyone in the small community in which he lived. He had just turned sixty-one when death suddenly interrupted his daily routine and without warning snatched away from his family a devoted husband, a loving father and a dutiful and deeply smitten grandfather.

Archie had just retired from his full-time job and was looking forward to enjoying a slow-paced life and more time to spend with friends and family. He had many plans for this next season in his life and was enjoying every moment of preparing for it.

Two weeks prior to his death, I visited with him and my sister briefly while they were vacationing at Disney World in Florida with their family. He beamed with pride as he showed me pictures of his grandchildren playfully posing with the Disney characters and told story after story of how enthralled they were by the themed attractions. He loved being a grandfather!

He expressed how much he was looking forward to joining me on an upcoming ministry cruise that I was hosting later that month. His final payment had been made, and he and my sister were counting down the days until the cruise.

Little did I know that this was the last time I would see him.

I was cooking dinner for my family one night when I received a phone call from my niece, Katie. Her voice, normally jovial and full of life, was unmistakably filled with panic.

"Aunt Rhea," she said, "I need you to get everyone you know to pray for my dad." Through tears she went on to tell me that her dad was missing. Her mother had spoken with him on his cell phone earlier that day while he was deer hunting by himself in a rugged wooded area adjacent to their home. He was excited because he was tracking a deer and expected to bring home some meat.

"We'll have venison for dinner," he proudly boasted.

"Oh, joy!" my sister sarcastically teased.

It was a brief conversation, and Archie ended it by telling my sister that he loved her and promised to have dinner ready for her when she arrived home from work that night. But dinner wasn't on the table when she walked through the door that evening. The fires were out in their wood-burning stoves, and there was no sign of Archie in the now frigid house.

His car was parked in the driveway, so she knew that he wasn't out running errands, nor had he been delayed visiting with a friend. She hurriedly called his cell phone, but the call went directly to his voicemail. Beginning to panic, she frantically raced throughout the house calling his name while continuing to call his cell phone over and over, each time with no answer.

Fearing that something had gone dreadfully wrong, she telephoned my youngest brother. My brother thought that maybe Archie had lost track of time or was struggling to get his deer out of the woods alone. He assured my sister that he and my nephew would search the area, but he was confident that it was nothing to be concerned about.

A layer of freshly fallen snow made it easy for my brother and nephew to track Archie's path. It wasn't long before they noted a trail freshly bloodied by the deer and Archie's footprints nearby. Fully convinced that Archie would be at the house when they returned, my brother and my nephew were about to turn back when they noticed Archie's lifeless body lying in the snow.

His cell phone was in his hand—evidently he had been attempting to call for help in the moments before he died. The paramedics were unable to revive him, and they reported to the family that he had suffered a sudden major heart attack.

Upon receiving the news, I immediately flew home to be with my sister, who, understandably, was in a state of shock, overwhelmed by sorrow and grief. As I sat at the kitchen table with her that evening, I noticed a Sunday school quarterly laying open on the table with Archie's handwriting meticulously scrawled across its pages. He had been a Sunday school teacher at the church that he and my sister attended and obviously had been working on his lesson earlier that day.

The verse he had been studying caught my attention: "Rejoice and be glad, for your reward is great in heaven" (Matt. 5:12). I was undone by God's timing. "Great is your reward in heaven" were the words that would have been fresh in Archie's mind as he took his last breath and stepped into glory.

Later that evening I walked into the bathroom and was overcome with sadness as I noticed Archie's toiletries strewn across the vanity. I thought about the brevity of life and how that morning had been no different from any other morning in his life. He had awakened, showered and prepared for the day just as he did on any other day. Only unbeknownst to him and everyone else, this day would be his final day on Earth.

I had the immense privilege of sharing the gospel message at Archie's funeral service. I spoke about life being a vapor and how all the days ordained for us were written in God's book before one of them ever came to be (see Psalm 139).

I pointed out that Scripture tells us that "it is appointed for man to die once, and after that comes judgment" (Heb. 9:27). This fateful day had been appointed in Archie's life long before he had ever been even born.

Being fully aware of this truth, Archie lived his life on Earth to the fullest for the kingdom of God. Knowing that his days were appointed and that life is short, he used the time he had been given wisely and carefully, and as a result, his reward in heaven was great.

Where Will We Spend Eternity?

Life didn't end for Archie the day he took his last breath; it only just began. For those of us who know Jesus Christ as our Lord and Savior, this world is not our home. We are just passing through this life to get to another. This life is brief, but the life that follows is eternal.

Where will we spend our eternal life? It's important that we ask ourselves that question, because death can interrupt life at the most inopportune moments. We never know when, like my brother-in-law, we'll wake up one morning and, unbeknownst to us, it will be our final day here on Earth and your first day in eternity.

Early one morning a number of years ago, my husband and I were driving to work together when an ambulance sped by us, lights flashing and sirens blaring. We followed the ambulance cautiously at a safe distance. Through the back window of the emergency vehicle, we could see the paramedics working diligently on a patient lying on a gurney.

Ahead of us, the ambulance approached a busy four-way intersection just as the traffic light was turning red. The driver slowed somewhat as he approached the junction but continued cruising through the light, evidently assuming that oncoming traffic would yield to the emergency vehicle. Tragically, that was not the case.

My husband and I sat horrified as the ambulance forcefully collided with an oncoming automobile. The force of the impact sent the car skidding across the highway and caused the driver of the ambulance to lose complete control of his vehicle. The ambulance became airborne, rolling several times before finally landing on its side in the middle of the highway.

When it eventually came to a standstill, fire was pouring out of the cab. Dave darted from our car, instructing me to call 911. In one colossal leap he scaled the side of the ambulance and began evacuating the crew from the smoke-filled cab.

In the meantime I ran to the back of the ambulance to check on the patient and the other crew members. I had difficulty accessing the patient compartment, as one of the rear doors was jammed from the extreme impact of the crash. As I looked inside, the gurney was lying on its side with the patient still securely strapped in; medical supplies were scattered throughout the compartment.

My eyes fell upon a crew member holding a white towel against her bloodied forehead. I couldn't help but observe the contrast between the stark white towel and the bright red blood saturating it. It all seemed like a bad dream. I grabbed her hand, and as I helped her over the jammed door, she asked me about the person they had hit. In my urgency to attend to the ambulance, I had completely forgotten about the other vehicle involved in the crash. Hastily I turned to check on the driver of the car and was completely stunned by what I saw.

The small sedan was crumpled like an accordion, its windows completely smashed. A wave of nausea rushed over me as I realized that the young driver, wedged between the steering wheel and her seat with her head back and eyes open, had clearly not survived the crash.

The girl was wearing tattered sweatpants and an old T-shirt. When she had gotten dressed that morning, had she realized that this would be the last day of her life? Had she realized when she had gotten in her car that morning that she had only moments left on Earth? Had she said her last words to her family in haste or anger, not that realizing they would be the last words they ever heard her utter?

Death had interrupted life at the most unwelcome and inopportune time, and in a flash, in the blink of an eye, life was snuffed out without the benefit of any notice. Yes, life is brief at best, and we must live it in the fullness of all Christ has for us. Eternity is forever, and where we will spend it is the most important decision that we will ever make.

The Essence of a Satisfied Life

As we have noted, God declares in Psalm 91:16, "With long life I will satisfy him and show him my salvation." But the reference to "long life" in this verse is not necessarily length of days; if that were the case, Archie and the young lady who collided with the ambulance were ripped off. They were both so young and had so much life ahead of them. God is not talking here about quantity of days but rather quality of life. He's talking about being satisfied in life and living in the fullness of it. "Satisfied" here means "sated, fulfilled, surfeited and to have life in excess."[1]

When I was younger, I thought that living life to the fullest meant sucking every bit of life out of every single day. My life was an endless string of parties, social engagements and living life in the fast lane. I didn't just want to party, I wanted to *be* the party. Material goods and worldly accumulation were vital to me—that is, until I realized how empty and fruitless that kind of life truly was.

Jesus told a parable about a man whose view of life was not so unlike many of ours. The man was rich in worldly standards, and he lived his life for the moment with no concept of eternity. He had an abundance of possessions and everything that the world said would provide life, and these things were the object of his attention and the focus of his energies. He gave no thought to his soul or the brevity of life. Eventually the man thought to himself,

> "What shall I do, for I have nowhere to store my crops?" And he said, "I will do this: I will tear down my barns and build larger ones, and there I will store all my grain and my goods. And I will say to my soul, 'Soul, you have ample goods laid up for many years; relax, eat, drink, be merry.'" But God said to him, "Fool! This night your soul is required of you, and the things you have prepared, whose will they be?" So is the one who lays up treasure for himself and is not rich toward God. (Luke 12:17–21)

"Let us eat and drink, for tomorrow we die" (1 Cor. 15:32). Isn't that the way many of us are tempted to live life—with no thought of eternity, no concept of the brevity of life? We suck every moment out of life that we can and live that way until, if we are lucky, something happens to make us realize that life is extremely fragile and alarmingly brief. We don't like to think about that though—we just want to do our own thing and forget about what happens after we die. We want to stubbornly ignore God's commands and give no heed to the voice of our Master.

I have a ten-year-old goldendoodle named Armani who struggles with a similar malady. Now all dog owners believe that their dog is the smartest, most brilliant animal alive, but mine truly is. Armani is the most intensely loyal and devoted dog I have ever known. Golden-doodles are widely used as service dogs because of their remarkable intelligence and excellent trainability. Armani fits the bill to a tee—he is brilliant!

Always eager to please, he has mastered an abundance of tricks that he is always happy to perform on command, especially if he is rewarded with a favorite treat.

Recently my daughter Kendal and I decided that we would teach Armani a new trick to add to his performance routine. We worked all day perfecting this trick, each time rewarding the dog handsomely with his favorite dog-bone treat.

When my husband arrived home from work that night, I was excited to have Armani demonstrate his show-stopping performance. I called Armani into the room and issued the practiced command. This time, however, instead of dutifully obeying me and wildly impress-ing Dave, Armani stubbornly turned his head to the side, making it clear that he had no interest or intention of following through with the covenanted performance. Thinking that he needed some positive reinforcement, I pulled a treat out of my pocket to assure him of the coming payoff. Once again I issued the command, and once again he obstinately turned his head away from me, watching me out of the corner of his sneaky eye as if to say, "You're crazy if you think I'm going to do this trick." Dave laughed heartily and walked away, obviously not nearly as convinced as I was of Armani's extreme intelligence.

As long as Armani refused to acknowledge me, he didn't have to follow through with what I was telling him to do. He turned a blind eye to my command and pretended that he didn't see me. We are no different. Sometimes we don't want to look at eternity or think about its reality. We'd rather obstinately turn a blind eye to the brevity of life and instead eat, drink and be merry, draining every moment that we can out of life while refusing to acknowledge the things above. But the reality is, a payoff is coming for those of us who run for cover and set our eyes on things above. Turning a blind eye to eternity doesn't change its reality.

Carpe Diem, "seize the day," is the motto of so many, but the problem with this idea is that it causes us to live for ourselves and for the moment instead of surrendering to the only true source of life, Jesus Christ. Jesus said in John 10:10, "The thief comes only to steal and kill and destroy. I came that they may have life and have it abundantly." The New Living Translation translates it, "The thief's purpose is to steal and kill and destroy.

My purpose is to give them a rich and satisfying life." Jesus wants to give us a rich and satisfied life, but we are deceived into believing that we can find that life in other sources.

But life is not about material goods, power or position. It's not about self-centeredness. It's about letting the Breath of life breathe life into us and impart His life-giving substance in and through us.

As one commentator said, Jesus came "not merely to preserve but impart *life*, and communicate it in rich and unfailing exuberance."[2]

What Are We Hungry For?

Are we living the abundant life that Christ came to give us? Are we letting the Breath of life breathe new life into us? Perhaps you work hard and have everything you desire in life—a beautiful home, expensive cars, a good education and well-behaved children. Maybe you have a great job and are fairly successful in it.

Perhaps you live comfortably, have money in the bank and even have a fairly good marriage. But most people would admit that, even with all these good things, something is still missing. Maybe we can't even put our finger on it, but we know that something is lacking.

The truth is, that something that is lacking is *life*. Not the life that can be found in the possession of things but the kind of life that Jesus came to give. We must not wait until our soul is demanded of us to come to that realization.

I have an insatiable appetite. I can eat and eat and never feel full. Food satisfies me temporarily, but before I know it, my appetite is back.

Part of the problem is that I try to satisfy my cravings with things like chocolate, breads and pastries when what my body desperately needs are vegetables, proteins and healthy fats. The empty things that I fill myself with only increase my cravings instead of satisfying them. Jesus once encountered a woman who had been feeding her appetite with empty things that provided only temporary satisfaction and left her longing for more.

Jesus went out of His way to introduce her to the true source of life and the only thing that could satisfy:

Jesus, wearied as he was from his journey, was sitting beside the well. It was about the sixth hour.

A woman from Samaria came to draw water. Jesus said to her, "Give me a drink." (For his disciples had gone away into the city to buy food.) The Samaritan woman said to him, "How is it that you, a Jew, ask for a drink from me, a woman of Samaria?" (For Jews have no dealings with Samaritans.) Jesus answered her, "If you knew the gift of God, and who it is that is saying to you, 'Give me a drink,' you would have asked him, and he would have given you living water." The woman said to him, "Sir, you have nothing to draw water with, and the well is deep. Where do you get that living water? Are you greater than our father Jacob? He gave us the well and drank from it himself, as did his sons and his livestock." Jesus said to her, "Everyone who drinks of this water will be thirsty again, but whoever drinks of the water that I will give him will never be thirsty again. The water that I will give him will become in him a spring of water welling up to eternal life." The woman said to him, "Sir, give me this water, so that I will not be thirsty or have to come here to draw water. (John 4:6–15)

This woman was a Samaritan, part of a culture that was greatly despised by the Jews. Jews had such disdain for the Samaritans that they would go miles out of their way to avoid going through their region.

But Scripture says that Jesus "*had* to pass through Samaria," or, as the Amplified Bible's classic edition puts it, "It was *necessary* for Him to go through Samaria." Geographically Jesus didn't have to go through Samaria—He chose to go.

Don't you love that Jesus doesn't hesitate to go places others avoid? He's not afraid to confront what others distance themselves from in our lives. He wants to put His finger on areas in us that others may have ignored or that we really would rather avoid. He is not turned off by our stuff or put off by our sin. He wants to confront these things so that He can set us free and truly satisfy us with life.

Not only was this woman born into a race that the Jews despised, but she also had a history of her own that wasn't anything to be proud of. She had been married, not once, not twice, not three or four times but five times, and the man she now lived with didn't respect her enough to marry her.

Her past clearly pointed to the fact that she was thirsty for more—but she sought to fill her hunger with empty things that did not satisfy. She had been rejected by the men she had hoped would satisfy her thirst, but that day at the well, she encountered the only One who could truly satisfy the longing inside her.

That's why Jesus had to go to Samaria.

Like this woman, we turn to so many other sources—sources that leave us thirsting for more and that fail to thoroughly satisfy our appetites. What is it that we are thirsty for? What is the one thing that we hope will finally satisfy us? Only Jesus can satisfy. Everything else will leave us empty and craving more.

When I was a teenager, I played on my high-school field hockey team. I was not all-star or MVP material, but I really enjoyed being part of the team. Practices were grueling and long and often took place in the middle of the hot summer day. At the risk of dating myself, let me add that this was before plastic water bottles had become a thought in some brilliant entrepreneur's mind. The closest thing my team had was a bright orange, not-so-clean team thermos that our coach rarely if ever remembered to fill.

Needless to say, I left practice each day parched, so I usually make a pit stop at a nearby convenience store and purchased a can of Coca-Cola to take the edge off my thirst before the long drive home. What

I didn't realize at the time is that the soda only dehydrated me more and failed to quench my thirst. What I really craved—but didn't know it—was water.

It never failed—by the time I reached my home, my thirst had returned with a vengeance, because I was settling for a cheap substitution instead of partaking of the one thing that would truly satisfy. Life is so similar. The things that we reach for to satisfy our thirst only leave us longing for more. That's because we are trying to fill a God-sized thirst with something that can only offer temporary satisfaction.

Jesus told the Samaritan woman that He could give her water that would make her never thirst again. Tired of searching and coming up empty, she was all in and wanted the water that Jesus was offering. So Jesus said to her,

> "Go, call your husband, and come here." The woman answered him, "I have no husband." Jesus said to her, "You are right in saying, 'I have no husband'; for you have had five husbands, and the one you now have is not your husband. What you have said is true." (John 4:16-18)

In one gentle statement Jesus encouraged her to go get the thing to which she had been looking to quench her thirst and to compare them to Him. He invites us to do the same today. It may not be "Go get your husband," but it may be

- Go get your alcohol
- Go get your heroin
- Go get your pornography
- Go get your credit cards
- Go get your fancy house and closet full of clothing
- Go get the thing that you are looking to give you life instead of Me.

Jesus, the One who is the way, the truth and the life, met this woman at the well that day. With one thought-provoking statement, truth exposed what was deep inside her (what she was trying to hide but that Jesus knew was there) and challenged her to face it. He touched the pain hidden in her inner man and quenched the thirst that kept her drinking from all the wrong wells.

What are we looking to, other than Jesus, for the satisfaction and fullness of life that can only be found in Him? What pain is buried deep within us that causes us to drink from all the wrong wells? Nothing can satisfy us and bring us fullness of life but Jesus.

A Satisfied Life

Imprinted in my mind is a statement that one of our church elders, Harvey Bickhart, made when I was just a little girl. One Sunday as he testified to God's goodness in his life and the contentment that he had found following Christ, he said, "If I die and find out that the Christian walk is a farce, that there is no heaven and that what I have believed about Christ is not true, even then I will have no regrets and will never wish that I had lived any other way."

Mr. Bickhart was saying that living God's way is a recipe for a satisfied life and that even if there was not a hell to shun and a heaven to embrace (there is!), he would still choose to live by the standards of Christ, for they are the only way to a truly full life. I couldn't agree more.

Jeremiah 2:13 says, "My people have committed two sins: They have forsaken me, the spring of living water, and have dug their own cisterns, broken cisterns that cannot hold water" (NIV). We look for refreshment from so many other sources, but only One can satisfy. All other sources are broken, leaky cisterns that cannot hold life. There is no other reservoir, no other source. Only Jesus.

One of the many fringe benefits of running for cover, abiding in the Lord's presence and holding fast to Him in love is that He satisfies us with long life. The life that we live in Him will be full and satiated with abundance and filled to overflowing with peace that passes all understanding. There is no better life and no deeper satisfaction. It will be a long life, because it won't end when we take our final breath—rather, our life will just be starting on the day that we step foot into eternity.

When we abide under the shelter of God's Word, looking only to the Lord, doing things His way and walking in obedience to Him, He increases the quality of our lives. Psalm 91:16 promises us that God wants to give us quality of life. We don't have to live miserable, defeated lives full of despair. We don't have to spend our days feeling angry, consumed by jealousy and full of hatred. The shelter of God's presence is a place of satisfaction and life abundant for us—and it will lead us to our true life in eternity.

Where are you going to spend eternity? Life is brief. None of us has the assurance of another day. Are you drinking from the spring of living water whose fountains never run dry? Have you accepted the gift of God—eternal life through Jesus Christ? It's a gift; we can't earn it, work for it or be good enough to deserve it. Our money can't buy it, and our church attendance can't secure it. We simply have to receive it. Come and drink of His living water, for Jesus Himself has said, "He who believes in Me [who cleaves to and trusts in and relies on Me] as the Scripture has said, From his innermost being shall flow [continuously] springs and rivers of living water" (John 7:38, AMPC).

Continuous, unending, fullness of life is found in staying under the cover of the shelter of the Most High God, seeking to do His will, longing to please Him and endeavoring to live our brief lives in light of eternity. We must always keep in mind the brevity of life, the certainty of death and the incredible length of eternity. We never know when death will interrupt our life and in a blink of an eye we will step from this world into the next. This world is brief at best; the next is eternal and irrevocable. Let's give careful thought to how we will live our lives on this earth and to where we will spend eternity.

AFTERWORD

Will We Be Found Faithful?

As we close, let's consider a final challenge from God's Word. Will we be dwellers? Will we be intentional about running for cover and abiding in God's holy presence, or will we dart in and out of His shelter, seeking pleasure and fulfillment in other things?

The Lord is a jealous God and will have no other gods before Him. Will we be purposeful about exalting Him and Him alone in our lives and looking to no other source?

Jesus once said, "When the Son of Man comes, will he find faith on earth?" (Luke 18:8). He wasn't talking about childlike faith; He was talking about faithfulness among people who *say* that they believe in Him. He will be looking not for Christians who claim to be followers of God but have no fruit to back up their declaration but rather for those who are hungry for His presence, sold out, laid-down lovers of Him who live according to His Word and are purposeful about abiding in His power and in His presence.

We all have a long way to go, but we should want the Lord to be able to say of us, as He did of Nathanael, "Here is a true Israelite, in whom there is nothing false" (John 1:47, NIV 1984). The Bible says that God knows what is in a man. He is not fooled by our spiritual façades or our religious posturing; He can spot hypocrisy a mile away.

We do not want to be numbered among those to whom He says, "I never knew you; depart from me" (Matt. 7:23).

In Luke 17 Jesus exhorts us to "remember Lot's wife" (Luke 17:32). In this passage the Lord is warning His followers about the world in its last days and how people will be unready for His return.

Jesus said that the last days would be "just as it was in the days of Lot—they were eating and drinking, buying and selling, planting and building" (17:28). He was referencing Sodom and Gomorrah in this verse, cities that are associated with sin and debauchery. "Sodom" has become a byword in our society for perversion and wickedness; it is from Sodom that we get our legal word "sodomy." But when Jesus mentions these towns in describing the unreadiness of the world in the last days, he never mentions their sin; rather He focuses on their busyness and preoccupation with the things of this world—things that clouded their vision and lured them away from the things of God. Jesus was issuing this warning to *His disciples*—to people who claimed to love Him and were committed to Him. These were the people He urged to be mindful of Lot's wife.

Lot's wife came from a religious and blessed family; the community of her time would have labeled her a righteous woman. She was related to Abraham, the patriarch of faith, through marriage; she also saw angels, which tells us that she witnessed the supernatural. But she was turned into a pillar of salt because of her unbelief. Religion will not get us anywhere—it's all about true and intimate relationship with God.

My friend, Beverly, called me one day recently and shared with me some thoughts from Matthew 3, a story about John the Baptist, in which John dealt with some people who were like Lot's wife— outwardly spiritual but inwardly faithless. John was calling people to repentance, and hordes of people flocked to the wilderness to be baptized. But when the Pharisees and Sadducees came to his baptism, John brought them a strong rebuke:

> You brood of vipers! Who warned you to flee from the wrath to come? Bear fruit in keeping with repentance. And do not presume to say to yourselves, "We have Abraham as our father," for I tell you, God is able from these stones to raise up children for Abraham. Even now the axe is laid to the root of the trees. Every tree therefore that does not bear good fruit is cut down and thrown into the fire. (Matt. 3:7–10)

John called them out on their presumptive behavior, informing them that just because they were in Abraham's line didn't mean that they were right before God. Family lineage, position in church and keeping up appearances were of no value. The Pharisees and Sadducees were highly religious people—the spiritual elite, if you will—but what they believed and confessed did not affect their heart condition, and as a result, very little fruit was produced in their lives. John challenged these men to bear fruit in keeping with repentance—to give evidence in their lives that lined up and affirmed what they confessed with their mouths.

Beverly reminded me that day that repentance has nothing to do with position, appearance or even right relationship with man. True repentance is about only one thing: right relationship with God. A truly repentant person no longer clings to self-preservation, nor is such a person concerned about what others may think of his sin. With true repentance comes a desire for freedom that is so strong that one would rather give up his own life than continue to be given over to a place of spiritual destruction and fraudulence.

True repentance will never allow us to justify or minimize sinful behavior by relying on a false understanding of grace. The Pharisees and Sadducees stood in their self-righteousness, relying on their family line and position, and today many stand in that same place of self-righteousness and call it grace. It is an absolute deception to believe that God's grace makes exceptions for sin that we claim that we cannot control.

God's Word clearly states that He has made provision for us to walk in holiness: "By his divine power, God has given us everything we need for living a godly life" (2 Pet. 1:3, NLT). We are without excuse. Romans 1:5 says we have been given grace *for* obedience and later adds that obedience leads to righteousness and that righteousness, in turn, will lead to holiness (see 6:16–19). We are either a slave to sin or a slave to obedience. Being a slave to sin leads to death, but being a slave to obedience leads to righteousness. The truth is, we will either be fruit bearers, or we will end up as fuel for the fire.

My heart is saddened by the complacency and mediocrity I see in the world today. Much of the church is asleep. Like Lot's wife and the Pharisees and Sadducees, many believers are going through the motions of Christianity and putting on a good front, but when the Son of Man returns, will He find faith—faithfulness to Him—on Earth?

> Oh, help us, Lord. Put a fire in our soul; ignite within us a passion and a desire for more of You. Strip away all that competes with our longing for You, all the fraudulent loves we turn to in lieu of You, and create in us a clean heart and renew a right spirit within us. Sharpen our ears to hear Your voice and awaken the sleeper within us. Soften our hard hearts; make them undivided so that we are not deceived by them. Open our spiritual eyes to see and our ears to hear. Don't let us be content merely to give You lip service, but rather may we exalt You in all that we say and do. Amen.

Daily, moment by moment, God issues us an invitation to come to Him and abide in Him. In His presence is fullness of joy and peace that knows no measure (see Ps. 16:11). He is our security, the only safe place. He wants to be our all in all, and He promises that as we put our hope in Him, we will not be disappointed (see Rom. 10:11).

Stay close to Him; cling hard and run for cover. Jesus will one day come like a thief in the night. "Blessed is the one who stays awake, keeping his garments on" (Rev. 16:15).

Notes

Chapter 1: God's Promise for Us

1. Blue Letter Bible, s.v. *emunah* ("faithfulness"), http://www.blueletterbible.org/lang/Lexicon/Lexicon.cfm?strongs=G1381&t=KJV (accessed January 21, 2016).

2. Edward W. Goodrick, John R. Kohlenberger III, *Zondervan NIV Exhaustive Concordance* (Grand Rapids: Zondervan, 1999), s.v. "dwell."

3. *American Heritage Dictionary*, s.v. "lip service," https://ahdictionary.com/word/search.html?q=lip+service&submit.x=0&submit.y=0 (accessed September 8, 2015).

4. Blue Letter Bible, s.v. "deceit," https://www.blueletterbible.org/lang/lexicon/lexicon.cfm?Strongs=H4820&t=KJV, (accessed August 29, 2015).

5. Blue Letter Bible, s.v. *chaqar* ("search"), https://www.blueletterbible.org/lang/Lexicon/Lexicon.cfm?strongs=H2713&t=KJV (accessed October 27, 2015).

6. *Greek-English Lexicon of the New Testament*, s.v. *koinonia* ("fellowship").

7. Blue Letter Bible, s.v. *yada`* ("know"), https://www.blueletterbible.org/lang/Lexicon/Lexicon.cfm?strongs=H3045&t=KJV (accessed August 30, 2015).

8. "Uses of Verbs," Grammarly Handbook, http://www.grammarly.com/handbook/grammar/verbs/2/uses-of-verbs/, (accessed August 29, 2015).

9. Peggy Joyce Ruth, *Psalm 91: God's Umbrella of Protection* (Kirkwood, MO: Impact, 2004).

Chapter 2: Hidden Securely in God's Shelter

1. Blue Letter Bible, s.v. *cether* ("secret place"), https://www.blueletterbible.org/lang/Lexicon/Lexicon.cfm?strongs=H5643&t=KJV, (accessed August 30, 2015).

2. Blue Letter Bible, s.v. *zoe* ("life"), http://www.blueletterbible.org/lang/Lexicon/Lexicon.cfm?strongs=G2222&t=KJV, (accessed September 2, 2015).

3. Blue Letter Bible, s.v. *elyown* ("most high"), http://www.blueletterbible.org/lang/Lexicon/Lexicon.cfm?strongs=H5945&t=KJV, (accessed August 30, 2015).

4. Kay Arthur, *Lord, I Want to Know You: A Devotional Study on the Names of God* (Colorado Springs: WaterBrook, 2000), 15.

5. Blue Letter Bible, s.v. *luwn* ("abide"), http://www.blueletterbible.org/lang/Lexicon/Lexicon.cfm?strongs=H3885&t=KJV, (accessed August 30, 2015).

Chapter 3: He Is Our Safe Zone

1. Matthew Henry and Thomas Scott, *A Commentary Upon the Holy Bible from Henry and Scott*, vol. 4, *Isaiah to Malachi* (London: Religious Tract Society, 1864), 143.

2. Blue Letter Bible, s.v. *'iyshown* ("apple" of the eye), http://www.blueletterbible.org/lang/Lexicon/Lexicon.cfm?strongs=H380&t=KJV (accessed August 30, 2015).

3. Blue Letter Bible, s.v. *kazab* ("lie"), http://www.blueletterbible.org/lang/Lexicon/Lexicon.cfm?strongs=H3577&t=KJV (accessed September 2, 2015).

4. Oxford Dictionary, s.v. "deceive," http://www.oxforddictionaries.com/us/definition/american_english/deceive (accessed September 8, 2015).

5. Blue Letter Bible, s.v. *mad* ("armor"), http://www.blueletter-bible.org/lang/Lexicon/Lexicon.cfm?strongs=H4055&t=KJV (accessed August 30, 2015).

6. Blue Letter Bible, s.v. *nacah* ("test"), http://www.blueletterbi-ble.org/lang/Lexicon/Lexicon.cfm?strongs=H5254&t=KJV (accessed August 30, 2015).

7. Blue Letter Bible, s.v. *batach* ("trust"), http://www.blueletter-bible.org/lang/Lexicon/Lexicon.cfm?strongs=H982&t=KJV (accessed August 30, 2015).

8. Blue Letter Bible, s.v. *shaphak* ("pour"), http://www.blueletter-bible.org/lang/lexicon/lexicon.cfm?Strongs=H8210&t=KJV (accessed September 2, 2015).

Chapter 4: Surely He Will Deliver Us

1. Blue Letter Bible, s.v. *yaquwsh* ("fowler"), http://www.bluelet-terbible.org/lang/Lexicon/Lexicon.cfm?strongs=H3353&t=KJV (accessed August 30, 2015).

2. Blue Letter Bible, s.v. *astheneō* ("impotent"), https://www.blueletterbible.org/lang/lexicon/lexicon.cfm?Strongs=G770&t=KJV (accessed August 30, 2015).

3. Albert Einstein, BrainyQuote, http://www.brainyquote.com/quotes/quotes/a/alberteins133991.html (accessed September 8, 2015).

4. Blue Letter Bible, s.v. *astheneia* ("invalid"), http://www.bluelet-terbible.org/lang/Lexicon/Lexicon.cfm?strongs=G769&t=KJV (accessed August 30, 2015).

5. Blue Letter Bible, s.v. *eidō* ("see"), http://www.blueletterbible.org/lang/Lexicon/Lexicon.cfm?strongs=G1492&t=KJV (accessed August 30, 2015).

6. Blue Letter Bible, s.v. *ginōskō* ("know"), http://www.blueletter-bible.org/lang/Lexicon/Lexicon.cfm?strongs=G1097&t=KJV (accessed August 30, 2015).

7. Blue Letter Bible, s.v. *thelō* ("will/would"), http://www.blueletterbible.org/lang/Lexicon/Lexicon.cfm?strongs=G2309&t=KJV (accessed August 30, 2015).

Chapter 5: Avoiding the Enemy's Traps

1. *International Standard Bible Encyclopedia*, s.v. "snare," http://www.internationalstandardbible.com/F/fowler.html (accessed September 2, 2015).
2. John Bevere, *The Bait of Satan: Living Free from the Deadly Trap of Offense* (Lake Mary, FL: Charisma, 2014), 6.
3. Blue Letter Bible, s.v. *brabeuō* ("rule"), http://www.blueletterbible.org/lang/Lexicon/Lexicon.cfm?strongs=G1018&t=KJV (accessed August 30, 2015).
4. Blue Letter Bible, s.v. *nephesh* ("soul"), http://www.blueletterbible.org/lang/Lexicon/Lexicon.cfm?strongs=H5315&t=KJV (accessed August 30, 2015).
5. Warren Baker and Eugene Carpenter, eds. *The Complete Word Study Dictionary: Old Testament* (Chattanooga: AMG, 2003), s.v. "deliver."
6. Ibid., s.v. "plunder."
7. Blue Letter Bible, s.v. *kleptēs* ("thief"), http://www.blueletterbible.org/lang/Lexicon/Lexicon.cfm?strongs=G2812&t=KJV (accessed September 8, 2015).

Chapter 6: Finding Refuge under His Wings

1. *Merriam-Webster Dictionary*, s.v. "pestilence," http://www.merriam-webster.com/dictionary/pestilence (accessed October 28, 2015).

Chapter 7: Fear Not!

1. Blue Letter Bible, s.v. *yasha`* ("salvation"), http://www.blueletterbible.org/lang/Lexicon/lexicon.cfm?strongs=H3467&t=KJV (accessed August 30, 2015).

2. *The Free Dictionary*, s.v. "courage," http://www.thefreedictionary. com/courage (accessed August 29, 2015).

3. Blue Letter Bible, s.v. *chets* ("arrow"), http://www.blueletter-bible.org/lang/Lexicon/Lexicon.cfm?strongs=H2671&t=KJV (accessed September 8, 2015).

4. Mart R. De Haan, *Our Daily Bread* (Grand Rapids: RBC Ministries), 90.

Chapter 8: Angels to Guard Us

1. http://youtu.be/OsgMXT7QBKk Online Video

Chapter 9: Made for Authority

1. Max Anders, *Holman New Testament Commentary: Galatians, Ephesians, Philippians & Colossians* (Nashville: Holman, 1999), 143.

2. Blue Letter Bible, s.v. *kephalē* ("head"), http://www.blueletter-bible.org/lang/Lexicon/Lexicon.cfm?strongs=G2776&t=KJV (accessed August 30, 2015).

3. Blue Letter Bible, s.v. *plērōma* ("fullness"), http://www.blueletterbible.org/lang/Lexicon/Lexicon.cfm?strongs=G4138&t=KJV (accessed September 8, 2015).

4. William Barclay, *The Daily Study Bible Series: The Letters to the Philippians, Colossians, and Thessalonians* (Philadelphia: Westminster, 1975).

5. Blue Letter Bible, s.v. *zēteō* ("seek"), http://www.blueletterbible. org/lang/Lexicon/Lexicon.cfm?strongs=G2212&t=KJV (accessed August 30, 2015).

6. Blue Letter Bible, s.v. *hypotassō* ("submit [one's] self to"), http://www.blueletterbible.org/lang/Lexicon/Lexicon. cfm?strongs=G5293&t=KJV (accessed August 30, 2015).

Chapter 10: Stomping on Serpents

1. Blue Letter Bible, s.v. *exousia* ("power"), http://www.blueletter-bible.org/lang/Lexicon/Lexicon.cfm?strongs=G1849&t=KJV (accessed August 30, 2015).

2. "Basic Facts About Lions," Defenders of Wildlife, http://www.defenders.org/african-lion/basic-facts (accessed August 29, 2015).

3. Blue Letter Bible, s.v. *pethen* ("adder"), http://www.blueletter-bible.org/lang/Lexicon/Lexicon.cfm?strongs=H6620&t=KJV (accessed August 30, 2015).

4. Blue Letter Bible, s.v. *tanniyn* ("dragon"), http://www.blueletter-bible.org/lang/Lexicon/Lexicon.cfm?strongs=H8577 (accessed September 8, 2015).

5. Blue Letter Bible, s.v. *exousia* ("authority"), http://www.blueletterbible.org/lang/Lexicon/Lexicon.cfm?strongs=G1849&t=KJV (accessed September 1, 2015.

6. Jesse Duplantis, "Learning to Resist: Never Fight an Enemy That's Already Defeated," *Voice of the Covenant*, May 2011, 8, http://www.jdm.org/magazine/jesse5.pdf (accessed August 29, 2015).

7. Blue Letter Bible, s.v. *distomos* ("twoedged"), http://www.blueletterbible.org/lang/Lexicon/Lexicon.cfm?strongs=G1366&t=KJV (accessed September 1, 2015).

Chapter 11: Holding Fast to God and Giving Place Only to Him

1. "The Camel's Nose in the Tent," Camelstories.com, http://camelphotos.com/tales_nose.html (accessed September 8, 2015).

2. Blue Letter Bible, s.v. *didōmi* ("give"), https://www.blueletter-bible.org/lang/lexicon/lexicon.cfm?Strongs=G1325&t=KJV (accessed September 1, 2015).

3. Blue Letter Bible, s.v. *topos* ("place"), http://www.blueletterbible.
   org/lang/Lexicon/Lexicon.cfm?strongs=G5117&t=KJV (accessed
   September 1, 2015).

4. Blue Letter Bible, s.v. *diabolos* ("devil"), http://www.blueletter-
   bible.org/lang/Lexicon/Lexicon.cfm?strongs=G1228&t=KJV
   (accessed September 8, 2015).

5. Rick Renner, *Sparkling Gems from the Greek: 365 Greek Word Studies
   for Every Day of the Year to Sharpen Your Understanding of God's
   Word* (Tulsa: Teach All Nations, 2003), 839.

6. The meaning of "give place" (*didōmi*), "The Location of Hell,"
   Hebrew Word Study—Skip Moen, February 15, 2010, http://
   skipmoen.com/2010/02/15/the-location-of-hell/ (accessed September 8, 2015).

7. "Zoologger: The Very Hungry Caterpillar Usurps a Queen,"
   New Scientist, http://www.newscientist.com/article/dn18439-
   zoologger-the-very-hungry-caterpillar-usurps-a-queen.html#.
   VR08e1yyiFJ (accessed August 29, 2015).

8. Renner, *Sparkling Gems from the Greek*, 603.

9. Charles Spurgeon, Exploring the Mind & Heart of the Prince
   of Preachers, http://www.spurgeon.us/mind_and_heart/
   quotes/a.htm (accessed August 29, 2015).

10. Blue Letter Bible, s.v. *pneuma* ("spirit"), http://www.blueletter-
    terbible.org/lang/Lexicon/Lexicon.cfm?strongs=G4151&t=KJV
    (accessed September 1, 2015).

11. Blue Letter Bible, s.v. *pisteuō* ("believe"), http://www.blueletter-
    terbible.org/lang/Lexicon/Lexicon.cfm?strongs=G4100&t=KJV
    (accessed September 1, 2015).

12. Blue Letter Bible, s.v. *homologeō* ("confess"), http://www.blueletter-
    terbible.org/lang/Lexicon/Lexicon.cfm?strongs=G3670&t=KJV
    (accessed September 1, 2015).

13. Blue Letter Bible, s.v. *batach* ("trust"), http://www.blueletter-bible.org/lang/Lexicon/Lexicon.cfm?strongs=H982&t=KJV (accessed September 1, 2015).

14. Blue Letter Bible, s.v. *leb* ("heart"), http://www.blueletterbi-ble.org/lang/Lexicon/Lexicon.cfm?strongs=H3820&t=KJV (accessed September 1, 2015).

Chapter 12: God's Conditional Promises

1. Blue Letter Bible, s.v. *chashaq* ("hold fast to"), http://www.blueletterbible.org/lang/Lexicon/Lexicon.cfm?strongs=H2836&t=KJV (accessed October 28, 2015).

2. James Hastings, ed., "God's Inner Circle" in *The Great Texts of the Bible* (New York: Scribner's, 1911), http://biblehub.com/commentaries/hastings/psalms/91-1.htm (accessed August 29, 2015).

3. Blue Letter Bible, s.v. *natsal* ("deliver"), http://www.blueletter-bible.org/lang/Lexicon/Lexicon.cfm?strongs=H5337&t=KJV (accessed August 30, 2015).

4. Blue Letter Bible, s.v. *palat* ("deliver"), https://www.blueletter-bible.org/lang/lexicon/lexicon.cfm?Strongs=H6403&t=KJV (accessed September 2, 2015).

5. Blue Letter Bible, s.v. *chalats* ("deliver"), http://www.blueletter-bible.org/lang/Lexicon/Lexicon.cfm?strongs=H2502&t=KJV (accessed September 2, 2015).

6. Blue Letter Bible, s.v. *shem* ("name"), https://www.blueletter-bible.org/lang/Lexicon/Lexicon.cfm?strongs=H8034&t=KJV (accessed September 2, 2015).

Chapter 13: He Will Deliver Us from Trouble

1. Blue Letter Bible, s.v. *praÿs* ("gentle"), http://www.blueletter-bible.org/lang/Lexicon/Lexicon.cfm?strongs=G4239&t=KJV (accessed September 2, 2015).

2. Blue Letter Bible, s.v. *thlipsis* ("tribulation"), http://www.blueletterbible.org/lang/Lexicon/Lexicon.cfm?strongs=G2347&t=KJV (accessed September 2, 2015).

3. Blue Letter Bible, s.v. *nikaō* ("overcome"), http://www.blueletterbible.org/lang/Lexicon/Lexicon.cfm?strongs=G3528&t=KJV (accessed September 2, 2015).

4. Martin Luther, *Concerning Christian Liberty; with Letter of Martin Luther to Pope Leo X* (Salt Lake City: Project Gutenberg, 2006), 3520.

5. Blue Letter Bible, s.v. *phroureō* ("guard"), http://www.blueletterbible.org/lang/Lexicon/Lexicon.cfm?strongs=G5432&t=KJV (accessed September 2, 2015).

6. John Phillips, *Exploring Ephesians & Philippians: An Expository Commentary* (Grand Rapids: Kregel, 2001), 164, s.v. "guard."

Chapter 14: Satisfied with Long Life

1. Blue Letter Bible, s.v. *saba`* ("satisfied"), https://www.blueletterbible.org/lang/lexicon/lexicon.cfm?Strongs=H7646&t=KJV (accessed October 28, 2015).

2. *A Commentary, Critical, Practical, and Explanatory on the Old and New Testaments by Robert Jamieson, A. R. Fausset and David Brown* (1882), http://biblehub.com/commentaries/jfb//john/10.htm (accessed August 29, 2015).

Founded by Rhea Briscoe, Snowdrop Ministries is a
non-denominational, Bible-teaching ministry in southeastern
Wisconsin. The ministry exists to passionately present the
Word of God in its fullness so that Christ may be glorified and
His work continued here on Earth.

To learn more about Rhea Briscoe and Snowdrop Ministries,
please visit www.snowdropministries.com.

PUBLICATIONS

Fort Washington, PA 19034

This book is published by CLC Publications, an outreach of CLC Ministries International. The purpose of CLC is to make evangelical Christian literature available to all nations so that people may come to faith and maturity in the Lord Jesus Christ. We hope this book has been life changing and has enriched your walk with God through the work of the Holy Spirit. If you would like to know more about CLC, we invite you to visit our website:
www.clcusa.org

To know more about the remarkable story of the founding of CLC International we encourage you to read

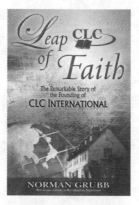

LEAP OF FAITH

Norman Grubb

Paperback
Size 5¹/₄ x 8, Pages 248
ISBN: 978-0-87508-650-7
ISBN (*e-book*): 978-1-61958-055-8

HEARTSTRINGS

Jill Briscoe

Jill Briscoe guides the reader through the "weeping willow trees" of conflict, grief and the daily grind that have caused Christians to "hang up" their joy like abandoned harps. She eloquently illustrates how Christians—like the exiled Israelites—can regain their joy in God's presence and play their harps in front of a watching world.

Paperback
Size 5^1/$_4$ x 8, Pages 243
ISBN: 978-1-61958-219-4
ISBN (*e-book*): 978-1-61958-220-0

IMPROVING WITH AGE

Stuart and Jill Briscoe

Improving with Age addresses the triumphs and challenges of aging Christians and examines the uniqueness of skills and resources they bring to their church communities. Through Scripture and story, the Briscoes assert that aging is not only normal, but it is a joyful and productive life season.

Paperback
Size 5¹/₄ x 8, Pages 254
ISBN: 978-1-61958-207-1
ISBN (*e-book*): 978-1-61958-208-8